STUDIES IN
AFRICAN MUSIC

PLATE I

Desmond K. Tay, master drummer

A. M. JONES

STUDIES IN
AFRICAN
MUSIC

VOLUME I

LONDON
OXFORD UNIVERSITY PRESS
NEW YORK TORONTO CAPE TOWN

Oxford University Press, Ely House, London W. 1

GLASGOW NEW YORK TORONTO MELBOURNE WELLINGTON
CAPE TOWN IBADAN NAIROBI DAR ES SALAAM LUSAKA ADDIS ABABA
DELHI BOMBAY CALCUTTA MADRAS KARACHI LAHORE DACCA
KUALA LUMPUR SINGAPORE HONG KONG TOKYO

ISBN 0 19 713512 9

First Edition 1959
Reprinted 1961, 1969 *and* 1971

PRINTED IN GREAT BRITAIN

'. . . neither are these drummes without dayly imployment, for this is their continuall custome every night after it seemes they have filled their bellies, they repaire to this Court of Guard, making fires both in the middle of the house, and in the open yard, about which they doe continue drumming, hooping, singing, and makeing a hethenish noyse, most commonly untill the day beginnes to breake, when as we conceive dead-sleepes take them. . . .'

RICHARD JOBSON, Gentleman, 1621,
in *The Golden Trade*

PREFACE

THIS book is addressed, in the first place, to musicians and, in the second, to those who, whether specialists in other fields of African life or as general readers, would wish to know what African music is like, and the social contexts in which it thrives.

The work falls into two separate volumes which are interdependent. Volume I is a series of essays on various matters connected with African music: it also contains detailed commentaries on the contents of Volume II which is a music book setting out full scores of songs and dances that belong for the most part to the Ewe people in Ghana.

This is the first appearance, as far as we know, of African music transcribed with precision and in full scores and printed *in extenso*.

In choosing the dances which form the major part of the study, Mr. Tay, our African master drummer, has selected a representative cross-section of the dance music of the Ewe tribe. Our African friends in Ghana may wonder why we have not included the interesting and highly skilled *Atsiagbeko* dance: the reason is that in this dance the movements of the dancers are intimately linked with the drumming in a special and standardized way. Thus to describe *Atsiagbeko* one would have to mark on the score in detail the choreography as well as the drums—a process too complex for inclusion in a book which covers so much ground.

The technical analysis of these dances, which forms the middle section of Volume I, will be too detailed, musically, for the general reader and may be omitted, though they are the very heart of the matter. While he skips the intensive musical *critique* he may yet find interest in the more general remarks which occur in these chapters.

Those who wish to make the attempt themselves to play some African music have been provided for. At the end of Volume I there are some performance scores which—when the main techniques as described in the text, and the scores in Volume II have been understood—should provide enough information to achieve at least a passable performance.

A word should be said about the orthography of the song texts.

Originally written out by Mr. Tay, some attempt has been made to bring them more or less in line with the standard orthography. But this process cannot be thoroughgoing. The meaning of many African songs is notoriously recondite even for Africans, and if the meaning is not indisputable, no hard and fast rules of orthography can be applied. We have done what we could, but in this matter it is impossible to please everybody.

We acknowledge with gratitude the generous grant made by the School of Oriental and African Studies towards the cost of the publication of this book.

It is our hope that these studies will help to bring African music to the notice of musicians outside Africa and that they will contribute in some measure towards the recognition and appreciation of a music which has, for far too long, flourished unheard and unobserved by the musicians of the world.

A. M. JONES

School of Oriental and African Studies,
University of London

May 1956

CONTENTS

PLATES

I

INTRODUCTION

IF one chances to find a novel object, the obvious and sensible course is to look at it carefully. Not only must the object be appraised as a whole, but each detail has to be studied separately, and its nature and function understood. A cursory glance is not sufficient to justify the finder's natural impulse to theorize on it or to jump to conclusions about it. This simple truism applies, of course, to all investigations of the unfamiliar and it certainly applies to the study of African music. Anyone who goes to Africa is bound to hear the music of the country and is equally certain to notice that it is not the same as our Western music. True, the people sing, in solo or chorus, as we do, and their instruments though lacking the precision of Western technology, will still recognizably belong to the familiar families of wind, string, or percussion. Yet the music produced is obviously not the same sort of music as that to which we in the West are accustomed. To take one example: a party of Africans sings first a European song learnt in school and then an African folk-song. No one could possibly be unaware that these two songs represent two different musical traditions. The plain fact is that African music is a strange and novel object when encountered by a Western musician.

To change the simile from objects to persons, one would have thought that a Western musician hearing the novel sounds made by a party of Africans singing, playing, or drumming, would pose to himself the extremely simple and obvious question, 'What exactly are these people *doing*?' following it up by the equally simple resolve, 'I must go and ask them.' Now, astonishing as it may seem, by and large this simple procedure is just the very one which we have not adopted. The available literature on African music, scanty as it is, is overweighted with descriptive prose, often rather sentimental, or else with a premature theorizing, while one looks almost in vain for the answers to that fundamental question, 'What exactly are the Africans *doing*?' This is not a biased and individual judgement, and indeed it is a healthy sign of the present critical attitude of scholars in this field that other writers also are beginning to take the same view. Ernest Borneman, himself a pupil of the Hornbostel school which laid the foundations of modern scientific ethnomusicology, is forced to remark, 'De tout ce mélange de rapports et d'observations accumulés pendant les derniers soixante-quinze ans par les anthropologistes, africanistes et musicologues dans leurs recherches sur la musique africaine, il ne surnage qu'un pitoyable fonds d'informations valables':[1] while Alan P. Merriam as late as 1953 complains,

Incredible as it seems, it may almost be flatly stated that we have no well-rounded information about the music of any African culture area save the Guinea Coast. As far as the Congo is concerned, while a rather surprising number of articles on the music of its peoples has appeared in diverse sources, examination reveals that most of them deal in vague generalities which leave the ethnomusicologist with little if any direct information about the music and musical styles. Unfortunately, the majority seem either to be romanticised accounts which rhapsodise on the beauties of the music, or rather solemn discussions which declare that 'the music of the Congo is functional': the first is fatuous, the second obvious.[2]

It is only fair to add, as indeed Merriam himself does, that there are a few works of value though even these avoid the basic principles of African music and are mostly concerned with the physical and musical characteristics of African musical instruments and their geographical distribution: they are not concerned with the actual music the instruments produce, and one can look in vain in the hope of finding reliable and helpful musical scores.

Most of the literature on matters of African music consists of essays in the journals of the learned societies or in journals produced in or relating to Africa. There are also references to the subject, as one might expect, in the volumes of travellers' accounts. If one of the hall-marks of scholarship in a book is the provision of a comprehensive bibliography, then the present work falls short of the ideal: but there seemed to be no point in drawing attention to published material which either is wrong or else con-

---

[1] E. Borneman, 'Les Racines de la musique américaine noire', in *Présence Africaine* (Paris), No. 4, 1948, pp. 576–89.

[2] A. P. Merriam, 'African Music re-examined in the Light of New Materials from the Belgian Congo and Ruanda-Urundi' in *Zaire*, vol. vii, No. 3, 1953.

tributes little or nothing of constructive value. In evaluating the scientific literature there is one unfailing criterion which is furnished by the musical transcriptions accompanying the text. If these musical examples do not show the fundamental rhythmic feature of African music—that is to say if they give no indication of the time-background of the music, be it a hand-clap or a pestle-beat or the swish of the paddles in a canoe-song, or whatever rhythmic background is used by the African for his song—then one can be virtually certain that the writer is not acquainted with this fundamental feature and therefore the whole of his article is suspect.[1] Similarly if he transcribes the melody of an African song without putting in the words which are sung to it, attaching each syllable to its appropriate note, he provides us with the information that he is not apparently aware that the words and the tune are inseparable. Such a transcription is again of no value and shakes our confidence in the rest of the text.

Among all the transcriptions we have seen, two and two only stand out head and shoulders above the rest. Both of them give clear and unmistakable evidence that other workers have, however brief and incomplete their illustration, independently observed one or other of the basic principles contained in this book. As long ago as 1920 Natalie Curtis, though she had never been to Africa, on meeting some African students in America attempted to study their music.[2] Working under this handicap she nevertheless transcribed correctly that widespread African clap- or bell-pattern which might well be described as the African signature tune, and which is this:

To her must go the palm for being the first to note down its time accurately, though she does not seem to have recognized its rhythm.

The second high-light is a short piece of music given by Brother Basile in his book *Aux rythmes des tambours*.[3] Here is the only piece

---

[1] Cf. Gilbert Rouget in *Les Colloques de Wégimont*, Brussels, 1956, pp. 132–44, especially, '. . . à des informations incomplètes — donc fausses — ne peuvent correspondre que des notions fragmentaires et par conséquent fausses, elles aussi'.

[2] Natalie Curtis, *Songs and Tales from the Dark Continent*, G. Schirmer: New York, 1920.

[3] Frère Basile, *Aux rythmes des tambours*, Les Frères du Sacré-Cœur, 2238 rue

of drumming we have seen in print, other than our own work, which shows clearly that the basic principle of African poly-rhythmic combination has been grasped. Since his book appeared Brother Basile has written to say that his work was done without knowledge of any other research on these lines.

Both these examples are printed at the end of the music-score book. Although they are short and in some respects not quite satisfactory, they are landmarks, and as they stand in a class by themselves they are worthy of special note.

Mention should also be made of an essay with transcriptions by Rose Brandel, published in 1952.[1] She makes the important contri-bution of the realization that the *pitch* of the drums and of their individual drum-beats is important.[2] She gives the actual pitch of one drum (B♭ below middle C) and is, as far as we know, the first person to have done so. For the other drums she gives the relative pitches of the drum-notes forming the musical pattern of each drum, but does not correlate the pitches of the several drums with one another. Both in the text and in the music she shows that she is aware of the 'polyrhythm of the drum music' though she does not seem to realize the fundamental principles involved and which Brother Basile clearly demonstrates.

Finally there is a short excerpt consisting of three bars of music from the Middle Congo transcribed by Herbert Pepper.[3] His scoring is somewhat unusual and difficult as his unit of time is not the same for each line of the score. What he has really given us is two drums playing 3 against 2, but he does not say so. Never-theless his transcription is to be noted not only because he realizes the conflict of polyrhythms in the music, but also because he goes a little further than Rose Brandel in indicating to some extent, the actual pitch of the drum-notes. He only gives two notes for each

Fullum, Montreal, 1946. He did not know of our own work published twelve years previously, viz.: A. M. Jones, 'African Drumming' in 'Bantu Studies', *Journal of the University of the Witwatersrand*, Johannesburg, vol. viii, No. 1, March 1934, nor of our subsequent essays.

[1] Rose Brandel, 'Music of the Giants and Pygmies of the Belgian Congo', *Journal of the American Musicological Society*, vol. v, No. 1, Spring 1952.

[2] In 1952 the present author in his *Icila Dance* (published by the African Music Society, Johannesburg) indicated in more detail than Rose Brandel the *relative* pitch of drum-beats and also their manner of production, but not their actual musical pitch.

[3] H. Pepper, 'Essai de définition d'une grammaire musicale noire', in *Problèmes d'Afrique Centrale*, No. 26. 4ème Trimestre, Brussels, 1954. This particular issue is described as *Numéro consacré à la Musique nègre*.

drum and these are identical in pitch for both drums, one of which is a slit-drum and the other an ordinary *tambour à membrane*, though he does say that what he has written are *sons approximatifs*.

The total amount of music in all these examples is very small. They are little to go on, perhaps, but still they are steps in the right direction.

As to the occasional references to music in travellers' tales, while they may provide us with valuable information of a historic or geographic nature, helping us to trace the incidence of a particular instrument or musical custom over perhaps several centuries, yet as the traveller is not engaged in musical research we shall not expect to find much detailed information of the sort we seek. There was, however, one traveller who, though living three centuries ago, still stands as an example to all who do research in the music of Africa, not because of what he wrote but because of what he did. This was Richard Jobson who travelled up the River Gambia in 1620 and 1621.[1]

I went likewise that night [says he], after we had supt, to the maister of the townes house; who had sent unto mee to mend my supper, a brace of Partridges, and finding there the Ballards [*sc.* Xylophones— *Ed.*], or best musicke, and the younger sort of women gathered together beheld their dancing, and for that they might see we had such pleasures amongst us; I tooke one of them by the hand, and daunced with her, whereof they gave great testimony of great gladnes, inviting the rest of my company to doe the like.

His contribution to our subject is that he took part with the Africans in their music and dancing. If all of us who wish to study their music were to do the same we should very soon become aware of the fundamental structure of African music: in fact we have no right to theorize about this music unless and until we have indeed had some practical experience of it.

Experientia docet, and no amount of theorizing can take the place of musical contact with living Africans. African music has been little served by writers who, following the lead of the Hornbostel school, tend to rely on their powers of abstract analysis largely from gramophone records, and whose articles though couched in learned language are based on no real first-hand knowledge. What

---

[1] Richard Jobson, *The Golden Trade or A Discovery of the River Gambra, and of the golden trade of the Aethiopians*. Reprint by Penguin Press. London, 1932. Original publication about 1621.

is scholarship in this field? Is it the ability to write in the idiom of professionalism? Or is it the possession of first-hand knowledge? Why should it not be possible to say in plain language just what the African does, provided we know what that is? Perhaps this is plain speaking: but it is needed.

The mention of Hornbostel calls to mind a theory he propounded concerning African rhythm. He held that in making the accented beats of a rhythm with a physical down-and-up movement such as is involved in hand-clapping, it is the up-beat which carries the stress in the African mind.[1] This idea seems to attract writers by its very novelty: it still reappears from time to time even in responsible quarters. But this odd notion must be killed dead, once and for all. The African, like ourselves, makes a clap to mark a rhythmic division and it is the clap that matters, i.e. the down-beat and not the up-beat. The pages of music in this book bear ample testimony to this fact. It is a pure invention on Hornbostel's part adduced to explain rhythmic features which he did not understand. Unfortunately this up-beat theory has been spread around and is not a little responsible, probably, for the failure of investigators to realize exactly what is the African's typical treatment of rhythm.

On the whole one is bound to admit that though the sum total of information would enable the interested inquirer to read round the subject yet at the end he would still not know what African music is really like. One main failure has been the tendency to take too wide a view and to try to arrive at definite conclusions without that essential preliminary phase of examining at first-hand and in detail. Only when, by such detailed investigations, we have attuned ourselves to the mind and the method of the African when making his music, are we in a position to make generalizations. In short we have been writing round the subject without taking the one and only step which will lead to the heart of it. That this is so can be easily seen by the paucity of the available

---

[1] E. M. von Hornbostel, 'African Negro Music' in *Africa*—Journal of the International Institute of African Languages and Cultures, vol. i, No. 1, 1928. The 'up-beat' idea lingers on: see Richard A. Waterman, ' "Hot" Rhythm in Negro Music', *Journal of the American Musicological Society*, vol. i, No. 1, p. 4, 1943; M. G. M. Lane, 'Music of Tiv' in *Nigerian Field*, vol. xx, No. 4, Oct. 1955; Alan P. Merriam quoted in *Ethno-Musicology Newsletter*, No. 6, p. 6, Jan. 1956; and especially John Blacking, 'Some Notes on a Theory of African Rhythm advanced by Erich von Hornbostel', *African Music Society Journal*, vol i, No. 2, 1955.

transcriptions of the music and the obvious inaccuracy of most of them. Surely by now we should have produced a corpus of transcriptions which would enable a student to understand the principles and technique of African music; but we have not done so.[1]

It is obviously impossible for most musicians to go out to Africa and study the music direct from the Africans in their villages. What we need are reliable scores of African music so that all musicians may see what it is like. This is precisely what has not been available. One can find in the literature of African music short isolated extracts illustrating this or that feature and perhaps a few songs. The usual musical example one meets with is of the same type as those little extracts printed in any textbook on the theory of Western music.[2] In the case of Western music, the short extract is admissible and useful because it is taken from the corpus of the whole musical tradition in which all the readers themselves live. To commend African music to the musicians of the world we need some full scores so that people may study whole complete pieces of African music. That is one main purpose of this present book. We have set out to provide eight examples of some length which will show the development of a piece of African dance music from beginning to end. It is, as far as we know, the first attempt at such a project and it no doubt suffers from the limitations and deficiencies which are the lot of pioneer efforts. It is, at any rate, an honest attempt, albeit restricted inevitably to a small part of Africa, to answer the simple but fundamental question, 'When the African makes music, what exactly does he do?'

The task has been a formidable one entailing first the difficulties of apprehending and of correctly transcribing the music, and second, the difficulty of trying to explain this novel realm of music to the reader. Let us consider these two matters separately.

[1] Joseph Kyagambiddwa, *African Music from the Source of the Nile*, Frederick Praeger: New York. 1955. Contains over 100 pages of interesting transcription. It may well be very valuable: but as the song melodies are not related to the music of the accompaniment and as there is no time-line such as a hand-clap pattern, it is impossible to assess its rhythmic accuracy. We have the impression that the song music is too conditioned by the European approach to rhythm and time-signatures, though in the absence of concrete evidence we admit that we may be wrong.

[2] With this big difference: these short extracts of African music are usually transcripts of very simple music. The total picture they give is nothing less than a travesty of the real African musical system.

African music goes fairly fast judged by Western standards of tempo: the average speed of drumming is seven unit beats per second, that is, to put it in a more familiar form, the speed of a succession of quavers played at ♩ = 140. This would be manageable if African music was susceptible of our divisive system of regular time-bars, 3/8, 4/4 time and so on: but it is not. As we shall see later, the African approach to rhythm is largely additive, and so one is confronted with a series of rhythmic motifs of ever-changing time-length which can only be intelligibly set down in a series of bars of continually changing value. In view of this technique, the real and at first blush insuperable problem is to be able to find out at all, and to be positively sure of, just what it is that the African is playing. After more than a quarter of a century of experience our difficulties in comprehending the music are often still great: and they would have remained insuperable had it not been our good fortune to have realized early, that the only possible way to capture these rhythms was to devise some apparatus which would operate mechanically and give an objective and analytical record of what was played. In both these ways it differs from conventional recording on a gramophone or with a tape machine; with an ordinary recording you can neither measure the distance of one note from another, nor can you see unmistakably just how one rhythm or one instrument is played in its time-relation with another. Our own apparatus can write down on a moving strip of paper every beat made by each instrument at the instant they are made, thus providing the transcriber with an indisputable record and an objective means of discovering not only the rhythm of each contributing instrument but also the rhythmic relationship that exists between them. Commenting recently on this apparatus, W. Tegethoff writes,

Le moyen pour reproduire visuellement l'image acoustique est fourni par des machines à noter électro-mécaniques qui marquent simultanément chacun des instruments. Il devient ainsi possible de rendre graphiquement lisibles d'une manière scientifiquement exacte les polyrythmes les plus compliqués. Personne ne contestera que cette méthode montrée par Jones est apte à résoudre le problème central de la musique africaine. Mais combien pourront l'utiliser?[1]

The reply to this last sentence is that no one *will* be able to

[1] W. Tegethoff, M.S.C., in *Aequatoria*, vol. xviii, No. 1, pp. 26–28. Published at Coquilhatville, Congo Belge.

penetrate and to transcribe African music unless and until he has some such apparatus at his disposal.

There are other matters which have to be discovered besides the purely metrical one of discovering the rhythms themselves. There is, for instance, the musical pitch of each drum-beat. When Africans beat drums they play *tunes* on their drums. One of the features of the transcriptions in this book is the scoring of the drum music to show not only the rhythm but also the tune which the drummer is playing. This is something which has never been done before *in extenso*.

Perhaps the most intractable problem of all is that of the master drummer's free variations. The difficulties already mentioned rather pale into insignificance when compared with those connected with the accurate transcription of a set of free variations which are the spontaneous creation of the master drummer at the very moment he plays them and are as quickly forgotten. How we came to capture them will be explained when we deal with them in the chapter on the *Agbadza* dance.

So much for the drumming. There are difficulties also which are attendant on determining the rhythm of the song in a dance and its incidence *vis-à-vis* the other instruments: while such is the unity of African music with African social life, that all sorts of subsidiary questions concerning the social setting of the music have to be considered before the music as a whole can be said to have been mastered. There has been too much to do and there is in these scores too much material for us to have had time to draw out all the lessons they have to teach even if we knew them. The pioneer work is done: it remains to discover all that lies hidden in these scores.

The second type of difficulty before us is that of trying to set down in language intelligible to the uninitiated, what is necessary by way of enabling him to understand the full scores. When one has studied for a long time in a world so remote from the musical world of the West as that of Africa, and when one has at last learnt to think of this music from the African point of view, there is the danger of taking things for granted and of missing out essential pieces of information. There is so much to be said on each small point and it all needs saying at once because all is interdependent.

In the third place, there is no avoiding the fact that in order to describe the musical features of an African dance so that what is happening musically shall be intelligible, one has to plunge into minute detail: and this is bound to put a strain on the reader. Anyone who hopes for an easy passage through this book had better put it down. The musical scores cannot be grasped without close study of the text: nor will the text be intelligible without frequent reference, as indicated, to the full scores.

The title 'Studies in African Music' was chosen deliberately. Though the major part is concerned with drumming and dancing which is at once the centre and climax of African music in the very large area where drums are used, the book is not restricted to matters of rhythm. We shall have to pay attention to features of musical typology, to the relation between speech-tone and melody in singing, while we thought it was time that someone made an attempt to analyse the problems of good transcriptions so as to help towards the much-needed raising of the standard in the future.

The enormous area of Africa and the multiplicity of tribes each possessing their own musical idiosyncrasies presents the musicologist who wishes to apprehend African music as a whole with a task so stupendous that he is tempted to try to take the wide overall view based on the study of recordings from representative tribes all over the continent. Yet it is the intensive and limited research that we would stress. When a person can transcribe an African song or drumming *and is able to prove that he is right*, he is well on the way to understanding the music. Note the emphasis on transcription all through this chapter. Unless a person can account for every note he has heard he has no right to expect anyone to believe that he has heard correctly, and the only way of accounting for all the notes is to write them down. This is the sort of study we deem essential. It would appear to be far more likely to produce sound results than the rather naïve attempt to get at the heart of the music by trying to deduce its essence from the sum total of its manifestations. The latter course is analogous to an attempt to discover what a molecule is by a superficial review of the characteristics of all known chemicals without first having carried out exhaustive experiments on the nature and properties of one or two chosen samples.

In preparing the full scores we were faced with a problem as regards the scoring of the drums. With melodic instruments such as we use in the West, the score of course indicates the exact pitch of the notes required. There is no need to show *how* they are produced for that is inherent in the art of playing the instrument anyway. Provided we show what note is required, the competent player will be able to produce it. With African drums the situation is different. In the first place a drum does not give out a clearly defined note which the ear can easily recognize as being of definite pitch. At the same time one is clearly aware of the existence of a difference in pitch between one drum note and another, a difference which in the case of the Ewe master drum extends over more than an octave. It is not difficult with the aid of an oscillogram or with our tonometer to find the actual fundamentals of the notes used by the drummer and so be able to write the drum-notes on an ordinary musical score. But when that has been done, a lot of essential information is missing from the score which is necessary if anyone is to play from it. African drumbeats vary not only in pitch but also in quality. If the wrong quality of note is played in any particular African drum-pattern, that pattern is no longer what it is intended to be and becomes another pattern. So it is much more important in the case of drumming, to know which hand a performer used for any given note, and how he played that note, than is the case with Western music. The score should ideally show not only the rhythm and the pitch of the notes but also *how* each note was made. The converse is true: in order to be able to place the drum-notes on a musical stave at all, one had to find out three facts about every single drum-beat: first, which hand played it; second, in what position on the drum-skin it was played, and third, whether or no the other hand was also employed simultaneously in producing it and if so, in what way.

So a decision had to be taken. What exactly shall be the aim of the full scores? If they are to be playing-scores then *ipso facto* in the case of the drums, they will have to include so much material that the general lines of the music will tend to be obscured. On the full score, therefore, we have omitted on the drum-staves the indications as to how the notes are to be produced and have confined ourselves to representing their rhythm and pitch. At the same time we have included one feature which seemed to be necessary if we are to be able to discuss the rhythm-patterns. While we have numbered the bars of the top line of music for ease of reference, yet in a polyrhythmic musical system this is not enough in order to be able to refer to a given bar or section of one of the other instruments playing across it. We want some way of being able to talk about the drum-patterns in the text without continually having to print *ad hoc* sections of the music. The obvious solution was to print on the full score the nonsense syllables of the patterns, and this we have done. By a reference first to the bar number printed at the top of the score and then to the nonsense syllables, we can pin-point any particular part of a pattern for discussion.

Nowadays there are some enterprising Western musicians chiefly of the jazz school but none the less musical for that, who are showing a desire to try to play some of this African polyrhythmic music. It would be a pity to whet the appetite with a music book giving some complete examples of African ensemble playing, without making it possible for musicians to have a shot at it themselves. So, in addition to the full scores, a few playing-scores have also been printed. From these, together with the full scores, with a good deal of persevering practice, it should be possible for musical people to make a very fair show at reproducing the real genuine African music. We could have given playing-scores for all the music in the full scores. But to print it all again as a playing-score seemed to be unreasonable not only because of the repetition involved, but also because we believe most of it is too difficult to be mastered by Western executants however keen their ardour.

The author has lived for twenty-one years in Northern Rhodesia where he had close daily contact with at least six tribes. This is a suitable country for the study of African music not only because it is free from the influence of Arab music, and until recently has been largely free from the influence of the music of the West, but also because it is an area where drumming is much practised: for drumming is at once the most difficult and yet the best form in which to study the subject. All kinds of African music exhibit in one way or another its peculiar characteristics but in the full symphony of the dance with song and claps and drums we have it in its most developed and complete form. What was learnt in Northern Rhodesia had to be acquired when it was possible during the many activities of a missionary life. On returning to England we set to work at the School of Oriental and African

Studies to investigate some of the music of West Africa. For this purpose we had as assistant Mr. Desmond K. Tay, a skilled master drummer of the Ewe tribe in Ghana. A large part of this book is the result of the research done with Mr. Tay but it could not have been accomplished without the previous knowledge and experience.

In London we were, of course, studying African music under abnormal conditions: for instance it was not possible to assemble a complete orchestra for the drum ensembles. But there were compensating advantages. The ordinary village drummer is quite incapable of giving a rational explanation of what he is doing: and to be surrounded by several such people at once is not at all conducive to clear and accurate work. Mr. Tay was able to reply in a reasoned way to the questions put to him, and after he had become accustomed to research technique was able to approach his art in a critical frame of mind which yielded excellent results. A master drummer combines in himself the complete orchestra and can demonstrate what any one player has to play. From the point of view of the investigator it is a great advantage to be able to deal with one master mind. What then of the cross-rhythms? It is one thing to know what is the rhythm-pattern of each instrument: it is quite another to determine their exact metrical relationship. Here we had good fortune owing to a peculiarity of Ewe music—a peculiarity shared also by a large number of tribes in West Africa. This is the use of a bell in most dances, which sounds a standard recurring pattern right through the dance. Though it would be wrong from the African point of view to single it out as the prime instrument on which all the others depend, yet for the researcher it acts as a yard-stick. One can ascertain the rhythmic relationship which exists between the bell and each drum or other constituent of the music such as the clapping or the song, by playing each of them one by one with the bell.

The prime task is to ascertain the exact rhythm of each instrument. For this purpose our drum recorder was adapted for laboratory conditions. It was provided with two small wooden boards on which were fastened some metal plates. One board was for the bell-pattern, and one for the drum or clap or other instrument. The two operators had in each of their hands a brass pencil. By touching the metal plates with the pencils an electrical contact was obtained. This in turn operated the drum recorder so as to make a mark on a moving strip of paper. Only a little practice was needed to familiarize Mr. Tay with this procedure and he was soon able to tap on his metal plates with accuracy and facility the rhythms of the drums. The rhythm of each instrument was taken in turn. It was played simultaneously with the bell-pattern into the drum recorder and so, after some twenty seconds, we had on the paper strip an unimpeachable record of what had been played. This we then converted to the conventional notation of music. It was in this way that we reduced the intangible, evanescent, counterplay of rhythms in an African dance to an objective, stable, and visible form.

To rely solely on a machine in analysing African problems of this sort is to court disaster. It is so fatally easy to conceive of their things from our own point of view, in fact it is inevitable unless we can inquire what their attitude to any particular point really is. The machine is essential: but so is the living African. One must be able to question him about what he has played or sung at the time he performs it while the problems and the performance are fresh in mind, and successful transcription springs from this fruitful trilateral collaboration between the researcher, the machine, and the African musician.

When reducing the African culture to music on paper we shall not expect it to look quite like our own music. We shall not be able to draw bar-lines right down the score as is our Western custom. To do so would be to produce a score showing accents and rhythms which would be a travesty of what the African played. Unfortunately this is what we instinctively hanker after: we would like to go on using our usual technique and force the African music to fit into our preconceived frameworks: on these grounds some musicians may at first sight resent the scores we have written. But let us plead our case: what is a music-score intended to accomplish? If it is to enable the reader to reproduce mentally or actually the music of which it is a transcript, then we submit that some such devices as we have used to secure this end will, in the case of African music, be found to be inevitable. There is no radical novelty in the scores except the treatment of the bar-lines.

Two possible ways of expounding the general principles and practice of African music suggest themselves. One would be to try and draw up a sort of musical grammar, taking each point in isolation and gradually building up the whole cultus. This seems to be too artificial a method: it would entail divorcing the music from its setting, neglecting all subsidiary details so as to adhere to a rigid and logical grammatical framework. The other way is to present a series of songs and dances and related subjects arranged as far as possible in order of difficulty from the point of view of the person new to the subject and, taking them one by one, to give a fairly full account of their musical characteristics. This is the method adopted in this book. It entails, no doubt, a certain lack of orderly progression in working out the principles of the music: yet it seemed better to invite the co-operation of the reader in finding out all that each piece of music has to teach us, rather than to give him a prefabricated theoretical scheme.

One last point. As we begin our study, we invite the reader to lay aside his own musical concepts and to approach this novel territory with an open mind. If by the end, he has begun to look at African music from the African's own point of view, that will be our reward and his enrichment.

2

PLAY-SONGS AND FISHING SONGS

EWE TRIBE—GHANA

A GOOD starting-point for our study is to consider some children's play-songs, because here, as we should expect, we find the characteristic African traits occurring in their simplest form. Like their elders, African children love to turn any physical movement into song. So when we speak of play-songs, the emphasis is on the play. These are, for the most part, children's games to which they sing. The singing is an integral part of the game, it is not just a musical version of a game which might be played without the song.

We could, if we wished, consider the music only: but this would be a pity as we should be divorcing it from its context. To understand it properly, we want to know the circumstances in which it is sung. Besides, as we are discovering just what the African *does*, it is worth while providing the necessary information to enable those interested, to play the games themselves or to teach them to a class of children.

The subject-matter of the songs is typically African and differs from the sort of things English children would sing about. The sentiments are strongly social: these are not songs about fairies: they comment on life as the children know it. There are references to the circumstances of birth: to poverty: to animals: to their religious cults: to the lagoon round which they live, and even to 'boy friends': or the songs may just refer to the game being played.

Like nearly all African songs, these children's songs are not easy to translate. They are full of allusions and hidden meanings, in fact they could not be translated so as to give the real sense intended without the help of an African. Sometimes no doubt the children sing a word just because they like the sound of it, as for example the word *Alada* which is merely the name of a town: but this is exceptional.

Song 1. For girls

> Agbaga lém(u) loo,
> Be Todzie lém(u) loo,
> Wobe amuya lém(u) loo:
> Wobe ʋeya lem(u) loo amewo nalém,
> Mawu nakplɔm loo!

> The Agbaga River has caught me, O
> I say that the Todzie River has caught me, O
> They say the wind on the lagoon has caught me, O
> They say the ʋeya breeze has caught me, O—people should
>   rescue me:
> And may God guide me!

Line 3. The wind on the lagoon does in fact frequently capsize boats.

Movement

There is no game here: the song is the game. The children form a ring. The cantor starts the song and the chorus joins in. All clap their own hands with a slow stroking movement, moving their bodies too, but without shifting their ground.

The music

The song is extremely simple and sounds quite European because not only is it in common time throughout, but the claps fall on the first beat of each bar. This is the usual clap for this song, but Mr. Tay says it would be quite in order to shift all the claps one beat backward so that they all fall on the fourth beat of the bar, though this clap could not be beaten simultaneously with the one given.

The song is repeated any number of times and consists of ten claps. We purposely avoid saying ten bars because *it is the claps which are the time-backbone of the song*: the bars do not exist so far as the African is concerned—the author put them there to indicate the lilt of the song. If we look at the words on the music-score we see that the first three lines of the song (up to bar 6) are parallels: the song here consists of 3 groups of 2 claps each. The rest of the song is one phrase of 4 claps. The total for the song is 10 claps. In our experience of African musical phrases, 10 is a number which does not exist in its own right. African phrases are built up of the numbers 2 or 3, or their multiples: or of a combination of 2 and 3 or of the multiples of this combination. A phrase

of ten might consist of two sections *A* and *B*, *A* having two claps
and *B* having three, which is all repeated—(2+3)+(2+3) = 10.
In the song we are considering, the division is (2+2+2)+4 = 10.

The first half of our melody, besides feeling very 'European',
suggests a simple harmonic sequence. This we must resolutely
lay aside, for Ewe music is melodic and not harmonic in its structure. Play-songs are always in unison: harmony is normally re-
served for less light-hearted occasions, for the times when the
music-makers really mean business, that is for the dances. Even
then, we shall see later that the harmony springs from the melodic
line, and the latter is not conceived of as arising from a sequence
of chord progressions. The second half of the melody is more
naïve: we might have expected the song to finish on the tonic,
but it does not, and why should it? Instead, the whole of bars
7–10 are made up of a pretty play upon just two notes, C and A.

Finally we note that the song is in 'Call and Response' form,
though on repeats the chorus sings the whole of it. Most African
singing is built on this cantor and chorus basis though there are
a number of different ways in which the principle may be developed. The song we are studying has the form (*A*+*B*): (*A*+*B*),
where (*A*+*B*) is repeated *ad lib*.

Song 2. For boys

> Tɔmelo le Ee
> Gotalo le Ee
> Sukuviwo mifu du
> Gbasasrã, gbasasrã.

> The Water-crocodile, Oh!
> The Land-crocodile, Oh!
> School children, run away!
> Swiftly, swiftly.

Movement

The game is a musical version of circular tag as played in England. Whether it was borrowed from us, and set to a genuine
African song, or whether the game is indigenous, it is not possible to say: we incline to the former view.

The boys stand in a circle facing inwards, one of them acting,
to start with, as cantor, and all the rest forming the chorus. When
the chorus reaches the last syllable of the song, i.e. when they
sing -*srã* at the end of the repeat of the second half (see music-

score), the cantor hits the buttocks of the boy either on his right
or left, and himself dashes round the outside of the circle. The
boy who was hit runs round the opposite way. He who gets back
first stays in the circle. The late one walks round outside the circle
as cantor. He starts the song again, and at *-srã* he hits another
boy. Each successive late arriver acts as cantor.

The music

There is no clap to this song. It has been superimposed in the
music-score in order to indicate the underlying time. In fact, in
order to determine the exact time of the second half of the song
there had to be some regular beat against which to plot it. We
do not infer that the song was thereby forced into an artificial
framework. Mr. Tay merely put in the claps to show where they
would fall in relation to the song. The result is instructive. There
is nothing to comment on in the first half of the song, but the
second has something typically African. The word *gbasasrã* in
bar 7 carries the melodic rhythm ◡－－. In order to preserve this
rhythm and join it to the preceding word which is sung to a
crotchet, we in the West would obviously shorten the crotchet to
a dotted quaver with this result:

If one listens to the song being sung without claps its time
sounds very much like this and the casual observer would write
it in this way. Yet however many times the song is sung it will
always sound just off time in exactly the same way. Once the claps
are inserted the reason becomes clear. The African is not in the
least attempting to sing in strict 2/4 time as in the above example.
Question him and he will tell you the syllables of the song on
which the claps occur. This is the key to the successful unravelling
of the time-values of African songs. To transcribe the melody
itself is simple: but to assign exact time-values to each note, it is
absolutely essential to discover right away the syllables on which
a clap occurs. The African finds little difficulty in supplying this
information because it is the essence of his time-keeping. His
only difficulty is that it is so natural and unconscious for him to
beat time in this way, that he has to make a conscious effort to

analyse just exactly what he is doing automatically. Yet for the European listener it is often very difficult indeed to perceive just where the claps fall in the song-words. Once one has found exactly where they do fall, it will be noticed that however many times the song is repeated, whether at the very time, or a week or a year later, the claps will always fall in the identical places. Now as the claps never give way but preserve an inexorably steady beat, we see that it is the song which depends on the claps and not vice versa. True, any song can be sung—and sung in perfect time—whether there is clapping or not: but that is because in the case of songs which normally have a clap, the singer, if no one claps, will be making the claps mentally. Oddly enough, we do not think that the African himself realizes the vital place that the clap-pattern occupies in his music, though at the same time he would immediately spot a mistake in singing which caused the clap to fall in the wrong place. We know further, that he does not realize that the *number* of claps determines within fairly defined limits the length of the phrases of the song, and certainly he has no idea, if he is asked, how many claps there are in a complete song. It comes as an amusing surprise to him when it is pointed out that all unconsciously he obeys a definite rule in the total number of claps which make a complete verse, the rule which, as we have stated, is founded on the numbers 2 and 3. A whole song will consist of a multiple of two or three claps or clap-patterns, or of simple combinations of multiples of these numbers. It is quite extraordinary that these apparently free songs should be found to rest on such a strict mathematical foundation.

Let us return to the Europeanized musical example above. In reality it is essentially un-African. The African is not concerning himself with preserving a regularly recurring divisive rhythm to which the inherent stresses of the melody shall agree. True, where there is a regular clap, there is divisive rhythm: but the African, while strictly regarding it as a metrical background, is not in the least using it to indicate any accentual stress in the melody. The clap has no such influence on the melody at all. The latter is perfectly free to pursue its own course, with its own accents arising from its form, so long as it fits the total number of claps required to make the song feel complete. So in our song, in bar 7 and the first half of bar 8, the melodic accent and the incidence of the clap part company. At this point the melody becomes additive in its rhythm. The repeated word *gbasasrã* requires two bacchics: very well, let there be two bacchics. We just 'add' these rhythms to the preceding music. This will cause the first clap in bar 7 to fall on an unaccented melody note, and the first clap of bar 8 to fall right between the syllables. We shall meet with this feature again and again. It is part and parcel of the African musical system. The claps carry no accent whatever in the African mind. They serve as a yard-stick, a kind of metronome which exists behind the music. Once the clap has started you can never, on any pretext whatever, stretch or diminish the clap-values. They remain constant and *they do not impart any rhythm to the melody itself.* The rhythm of the melody is derived partly from the rhythm of the words as they would normally be spoken, and partly from the rhythm naturally produced by imitative sequences and, as in the West, by the whole build of the tune.

Obviously this way of singing presents problems to the transcriber. There is going to be one kind of bars for the claps and a varying bar-system for the melody so as to indicate where the melodic stresses lie. This we think is inevitable in dealing with additive music. The music printed in this book is set out on that principle. To help the eye still further, in cases where for example a single bar contains both a duple and a triple motif, intermediate bars of dotted lines have been drawn.

The particular device used by the African in bars 7 and 8 is of very frequent occurrence. When he wants to insert a triple motif into what would otherwise be a duple rhythm, normally he does not do what we should. He does not shorten the preceding note as we have done in the example above. He nearly always gives the triple motif, and the preceding duple time their full values regardless of what to us is the upsetting of an orderly time-sequence. To him a regular time-sequence in a melody would be banal. It is spice to the African to do just this very thing which makes the lilt of the music so difficult for us to catch. A little practice at singing bars 5 to 9, while beating out a tap of quaver value, will introduce the reader to this attitude to music. After a time one gets accustomed to it. The system makes for far more rhythmic variety than we normally use in Western music.

This delightful flexibility of rhythm is not the end of the matter. Bars 5–9 are also illustrative of another cardinal principle of African music. The melody being additive, and the claps being divisive, when put together they result in a combination of rhythms whose inherent stresses are *crossed*. This is of the very essence of African music: this is what the African is after. He wants to enjoy a conflict of rhythms. As this is a children's song it is a very simple example. In the whole of the first half of the song there is no conflict at all: but this is just an accident of the words and melody—they happen to fall in with the claps. The typically African part of the song is the second half where the cross-rhythms appear. The reader may finally be reminded that the claps are not used in practice in this song: but they provide a simple introduction to features which we shall later meet in far more complex form.

As can be seen by the phrasing on the score, together with the repeat of the second half, the song is in the form

$$(A+B)+(C+D)+(C+D).$$

The total number of claps is sixteen which is divided thus: $4+4+8 = 16$. In the score we have phrased the last eight claps according to the cantor and chorus divisions, that is, $3+5$. Looking at bars 7, 8, and 9, we can see that this latter group of five claps is susceptible of division into $3+2$ which is indicated not only by the rhythm of the tune which consists of the two bacchics, but also by the words: *gbasasrã* is sung twice, the first time to three claps, the second time to two. The complete analysis of the claps will thus be:

$$4+4+3+(3+2) = 16.$$

This again confirms the rule we have given both as to the number of claps per phrase and also as to the total claps in the song.

Song 3. A lullaby

Đevi mase nua ɖewo danɛ
Ʋlaya, ʋlaya, ɖewo danɛ.

A naughty child is usually rocked to and fro
Swing! swing! he is usually rocked to and fro.

Note. *Nua* is a bold, unbiddable infant.

Movement

Among the Ewe, people will do anything to stop the baby crying, and this lullaby is an example of what can be done. The father holds the baby either by its two arms or its two legs: the mother holds the opposite limbs, the baby facing upwards. They swing the baby slowly and alternately to the left and right in the following manner: first, swing to the left then, without pausing, swing to the right, and again without a pause swing to the left where they hold the baby for about two seconds: then to the right, then left, then right where they again pause for some two seconds. This is repeated as long as is desired.

The music

There is no melody and for that reason we have scored the song on an open stave. The words are merely spoken in a crooning manner. Such a simple performance would not appear to hold much for the musician yet it has at least three points of interest.

We see that on the score, the crooning is set to a definite time and rhythm. This is not just an approximation. The note-values we give are strictly adhered to. The time-signatures call for comment. The European listener would be inclined to think that the first half of the song is in 2/4 time, thus:

De - vi ma - se nua   de - wo da - ne

but if the meaning of the words be taken in conjunction with the rocking movement we find that the first two bars are in 3/4 time. This view is confirmed by bars 3 and 4 where the second half of the lullaby is clearly divided into two, of which the second piece, three crotchets in value, is a repetition of bar 2. One must constantly bear in mind that bar-lines are an importation into African music, used in order to show the lilt of the music as it is sung. This brings us to look at bar 3. Why complicate matters by introducing a 6/8 signature? Why not keep on with the 3/4 time right through the song? The answer is that this would make the rhythm in bar 3 sound as if it were syncopated, which it is not. It would further indicate that the rhythm of this bar would cross that of the rocking motion, which again, it does not. Further, the easy movement from 3/4 to 6/8 time is completely familiar to the African: we shall meet it frequently and as it is a definite factor in the construction of their music, it should be plainly indicated on the score. So the song consists of two bars of 3/4 time, one bar of 6/8 and one bar of 3/4. But that is only part of the truth for this is not the whole song. This introduces us to another rule of African music which we might call the Rule of Repeats. On the score, the first half of the song is repeated and is then followed by the second half which is performed three times in all. This complete performance makes *one unit*: this is the song and anything less is not the song. *The repeats within an African song are an integral part of it.* This principle has to be constantly remembered in determining the total length of a song. If it is neglected we may find ourselves presented with songs which apparently break the 'multiples of 2 and 3' rule. Thus it is quite wrong to say that this Song 3 is in $A+B$ form: it is, in fact, in the form

$$A+A+B+B+B.$$

Note that there are TWO of A and THREE of B: this is our first rule at work again.

The swings are scored in 6/8 time. Why not in common time as the actual rhythm of the swings is duple and has nothing triple about it? The obvious answer is that the incidence of the swings *vis-à-vis* the crooning demands that each swing should have a time-value of a dotted crotchet. This is true, but as it illustrates the 'Unit of Time' rule in African music, we will enlarge on the point. Normally speaking, African music is all built up on a basis of small equal time-units. The author reckons these as quavers which is quite arbitrary but produces a page of music reasonably easy to read. There are, however, two exceptions which will be dealt with when we meet them: they are the playing of 3 against 2 and of 3 against 4. In spite of these, to understand African music and especially the drumming, the broad principle must be accepted that, to put it succinctly, a quaver is always a quaver wherever it occurs in the score. This looks like a platitude; yet the vagaries of African rhythm even in a simple linear case like the time of a song are such as to prompt the use of a jumble of different basic time-values in a confusing medley which might lead the student to wonder if there really is any rhyme or reason in this music. It is not a platitude to insist that normally in African music all rhythms are compounded of notes whose value is a simple multiple of the basic unit of time, and that the whole complex structure rests on this simple mathematical basis.

Returning now to the score of Song 3 we review the rhythm of the swings *vis-à-vis* that of the words. The swing being duple, is going 2 against 3 of the words. If, in order to show this, one were to write out the crooning line using the conventional short triplet bracket in each bar, this would infer that the crooning line was behaving *abnormally*, departing from the standard unit of time. But it is not: the African would stoutly deny any such imputation. So the choice of 6/8 time for the swings is no caprice.

Song 4. For little boys and girls

> Ahiãvia yeye
> Tsoe da ɖe abatia dʒi nam loo
> Ahiãvia gbɔgbɔ, tsoe da ɖe abatia dʒi nam loo.

> My small lover, you are welcome:
> Put it on the bed for me:
> My small lover you are welcome, put it on the bed for me.

Line 2. 'It' refers to some cloth or perhaps a head kerchief which the boy says he has brought as a present.

Movement

All form a circle. One child acts as cantor and starts singing. At the word *yeye* all start clapping. At any time after the song has started, anyone who feels like dancing will leave his (or her) place in the ring and move into the area enclosed by it. They do this one at a time or two at a time and it is all done quite informally with no regard to a strict rotation: but there will not be more than two dancing at any one time. The pair or the person who has come out dances for about three repeats of the song and then dances out to their former place in the circle. Then another one or pair comes in to dance. When dancing, any step (e.g. *Gumbe*) may be used, but it must be done in a stylish way.

The music

Let us first look at the music of the song. It has one feature which should be noted. This is at the word *yeye*. The syncopation here occurs three times again, each time at the beginning of the bar and nowhere else, so that the syncopations are evenly spaced through the song.

There are two claps to this song and they are performed simultaneously, some children doing one and some the other without pre-arrangement. The first is a regular succession of claps of crotchet value. They have no accent and therefore from the point of view of listening, there is nothing to indicate that they should be grouped in bars. They just go on and on, all being of the same intensity.

If the second clap is performed by itself and without the song, it appears to be:

$$\frac{4}{4} \mid \, \downarrow \quad \downarrow \quad - \mid \, \downarrow \quad \downarrow \quad - \mid$$

but one feels that it is not quite this. Mr. Tay said that in order to get the rhythm of the second clap, the performer adds silently in his head some extra claps during the rests in his pattern, and mentally plays the following pattern in combination with clap 1:

Clap 1

Clap 2

What the second clapper is really thinking about and mentally producing is the resultant pattern emerging from the combination of the claps which is of course this:

If now, while *thinking* of this, in actual clapping he omits everything but the first two notes (which he ties) and the last note, he will be clapping a regularly recurring pattern which is this:

$2\frac{1}{2}$ *crotchets rest,* $2\frac{1}{2}$ *crotchets rest,*

and so on: and that is how the African thinks about it. Once the clappers have established this rhythm, it starts to exist in its own right as a pattern which has two claps then a pause, two claps then a pause and so on. The obvious way to bar this rhythm is to do what we have done on the score, and having done so, we find that this 4/4 barring also agrees with the accented notes of the melody. We also find that the syncopated clap falls each time on the syncopated melody notes.

Looking back at the example printed above, showing how the second clapper thinks of his pattern *vis-à-vis* the first clap, we see that he conceives of the first clap as existing in groups of four, i.e. in 4/4 time, and further, that the first clap of his phrase of two claps actually coincides with the last of the four claps of clap 1. Thus we have both claps in 4/4 time but the second clap's bars are continuously one crotchet ahead of those of clap 1. This is a true crossing of the rhythms, and by how ingenious a process of thought is it arrived at! Lastly, when we consider this simple example of cross-rhythms, and when we remember that the syncopated notes in the melody help the second clap to come in at the right places, we feel inclined to wonder if we have not here a charming example of how children in Africa are introduced to the cross-rhythms of their music.

The form analysis of the clapping is this: both patterns are played four times to each verse of the song, i.e. there are sixteen crotchets to the whole song: so we get $4+4+4+4 = 16$.

The song is in the simple form $A+B+C+D$, the whole of which is repeated *ad lib.*, and therefore the law of repeats does not operate in this case. That law applies to repeats within a song, and not to cases where the song is repeated in its entirety.

Song 5. For boys and girls: a play-dance

> Ta avɔ na legba, yiye
> Tamakloe hotsuitɔ neta vɔ na legba
> Legba le avi dʒi be avɔ la mesu ye-o, yiye.

> Clothe the idol: well done!
> The worthy Chief Tamakloe should clothe the idol
> The idol tearfully complains of insufficient clothing.

Line 2. Tamakloe is an actual chief, and is a member of a well-known family.

Movement

This is a play-dance for boys and girls up to the age of about fifteen years. Like all the play-songs it is performed in the evening by moonlight.

The children form a circle. One of them acts as cantor and starts the song: the rest sing the chorus. The song is repeated continuously throughout the dance. When the song is established, anyone (alone, or with a partner of either sex) enters the ring and dances for two or three verses and then retires to place. Someone else now comes in to dance, and this goes on similarly till all have had enough. There is no order of entry nor are the partners organized: it happens spontaneously.

For this dance there is no clap. Instead, a regular Ewe dance movement is used. It consists of a combination of foot-work and a regular movement of the shoulder-blades. The former is very

simple: the weight of the body is regularly transferred in a swinging movement from the right foot to the left and back again continuously, producing a slow steady treading sound. Everyone is
doing this right through the dance. The shoulder work is performed as follows. Both forearms are bent from the elbows in
a forward direction so that they are more or less parallel with the
ground: the palms face downwards, and both arms and hands
are relaxed and flabby. By an up and down movement of the forearms both working simultaneously, you alternately raise and lower
these flabby hands in such a way that at the same time you close
and open the shoulder-blades. It is this bringing together and
separating of the shoulder-blades which is the essential movement.
All this is done in strict time: the shoulder-blades are closed with
a sharp movement on each foot-beat, and are slowly opened during
the intervening time. Thus the shoulder-blades take the place of
a regular hand-clap. On the last word of the song and of its repeats, the shoulder-blade action is doubled in speed, so that on
this particular foot-beat the shoulders go—close, open, close,
open. On the two foot-beats following, the shoulders do nothing.
This is all set out on the music-score. Every time the song is
repeated, the same thing happens at the end of the verse.

The music

This cheerful and rather charming song is in a mixture of 6/8
and 3/4 time. We are not the first to observe that for some curious
reason, Africans do not appear to recognize the characteristic lilt
of 3/8 or 6/8 time and yet they frequently make use of it both in
song and in drumming.[1] In Northern Rhodesia, we found in
teaching Morris Dancing to Africans, that in spite of rigorous
measures to stop it, the dancers would in a matter of seconds
reduce a triple step to a duple one. They would insist on dancing
2 against 3 to the accordion accompaniment. Yet in a song of
this sort, the 6/8 pieces will be sung with a splendid triple swing.
It is all very puzzling.

As to the melody itself, we see that there is in bars 3 and 4 an
imitation of bars 1 and 2, and bar 7 is imitated at bar 9; the song
ends on the dominant, which makes a fine exhilarating finish for
a chorus.

    [1] W. E. Ward, 'Music in the Gold Coast', in *The Gold Coast Review*, vol. iii, No. 2,
1927.

The cantor only sings the first phrase: thereafter during all repeats, the chorus sings the whole song. How should we analyse its form? As the chorus sings it all we have not got the easy division provided by the alternation of cantor and chorus to help us. We could of course divide it as seems best to ourselves. But if we want to know the real division, we must find out how the African conceives of his own music. Mr. Tay says the song falls into the sections marked *a*, *b*, *c*, and *d* on the score. Section (*a*) looks as if it should really be two: Mr. Tay, however, says that if you take a breath in the middle where the chorus enters 'it makes it jump', which clearly indicates that in his mind the whole is one unit. He says that section (*c*) belongs to section (*b*) and that if you breathe between them you make a jump as in the case of subdividing section (*a*). So sections (*b*) and (*c*) are really one unit. This song is rather different from those we have studied because it does not divide naturally into clearly defined sections. We omit therefore to provide it with the usual formula. However, Mr. Tay's analysis gives the key to its metrical division, that is, the grouping of the foot-beats. Section (*a*) has 4 foot-beats, (*b*) has 3, (*c*) has 2, and (*d*) has 3. Thus the grouping of the foot-beats is: 4+(3+2)+3 = 12. Once again the rule of 2 and 3 is vindicated and this time by the African himself though we are certain he was thinking of the words and tune and not of the number of foot-beats when he made his analysis.

There are two foot-beats in silence after the song has finished and before it repeats. These have been counted as belonging to section (*d*). The rests between repeats are part of the length of the song and must always be included. The fact that Africans are very particular indeed as to the length of time (measured in claps, &c.) which elapses between repeats, shows that there must be something important here. Adding to this the observation that if one counts the total length of a song including the rests one gets a number which follows a clear rule, and if the rests are not counted the lengths of songs would seem to be arbitrary, we have a fair case for insisting that the rests are part of the song.

Let us now review the relationship between the rhythm of the melody and the incidence of the foot-beats. In bars 5–9 the melody is partly 3/4 and partly 6/8 but nevertheless its accents coincide with the foot-beats so that the first beat of the melody-bar falls on the first beat of a foot-beat bar. The case is very different in bars 1–4. Here, while the melody is all in 6/8 time, its accents are staggered with the foot-beats so that the foot-beat falls on the sixth beat of each melody-bar. This is a typical African cross-rhythm. The critic might say that we have mistaken the accent in the melody here and that obviously the bar-lines should go right down the score including the melody. But that is quite impossible. The melody as sung by the African has a clear rollicking 6/8 time as we have written it. There is no avoiding the fact of the cross-rhythms. So now we have the first half of the song in cross-rhythm and the second half with no cross-rhythm. How is this brought about? For the answer we look at bar 9 and the first note of bar 10. Here is something interesting. The last note of bar 9 and the first note of bar 10 make a triple motif. We in the West would deal with this situation by writing either

Not so the African. If he wants a triple motif he just uses it, compounding his music of varying combinations of a standard unit of time. The effect of doing this is to establish at the end of bars 5–9 which have no cross-rhythm, the cross-rhythm which will be needed for bars 1–4. It also secures that the word *yiye* in bar 10, which is a repeat of the same word in bar 4 and has almost the same tune shall, like the latter, be staggered with the foot-beat. So the whole song which at first sight appears to be irregular turns out to be a simple, consistent, and well-balanced piece of music.

Song 6. For little boys and girls

> *Verse* 1. Abaye loo, Abaye, Kunu bayee
> Aya ḍu gbe
> Abaye nefui 'ta', fui 'ta', Alada!
> Gidigo gidigo, Alada!

> *Verse* 2. Bentsye bentsye
> Akumanu bentsye bentsye
> Akumanu ȝoga ȝoga.

> 1. Oh, Miss Abaye, Abaye the daughter of Kunu
> There is a poverty which drives one to eating grass
> Abaye, beat 'TA', beat 'TA', Allada!
> Ting, ting, Allada!

2. This is not in Ewe, and Mr. Tay could not translate it.

Line 3. 'TA' is onomatapoeic for the sound of clapping.
   Allada is the name of a town on the railway, north of Whydah in Dahomey.
   Used here probably because the children like the sound of the word.
Line 4. *Gidigo*: onomatapoeic for the sound of a bicycle bell and used here by
   analogy for the sound of the hand-claps.

Movement

This is a hand-patting game for small children up to say eleven years of age and of either sex, though girls are more fond of it than boys.

All stand in a circle with the sexes mixed anyhow. The hands are held out sideways, left palm facing up, right palm downwards, so that one's left palm is below the right palm of the child to one's left and vice versa on one's right side. In bars 1–7 you stroke your partners' hands with a soft sliding action on the six dotted minims marked *P* on the score. Both left and right hands of all players are making the stroking movement. At bar 8 they start clapping thus:

(*a*) left palm facing up claps partner's right palm facing down;
(*b*) clap your own hands together in front of you;
(*c*) right palm facing up claps partner's left palm facing down;
(*d*) clap your own hands together in front of you.

This is repeated, and then verse 2 is sung. The clap-line in the score shows that the action in verse 2 is more difficult than in verse 1. The quick movements of bars 8–13 are continued from bar 14 to bar 25. In bars 26–30, instead of clapping one's partner's hand, one hits the right elbow on his left palm. This section is repeated.

The object of the game is to find the champion. It is all repeated again and again and the tempo of bars 7 to the end is increased till someone makes a mistake. He stands out and so on till only two are left. They perform the championship round facing each other.

The music

Turning to the music-score we look first at the clap-line in verse 1. The reason why the signature 3/4 is necessary is, of course, because if one takes the quaver as the basic unit of time and one writes the melody of the song on this basis, it is found that a clap

occurs after every third crotchet. Now the time of the song in
the first verse is very tricky, and the widely spaced claps in bars
1–7 are too far apart to enable the transcriber to be certain of the
melody-note values. We therefore asked Mr. Tay to use a quicker
clap (which was perfectly easy and natural to him) so as to have
more fixed points as guides. He clapped in crotchets. These are
inserted in the score though it must be understood that they do
not belong to the game and are never used, and are only placed
on the score to show how it is possible to arrive at a correct
transcription of the melody as we shall see in a moment.

The clap-line in verse 2 follows the rhythm of the latter half
of verse 1, the only difference being the use of the elbow in bars
26–30. We can now see the rather interesting layout of the song.
It starts with six bars of slow claps, followed by a sentence consisting of a short clap-pattern played twice. This sentence is repeated. Going on to verse 2, we find the same short clap-pattern
played 4 times and then a modification of it played twice to form
a complete sentence, which sentence is then repeated. So the song
is in the numerical form:

$$\text{Verse 1.} \quad 6+(2+2)+(2+2)=14$$
$$\text{„} \quad 2. \quad 4\times2+(2+2)+(2+2)=16$$

Both verses follow the rule of 2 and 3. Verse 1's total of 14 which
at first looks peculiar, turns out to be a perfectly regular combination of 6 with sets of 2.

We now look at the melody. There are several points of interest. In bars 1 and 2, the word *Abaye* which, in speaking, has
a stress on the second syllable, is arranged so that this stressed
syllable -*ba*- coincides with a clap; this happens twice. But in bar 3,
the word *bayee* which is still the same word minus its initial vowel,
falls so that its stressed syllable -*ba*- is off-beat with the clap. The
result is that we have a bar of five quavers in bar 2, and a bar of
seven quavers in bar 3. This cannot be avoided if the scoring of
the melody is to indicate how the African actually sings it: but
it shows the African love of a cross-accent. Coming to bars 4 and
5 we find the time changes to an unmistakable 3/8. Two 3/8 bars
make one 3/4 bar but were we to continue in 3/4 time the score
would indicate a syncopation on the words *Aya ɖu-* which simply
does not exist. These words are sung in a *forceful* triple time.

The next point to note is a melodic one; it occurs in bars 7 and 8. The last two notes of bar 7 and the first note of bar 8, give us a tritone fourth from B to F. This is in our experience most unusual in Africa. Every time Mr. Tay sang this song, the tritone fourth was there. Looking at the whole melody of both verses 1 and 2, it would be natural to conclude that the song starts on the dominant and that it should have been written in the key of F major. This sort of thing often happens in transcribing African songs. They appear to be in a diatonic major scale, starting possibly on the dominant and ending on the tonic: but careful study of the details not infrequently shows that the song actually starts on the tonic and finishes on the subdominant. Here is a case in point. The presence of B♮ seems to indicate that the note C is not the dominant but is actually the root or tonic of the melody. This melody ranges from C, a diatonic fourth upwards to F and a diatonic fifth downwards to the F below. Confirmation is provided by the B♮ in bar 1. Instead of being an accidental grace note, which would be possible in Africa, though unusual right at the start of a song, it now appears as a regular and essential melody note. The B♮ occurs also in bar 12.

From bar 8 onwards to the end of the verse, the melody changes to a strong duple rhythm yet even this contains a typically African twist to avoid its monotony. This 'twist' is sung twice, and occurs between bars 9 and 10, and between bars 12 and 13. The word *Alada* as spoken, has an accent on the middle syllable. It would be natural therefore, to expect that the syllable -*la*- would fall on the clap, thus:

Clap

fui   'TA',   A - la - da,

But however many times we tried this passage, the clap did NOT fall on *A-L'A-da*, but between the -*la*- and -*da*. This might have been an (unlikely) inaccuracy on Mr. Tay's part. Here is a case which shows the value of the technique of trying the melody against a different clap. When Mr. Tay used the crotchet clap (clap 2 on score), there was a clap *after* the first syllable *A*- but *before* -*la*-; and again a clap very near to, but just after the final syllable -*da*. Now in such a case one has to remember that in

African music the problem, however apparently difficult, will turn out to have a solution which is perfectly simple and in accord with the general principles of African practice observed in countless other and less recondite examples. The solution we have adopted accounts for all the phenomena, and it is so typically African. It turns out to be merely the use of short triplets, a fairly common African device in melody. The difficulty was only caused by the fact that the last note of the first triplet and the first note of the second are ties.

In verse 2 we have a completely duple melody sung against a triple clap. But this emphatically is not a case of playing 3 against 2. The unit of time in both clap and song being the same, the combination results in the overlapping of bar-times, which coincide at the beginning of each repeat of the clap-pattern. It all goes perfectly naturally in performance and there is, as we know by having taken part, no sense of clash, except during the word *Akumanu*. This duple-rhythm word is accompanied each time it occurs, with a clap which falls on what in speech appears to be a very unaccented syllable.

Lastly, the build of the song, as distinct from that of the claps, is: (v. 1) $A+B+B$; (v. 2) $(C+C)+(D+D)+(D+D)$. This is not a call and response song: the whole of it is sung by all.

Song 7. For little boys and girls

> Yɔe nam(a) yɔe nam(a) KOTE
> Miyɔe
> KOTE nɔ yiyim ale, KOTE nɔ yiyima
> Nɔvia KOLE hekploe ɖo,
> Wòbe nuwɔnue le yewɔm—MIYƆE!

Call $\begin{cases} \text{him} \\ \text{her} \end{cases}$ for me, call (any name as e.g.) KOTE
Call him (her)!
KOTE walks like this
His relative KOLE has followed him (sc. joined him)
And he says he is still in need—Call him!

Line 4. 'His relative.' If there is no relative present they substitute 'his friend'.

Movement

Here is a little children's play-song for learning who your relations are. This is an important social matter. Anthropologists have dealt in detail with the subject of 'joking relationships'. The writer has given a musical example in a previous publication.[1] The position is that in African society there are certain relations with whom you are entitled by custom to be on friendly terms (joking relationships), even if they are your seniors, and others whom you treat with great respect even if they are your juniors. Again in African society there are strict laws of marriage in respect of kindred and affinity. The first step in becoming a socially educated African is obviously to learn who your relations actually are. That is the point of this game.

The children form a ring, one child acting as cantor and the rest as chorus. The cantor calls one child by name (e.g. *Kote*). While the cantor repeats this line, Kote goes to the centre of the circle, and walks about in a stylish way which the rest of the children imitate. The cantor, in line 4, calls out the name of one of Kote's relatives (e.g. Kole) who then joins Kote and walks up and down with him. At the end of the song, these two retreat to their places, and another pair is called out in a similar way; and so on.

The music

On the score, for convenience of reference, it is the song-bars which are numbered and not the clap-bars. Reviewing the melody as a whole we find it undistinguished, in fact rather dull, but yet it is well balanced and closely knit: for example, the rhythm of bar 1 is repeated on different notes in bar 2 and extended in bar 3. The sequence of the two dotted quavers on A and B in bars 3 and 7 reappears in quaver form in bar 9. The whole phrase of bars 9 and 10 is answered in rhythmic imitation in bars 11 and 12, while the melody of bars 9 to 13a is well answered by bars 13b to the end; they begin by repeating the rhythmic formula of bar 9 (two quavers and a crotchet) and repeat this motif in the middle of bar 15.

When, however, we look at the time and the melody as a whole, and better still, sing it, it gives the impression of being in free rhythm. Yet it is not: it is inexorably governed by the claps which *ipso facto* reveal that it must be really in strict time. True, there are many songs to which it is not possible to clap: these are real

[1] A. M. Jones, *The Icila Dance*, pub. by the African Music Society, P.O. Box 138, Roodepoort, S. Africa.

free-rhythm songs. But normally, and wherever there is dancing, the song has to express this love of freedom within the limits of an underlying metrical pattern such as is provided by hand-claps or any other metrical accompaniment. The song we are studying is sung *legato* and ambles along in a pleasing undulating way which quite belies the fact that it is compounded of definite but varying rhythmic motifs set in irregular juxtaposition.

The form of the song, if we counted the chorus's spoken exclamation as a separate section as indeed it is, will be

$$(A+B)+(A+B)+(C+B).$$

Looking now at the clap-line on the score, the question at once arises 'Why is the first clap phrased so that it apparently belongs to the last clap of all in bar 18?' The reasons are two: first of all, because Mr. Tay said it belongs to the last clap, and secondly, because the following analysis confirms that it must. In practice there is no hint at all given by the African that the claps fall into phrases: he just claps steadily on. But if we want to arrive at the inner structure of the song we shall find it expedient to relate the claps to the words of which they are the background. The first line of the song plus its answering chorus, if one omits the preceding clap in bar 1, has three claps. The second line likewise has three claps which fall in the same relative positions *vis-à-vis* the words. The third line says the same thought twice, but the second statement is extended in the melody to make one sentence with the fourth line. To show the musical division it should be set out thus:

> KOTE nɔ yiyim ale
> KOTE nɔ yiyima, nɔvia KOLE hekploe ɖo.

This gives us two claps for the first of these two lines, and three claps for the second. The concluding line of the song has three claps, and *then there is a solitary clap on the rest in bar* 18. What is this clap doing? By all we know of African music it cannot stand in isolation: and it does not, for together with the first clap (in bar 1) which is also on a rest, it forms a group of two. This is why Mr. Tay said the first clap belongs to the last one. The whole structure of the song becomes clear when set out thus:

$$(3+3)+(2+3+3+2)=16$$

Perhaps more than any of the previous songs this one shows

the independence of the melody rhythm from any sort of accent induced by the claps. They just go on regularly in the background to keep the music in time, and all the accents are produced by the melody and words which mutually interact just as in plain-song, though one is inclined to feel that the rhythmic accentuation of the melody has the upper hand.

Song 8. For boys

> Nane do ŋku ḍa—fiḍo!
> Baba ḍui wotso ka—fiḍo!
> Kpatsi, kpatsi eka—fiḍo!

Something is peeping (*sc.* there's a *hole in the fence*)—Peep-bo!
Maybe white ants have eaten it—Peep-bo!
Place a stick, and get a rope (*sc.* to repair the hole)—Peep-bo!

As with most songs,[1] this song has a hidden meaning. In this case it is a perfectly simple one. The song is about a fence which has a hole in it and needs to be repaired.

Movement

This is a memory-testing song for boys and is of the eliminating type which ends in finding the champion. The boys make a circle with one of them acting as cantor, standing in the centre of it. He adjusts his position so that he can keep an eye on everybody so as to spot any defaulter. He starts the song and the boys respond '*Fiḍo*' at the right points. At the end of the song the cantor alone says '*EVIM*' while the rest merely make a humming *soto voce* grunt. The object of the game is to try and trip the boys so that they inadvertently say '*Fiḍo*' where they should grunt at '*EVIM*'. To this end the cantor may, if he wishes, suddenly decide to omit the first line altogether, thus reducing the number of times '*Fiḍo*' has to be repeated before the grunt. As can be seen from the repeat marks on the score, this is quite a tricky little song. While the first and second lines are both repeated, making four '*Fiḍo*'s' in all, the third line is not and has only one of them. As the song is repeated any number of times, someone is sure to make a mistake, causes a burst of laughter and is out. They go on till the winner is found.

---

[1] Mr. Tay once said that his people want at all costs to avoid singing *directly*. 'They always want to sing in parables.'

The music

This song is not actually sung but is rather spoken in a sing-song fashion. In spite of this it is performed strictly to time. There is no clap or any other accompaniment to the song and so, when Mr. Tay first sang it, there was no way, other than guessing, to find out the exact length of each melody note. Now guessing will not do: accordingly we asked Mr. Tay to provide two check-rhythms against which to measure the time-values. One check-rhythm was a steady clap, the other was a standard bell-pattern which we shall meet with again and again when we come to the dances. These form no part of the song and are never performed with it. If the eye is run up and down the score it will be seen that either the clap-beats or the bell-beats fall mostly on syllables, the remainder of which falling mid-way between bell-notes are easy to assess. We have taken the trouble to demonstrate all this because of its value to anyone who wishes to transcribe African music. One simply cannot transcribe irregular time-values *in vacuo*. There *must* be a *regular* counter-rhythm against which to measure them, and this counter-rhythm must be supplied by the African. If the transcriber attempts to beat time himself he will get hopelessly lost owing not only to the subtlety of African additive music but also to the absolute exactness of his time-keeping. When we Europeans imagine we are beating strict time the African will merely smile at the 'roughness' of our beating. One might object to this procedure that it forces a free song un-naturally into a metrical mould. In this case, however, it is not so. For Mr. Tay said that while for this song there is no ostensible clap, yet it is built on such a time-basis and in singing it you 'hear the time in your mind'.

Let us look at the score. Were it not for the accentuations in the melody falling as they do, it is quite easy for a European to clap to this tune. The reader is invited to try clapping and singing: first, accenting every melody note which coincides with a clap and then, accenting the melody as indicated in the score. When he succeeds in doing the latter exercise with facility he will ex-perience that curious sensation of being able to sing in the African way, with an awareness of two separate but interdependent rhythms.

The song is in the form $(A+A)+(B+B)+(C+C)$.

We next observe the bell-pattern *vis-à-vis* the song. We see that the song does not start at the beginning of the bell-pattern, it starts three quavers later; and we see also that the song does not end on the last note of the bell-pattern phrase, but on the first note. We merely make mention of this phenomenon now: we shall later, when dealing with the bell-pattern, see the reason for this way of ending a verse: but as the claps usually go to the bell-pattern in a dance, it can now be understood why we have barred the claps in groups of four, with the song starting on the second and not the first clap of a group.

The metrical form of this song is extremely simple. If we look at the words, together with their claps we see that counting repeats, the claps are grouped thus:

$$4+4+4+4+4+4=24$$

This concludes the review of children's songs. Right from their tender years, African children become familiarized through their play with this fascinating music. It is an interesting reflection whether or not we Westerners, had we been surrounded by the same music in childhood, would be able to assimilate their cross-rhythms so as to perform them with that grace and facile ease which are so delightful to watch in Africa.

FISHING SONGS

Song 1. Sprat-catching song—for lagoons only

> Miḍo ka ḍa, miḍo ka ḍa
> Kpaviawo naḍo ba, E akpagãwo naḍo ba
> Miḍo ka ḍa, miḍo ka ḍa-ee
> Kpaviawo naḍo ba, E akpagãwo naḍo ba

Give space for the rope (*sc.* do not follow it too closely)
So that the *small* sprats will sleep in the mud; yes, so that the
   big sprats will sleep in the mud
Give space for the rope
So that the *small* sprats will sleep in the mud; yes, so that the
   big sprats will sleep in the mud.

The occasion for the song

The song is used for sprat-catching on the edge of the lagoon (cf. Song 2 which is for sea-going craft). Often on Saturdays, young folk—schoolboys and girls, &c.—when the water in the lagoon is at low tide, will go all day on a sprat-catching expedition.

For this purpose a special rope is required. Being about ¾ inch in diameter it will be from 50 to 100 yards long; it is bought second-hand by a party of boys from European or African fish-net owners and it is these boys who organize the expedition. Palm branches are cut down, split down the main rib into two fronds, and these fronds are tied one behind the other along the rope which thus becomes a long sweep. In its completed state it is called *Tekali*. With one boy at each end, the rope is dragged along in the lagoon where the water is about 9 inches deep. The rest of the party, carrying baskets, spread out behind the rope and follow it, but not so closely as to spoil the chances of a catch. The sprats in the water take cover from the rope by digging their heads in the mud and can be caught by hand. The boys keep some of the fish for their mothers and sell the rest, making anything from 3 to 10 shillings each in a day's fishing. To lighten the toil while following the rope they sing this song.

The music

This song has no rhythmic accompaniment at all, but yet it is sung in strict time. In order to plot the time-value of the notes, Mr. Tay was asked to sing the song to the standard bell- (Gankogui) pattern and also to clap to it.

Looking at the score, we see that the song is mostly in triple time with two duple bars and one 5/8 bar. These three bars are instructive. They all occur at the end of a line of the song. In Western music, in singing a song of this type, when we reach the end of the lines we can do one of two things. We can go on rather breathlessly and unmusically in strict time with no break at all: or we can pause between each line to give some relaxation. These pauses of ours having no fixed time-value depend on the aesthetic sense of the singers. In African music, except for purely free-rhythm songs, the use of a *fermata* is impossible. It would upset the claps: it never happens. Nevertheless the African being just as musical as we are, instinctively feels where relaxation is required. With this in mind, the reason for the duple bars 5 and 16, and the 5/8 bar 12 is clear. It seems to be the African way of prolonging the triple rhythm where he needs a pause and yet preserving the strictly metrical structure of the whole song. The remarkable feature of this technique is that he does not thereby lose sight of the main accents of his song. Look at bar 2: the first syllable of *Miɖo* is sung to the second clap of the 4-clap bar. When the cantor repeats this line in bar 13, the first syllable of *Miɖo* falls in precisely the same place *vis-à-vis* the clap. The same happens with the entry of the chorus. In bar 6 it enters on the quaver-note of the bell-pattern; on its re-entry in bar 17, it comes in on exactly the same bell-note. This all tends to show how closely knit these songs are: they are anything but primitive. Yet they are certainly very far from being sophisticated. They are the folk-product of a musical aesthetic which has a highly developed sense of time.

This song shares a feature in common with Song 8 of the children's songs: it is the way in which the song starts and ends with reference to the bell. The whole song occupies six bell-patterns and therefore, theoretically, if it were written so as to start simultaneously with the start of the bell-pattern it would end at the end of the sixth bell-pattern. This would be so tidy but it cannot be right, because Mr. Tay performs it as written on the score. The point to notice in both these songs is that the song *ends* on the bell-beat which *begins* the bell-phrase. There is no doubt that the proper END of a phrase or a piece of music is of importance and significance at least to Ewe musicians.[1]

This feature occurs not only at the end of our song: it can be seen at the end of the chorus phrases (bars 12 and 1) and at the mid-point in these phrases (bars 8 and 9): and the cantor's lines both seem to work towards the low bell-note (bars 5 and 16).

In bar 8 we encounter the first indication of Ewe harmony. The note F with its inverted tail is a harmony note, the melody descending to C. This matter will be dealt with in the chapter on African harmony.

There remains only to find the form of the song and its metrical divisions. It is of the call and response type and in this case the response is the same both times it is sung. The response itself is subdivided, both words and tune being nearly identical in both halves (bars 6–8 and bars 9–12, duplicated in bars 17–19 and 20–24 (= 1). So we get the form

$$A+(B+B')+C+(B+B').$$

---

[1] This is of course a masculine ending if you reckon the whole of the bell-pattern to form one bar. But merely to dub a phenomenon with a name does nothing to explain it. We have failed to find any full discussion of the aesthetic, psychological, or physiological *raison d'être* of the rhythmic endings used in Western music.

To find the metrical structure we look at the song-phrases and count the claps which accompany them. What shall be the principle of counting at bar 6? Shall we count the previous clap as belonging to the phrase of bars 6–8 or to the previous phrase? This is a case of *experentia docet*. When one is familiar with the metrical build of songs there is little difficulty. The answer here is that the previous clap (occurring on the last quaver of bar 5), belongs to bars 6–8. Look at the syllable *kpa-* in bar 6, immediately preceded by a clap: now look at bars 9 and 10, at the syllable *akpa*, where the *kpa-* is also immediately preceded by a clap. There is your parallelism and there is the clue to the division of the claps. Starting from the beginning of the song, we thus get the following numerical division, measured in claps:

$$\left\{ \begin{array}{cccc} \text{Cantor} & \text{Chorus} & \text{Cantor} & \text{Chorus} \\ 4 & + (4+4) + & 4 & + (4+4) = 24 \end{array} \right.$$

Song 2. Paddle song

> Yevuḍɔ nenye nù maḍu, Sogã (kpa, kpa,)
> Nenye avɔ mata, Sogã (kpa, kpa).

> The European fish-net should be food for me, Sogã
> (rhythm noises)
> Should be a cloth for me to wear, Sogã
> (rhythm noises).

Occasion for the song

This and the two following songs are sung by adults. The song is used in connexion with fishing where a surf-boat and a seine-net are used. To make clear the text of this and the following song we must describe the net and the process. A long rope is needed such that when the net is fixed to the middle of it, there will be a long strand of rope at each end which can be fixed on shore. The main net, which is a long one, is attached along its upper edge to the rope and hangs down below it. It has a fairly coarse mesh and is called *Agu*. Fixed along the centre portion of the bottom edge of this net and hanging down below it is another net with a fine mesh: this is called *Ðɔvoku*. Attached to the rope and at the sides of the net are sticks, with buoys attached at each end to keep the net afloat. These are called *Kpoti*. To set the net the whole apparatus—rope and net—is piled on shore near the water and one end of the rope is tied to a tree or other firm anchor.

The other end of the rope is given to a boy stationed in the prow of a surf-boat. Besides this boy, who must be a good swimmer, there are in the boat the paddlers and the steersman who, armed with a special long paddle, stands in the stern and usually acts as cantor for the song. The surf-boat goes out, the rope and then the net paying out as far as they will go. Then the boy in the prow, taking the end of the rope, jumps in and swims ashore and hands it to people there who fasten it to a coconut tree or some such object. Meanwhile the surf-boat returns to shore and there they wait for anything up to an hour, the time depending on the state of the tide. Our song is sung by the surf-boat crew as they are setting the net.

There are two ways of paddling a surf-boat. It can be done either by the synchronous or by the alternate paddling of port and starboard paddles. On the score we have marked the paddle-strokes for synchronous paddling. The song can equally well be used for alternate paddling: in this case the paddle-strokes will be doubled in number and would thus be scored as dotted crotchets. It does not matter, as far as the song goes, whether in this case you start with a port or a starboard stroke.

As the paddle-strokes on the score are few and far between, we adopted our usual technique for fixing the note-values. Mr. Tay sang the song to the accompaniment of the bell. This is marked on the score but of course is not actually used. In this song the paddle-strokes take the place of hand-clapping.

The song is sung in this way: a cantor starts off and the verse is sung in call and response as on the score. At the end and without any pause, the cantor repeats only his second line (end of bar 5 and bar 6) and the chorus replies. He keeps on repeating this section as long as he likes. When he gets tired of so doing he suddenly reverts to bar 1 and the song is sung right through, followed again by as many repeats of the second half as the cantor desires. We thus get the form A+B+[C+B repeated *ad lib.*]. The melody is a very jolly tune. It really consists of only two phrases, each of which though started by the cantor is completed by the chorus. These two phrases are separated by what is, musically speaking, merely a long rest, though in practice it is broken by the words *kpa, kpa*. These words are not really part of the song proper: they are exclamatory rhythmic noises sung on the note C, to keep the rhythm going during the rests. While looking at the melody we notice the presence of harmony in bar 7: once again it is a fourth, the melody descending to C and the fourth superposed. We also observe the sharing of the time between 3/8 and 3/4. The singing is so smooth and easy that it is only when one puts the music on paper that this change of rhythm reveals its exact nature.

Let us now review the relation of paddle-strokes to melody. The best points to look at are the end of bars 4 and 7. Here we see that the melodic accent is one quaver late on the paddle-stroke. To make the situation clearer, let us imagine that the paddlers are using the alternate port and starboard method. This will give an extra paddle-stroke between each of those marked on the score. If these are pencilled in we can see at once that the accents of the whole song are consistently one quaver late on the paddle-rhythm. So here we have a true cross-rhythm, both voices being essentially in 3/8 time with the bar-lines of one voice moved consistently one quaver to the right. This throws into prominence the significance of the words *kpa, kpa*. In the silence after the chorus there is an off-beat swish of the paddles, followed immediately by the reassertion of the rhythm of the song by singing *kpa, kpa*: it is a thrilling little piece of cross accents.

The metrical form of the song is reckoned by the paddle-strokes. The first half (as far as *Soga*) carries two strokes: this is followed by the rest (punctuated by *kpa, kpa*) and the second half of the song, all of which is again covered by two paddle-strokes. These latter strokes with their accompanying singing are repeated *ad lib.* This gives:

$$2+(2+2+2\ldots ad\ lib.)$$

The total length is indefinable but the song still follows the rule of 2 and 3.

Song 3. *Hauling in the fish-net*

> Alăgawo gbɔna solăgawo gbɔna da
> Kliya kliya alăgawo gbɔna.

The fish are coming, the fish are coming from afar
They are coming all higgledy-piggledy.

Line 1. *Alăga* is the name given to a man or woman, usually a member of a religious cult, who has been offended. The sense of being offended strikes deep in these people. This person is likely to leave his house, put leaves on his body

and twigs of leaves on his head and live in the bush till the offender is caught.
In the song, the fish are likened to this person, and so in this context *Aläga*
means 'fish'.

Line 2, *Kliya* is the ragged condition of the dress of an *aläga*: hence 'raggedly',
'higgledy-piggledy'.

Occasion for the song

The fish-net has been put out during Song 2. After a suitable
interval, the fishermen assemble in two parties one at each end of
the rope and lay hold on it in preparation for hauling in. When
the leader, who acts as cantor, sees that all are ready he starts the
operation with the following yell:

Cantor.	DZOBOE:	*Chorus.*	HEE
„	WOYIE AHOBA:	„	AHOOBA
	Get ready:		O.K.!
	Heave ho!		HEAVE!

The cantor then starts the song, during the singing of which the
fishermen pull backwards, moving their feet in time to the song.
They keep on repeating the song till the net is hauled in.

The music

In scoring the melody we have put it in 3/4 time. This time is
not at first apparent if we look at bars 1, 2, and part of 3: but if
one sings the chorus, the 3/4 time is unmistakable, and the rest
of the song is found to follow suit. Corroboration is found in
that the word *gbɔna* in bars 2, 3, 7, and 1, each time falls at the
beginning of the bar. It is a jolly song with a very singable chorus
whose strength lies in the syncopation in bar 4.

The form of the song is clearly indicated both by the melody
itself and by the divisions between cantor and chorus. It is this:

$$(A+B)+(A+B').$$

We look now at the foot-beats. The feet fall on every third
quaver of the song and as the feet go alternately left, right, . . .,
and so on, it is natural to bar them in 6/8 time. What of their
relation with the song-rhythm? It is seen clearest in bars 2, 4, 6,
and 8. The first beat of the bar of the 6/8 foot-beat time falls in
the *middle* of the 3/4 song-bars. This might be objected to as
arbitrary, for the feet are going steadily without accent and there

is apparently nothing to indicate this barring. It is to a certain extent arbitrary but the barring is linked with the phrasing of the foot-beats. There are sixteen of them in the song and our own inclination was to phrase them in four sets of four: but Mr. Tay disliked this. If you do it this way, then the foot-beat in bar 3 becomes the first beat of the second group of four beats, being anticipatory to the word *Kliya* in the chorus. Mr. Tay said that, on the contrary, this foot-beat belongs to the previous word. In view of this it seemed that the phrasing should be two groups of eight foot-beats. Mr. Tay, however, maintains that the proper phrasing is that given. This all shows how impossible it is for a European to arrive at the truth by relying on his own judgement. In actual fact therefore, the metrical build up is:

$$(2+3+3)+(2+3+3) = 8+8 = 16$$

To return to the question of barring. Whatever way you bar it, whether in 6/8 or 3/8 or a combination of 6/8 and 9/8 the fact remains that the feet are moving against the song continuously in the relation of 2 against 3. This is a cross-rhythm familiar to us of the West, though whereas we use it as an exceptional device, in Africa it is part and parcel of their musical vocabulary. To beat 3 against 2 is to them no different whatever from beating on the first beat of each bar. In fact, to illustrate to an inquirer the rhythm of a triple piece of music, Africans will as often as not accompany it, not as we would, by beating on every third beat, but by playing 2 against 3.

Song 4. Fish-collecting song

> Anipaye loo!
>   Nyemanɔ kpotia nu, hee!
> Anipaye loo!
>   Nye ŋutɔ manɔ kpotia nu lã yi vo gɔme.

> (Name of a fish) ho!
> I shall stand by the buoys, ho! ho!
> (Name of a fish) ho!
> I myself will stand by the buoys, the fish
>   will go to the fine mesh.

Note. The fine mesh (see Song 2) is in the centre of the seine-net. The buoys are at the ends of the net.

Occasion for the song

This song follows the completion of the hauling in which is done during Song 3. When the net reaches the shore, most of the fish will have collected at the middle of the net where the net is wide and the lower mesh is fine, but some are caught by their gills in the sides of the main net. The people pull them out and toss them into baskets. There is of course all the excitement of a catch, which expresses itself in this song, sung while the fish are being collected. Part of the operation is to shake the net and it is the regular net-shaking which forms the time-background of the song.

The music

The melody has a wistful and satisfied air about it as much as to say, 'Well, that is the end of a good fishing'. Its time is irregular, being a mixture of duple and triple time, and yet with a little practice one will find it goes perfectly smoothly and rhythmically. This sort of song shows how unnecessary it is to use a divisive rhythm of regular bars in order to make a rhythmically satisfying melody. Once one becomes accustomed to the additive attitude, a divisive rhythm tends to feel puerile and banal.[1]

The melody is characterized by the frequent use of the quaver and crotchet motif seen in bar 2, which occurs again in bars 3, 5, 6, 10, 11, and 15, and gives homogeneity to the shape of the song. The only other feature calling for comment is the presence of an accidental B♮ in bar 7. As B♭ nowhere appears in the tune, should it not have been written in key C, thus starting and ending on the subdominant? This would have been possible and entirely African and it may indeed be correct. But another factor in African melody has to be taken into consideration before a judgement is made. Normally, the African does not sing accidentals: but there are one or two exceptions. The most frequent is this: in a tune which by its notes shows itself plainly to be, say, in the key of F major, there will often occur the sequence Dominant—sharpened Subdominant—Dominant. The sharpened subdominant in our experience never occurs except in this combination. It is this very sequence which is seen in bars 7 and 8. As B♭ does not appear in the melody, we have no means of knowing whether the song in

---

[1] For the terms 'divisive' and 'additive' see Curt Sachs, *Rhythm and Tempo*, pp. 24 and 25.

the African mind belongs to the category which contains an accidental or not. He is not himself aware of this organization of scales and keys. So it really does not matter in this case whether we write the song in key C or key F.

The phrase-form of the song is obviously $A+B+C+D$, following the cantor and chorus sections. When we look for the relation between the net-shaking beats and the song-rhythm, what are we to say? As the song's bars are so irregular, there can hardly be a consistent relationship. But a study of the score will show one interesting fact which is that of all the fifteen organic accents of the melody, i.e. the notes at the beginning of each bar, not a single one coincides with a net-shaking beat. Once again and this time in a slightly different form, we see the African's intuitive desire to stagger the beats. It cannot be accidental: with such a closely knit tune, there must be definite design here. Suppose now, we were to imagine the time of the net-shaking to be speeded up so that there were double the number of net-shakes: again not a single net-shake would land on an accented melody note. We may conclude that this off-beat singing is a definite feature of the song. It provides two sets of rhythms to enjoy, each independent and complete in itself and yet linked intimately with the other. This is of the essence of African polyrhythm.

Lastly, we consider the phrasing of the net-shakes. This was not done so as to make the phrases correspond to the cantor and chorus sections. They are Mr. Tay's own phrasing. The technique of discovering this phrasing, which is a fact of his music quite novel to the African when pointed out to him, and yet which he recognizes quite easily as being present, is to ask him either where you can 'break' the net-shaking or clapping, or else to ask which net-shakes belong to which words. Were one to seek the metrical build of the song from the melody itself, one would never arrive at the true answer. So, following Mr. Tay's own analysis and taking the call with its response to form a natural larger unit within the song, we find the song is in the metrical form

$$(2+2)+(2+4) = 10.$$

* * * * *

This fairly detailed study of songs both for children and adults, both for play and work, has brought to light many of the distinctive features of African music. Without this close attention to detail they probably would have escaped us. There remains to summarize what has been extracted from them.

FEATURES OF AFRICAN MUSIC

1. Songs appear to be in free rhythm but most of them have a fixed time-background.
2. The rule of 2 and 3 in the metrical build of songs.
3. Nearly all rhythms which are used in combination are made from simple aggregates of a basic time-unit. A quaver is always a quaver.
4. The claps or other time-background impart no accent whatever to the song.
5. African melodies are additive: their time-background is divisive.
6. The principle of cross-rhythms.
7. The rests within and at the end of a song before repeats are an integral part of it.
8. Repeats are an integral part of the song: they result in many variations of the call and response form (see summary).
9. The call and response type of song is usual in Africa.
10. African melodies are diatonic: the major exception being the sequence dominant—sharpened subdominant—dominant.
11. Short triplets are occasionally used.
12. The teleological trend: many African songs lean towards the *ends* of the lines: it is at the ends where they are likely to coincide with their time-background.
13. Absence of the *fermata*.

SUMMARY OF THE PHRASE-FORMS

Play-songs:
1. $A+B$: ($A+B$ repeated *ad lib.*)
2. $(A+B)+(C+D)+(C+D)$
3. $(A+A)+(B+B+B)$
4. $A+B+C+D$
5. Indivisible
6. $\begin{cases} \text{v. 1. } A+(B+B) \\ \text{v. 2. } (C+C)+(D+D)+(D+D) \end{cases}$
7. $(A+B)+(A+B)+(C+B)$
8. $(A+A)+(B+B)+(C+C')$

Fishing songs: 1. $A+(B+B')+C+(B+B')$
2. $A+B+(C+B$ repeated *ad lib.*)
3. $(A+B)+(A+B')$
4. $A+B+C+D$

SUMMARY OF METRICAL FORMS

Play-songs: 1. $(2+2+2)+4 = 10$
2. $4+4+3+(3+2) = 16$
3. $(1+1)+(1+1+1) = 5$
4. $4+4+4+4 = 16$
5. $4+(3+2)+3 = 12$
6. $\begin{cases} \text{v. 1. } 6+(2+2)+(2+2) = 14 \\ \text{v. 2. } 4\times2+(2+2)+(2+2) = 16 \end{cases}$
7. $(3+3)+(2+3+3+2) = 16$
8. $4+4+4+4+4+4 = 24$

Fishing songs: 1. $4+(4+4)+4+(4+4) = 24$
2. $2+(2+2+2 \ldots ad\ lib.)$
3. $(2+3+3)+(2+3+3) = 16$
4. $(2+2)+(2+4) = 10$

3

THE INSTRUMENTS OF THE ORCHESTRA

EWE TRIBE—GHANA

THE norm of African music is the full ensemble of the dance: all other forms of music are secondary. If an African wants to explain his music to the outsider, it is the full dance which he will take as his example. If the drums are beating but there is no singing or dancing Africans will think 'there is nothing happening': so too, if there is music and the performers 'really mean business' it is essential to have the full ensemble. This consists of the instruments of the orchestra, the hand-clapping, the song, and the dance. All these four ingredients combine to form the central act of African music-making, the equivalent of our Western symphonies. In the performance of the full dance with singing and drumming we have the flower of African musical genius, the highest manifestation of his art, and the most spontaneously creative expression of the soul of music within him. We have nothing like this in the West: the nearest equivalent would probably be a very expert and free jazz dance. What exactly happens will become clear when we deal with the music of their dances: but first of all we must review the orchestra itself. For this purpose we take the practice of the Ewe tribe again. Details differ quite a lot from tribe to tribe: different tribes may use different instruments: some use more drums than others, some may not even use them at all. The latter are exceptional, taking Africa as a whole. Yet beneath all this diversity, is a unity of attitude to the dance and what is true for the Ewe is, by and large, the same for a large part of the African continent.

The Ewe orchestra consists of three sections: these are the background-rhythm section, then the drum section, and lastly the claps and song. In this chapter we are chiefly concerned with the first two, though some consideration of the claps and song cannot be avoided. Plate 2 gives us a general picture of the orchestral instruments together with Mr. Tay in the official costume of a master drummer. Notice the drums with their appropriate drum-sticks, and in the front, the background-rhythm section. Standing in the centre foreground is the double bell, called *Gankogui* by the Ewe but popularly spoken of by Europeans as the gong-gong, with its playing-stick lying in front of it. On either side are two rattles, called *Axatse*: and right in front are two special high-pitched gongs called *Atoke*, each having its playing-rod made of iron. We will deal first with the *Gankogui*.

THE BACKGROUND-RHYTHM SECTION

With the Ewe, the *Gankogui* is the foundation, *par excellence*, of the background-rhythm section. The best ones are made of iron smelted in the traditional African way: this gives the best tone. The *Gankogui* is a double clapperless bell, the two bells welded at the top to form a tine by which to hold it. It is not cast but is beaten into shape. The two notes it gives vary from instrument to instrument. The two which we used gave respectively an octave and a minor third, i.e.

1st Gankogui   2nd Gankogui

As we shall see in the *Adzida* dance, for the right effect it is necessary that the pitch of several *Gankoguiwo* when used in combination should be different. The instrument is played with a wooden stick, of which the best are made from the solid branches of the *Eklï* or the *Exe* trees. It gives two clear notes in which the upper partials are surprisingly inaudible. It produces a purer tone than an ordinary Western cast bell. The *Gankogui*, with its stick and the method of holding and playing it is illustrated in Plate 3.

If you want a *Gankogui* it *is* possible to buy one in the market: but if you would have a really good one you go to the blacksmith. He will ask what dance it is for: he will like to know if it is to accompany the songs of a well-known composer, and if so, who. He will then know the suitable tuning. He will show you several instruments: you will choose one you like and he will then make one which sounds just the same.

In the *Hatsyiatsya* or songs which precede certain club dances, sometimes as many as sixteen gong-gongs will be used, but in the main dance there will be only one or two. If there is a funeral procession for a member of a religious cult, maybe four or six gong-gongs will be used.

Each musical member of a cult will probably have his own *Gankogui*. If it has a poor sound and spoils the ensemble he will be asked to stop playing: but members like to possess a clear-sounding instrument.

Normally the *Gankogui* plays steadily and continuously right through a dance. It provides a background rhythm which keeps the whole orchestra in time. Not that the *Gankogui* player is in any way responsible for the actual tempo of the dance. This is the responsibility of the master drummer. If the *Gankogui* is too slow or too fast, the latter will indicate by his beating, the time required and the *Gankogui* will come into line: but apart from this, the *Gankogui* goes on inexorably with neither *accelerando* nor *rallentando* unless the special circumstances of the dance require it.

What *Gankogui* plays is a rhythm-pattern and not a succession of regular beats. There are several of these patterns whose length lies from 8 to 12 quavers. The pattern is repeated over and over again. In studying the drumming of the Ewe it is absolutely essential right at the start to determine with exactitude the rhythm of the *Gankogui*: on this will depend the accuracy of the whole music-score. It is by no means easy to determine an irregular rhythm of this sort played *in vacuo*, and it is worth while considering the matter so as to show how the truth may be arrived at. Each of *Gankogui's* several patterns is used for a specific dance. One, however, is used much more than the others: it figures in most of the dances in the score-book, and for this reason Mr. Tay calls it the Standard Pattern. It is this:

Gankogui

Clap

Resultant

GO-dzi GO-GO·dzi GO - dzi   GO-dzi.

In this example the top line represents what we hear on the bell but which we cannot at first transcribe with certainty. We ask Mr. Tay: he says that you can clap to this bell-pattern and that his people have a jingle of nonsense syllables as reminders of the rhythm. When the African hears the bell together with the clap, he also hears a new pattern emerging from the combination of the two. The reader will see that there are a number of possible resultant patterns depending on where one starts the pattern *vis-à-vis* the bell. We in the West would hear the resultant as co-terminus with the bell, i.e. as:

in which the claps reinforce the first beat of each bar and the resultant pattern itself starts on the first beat of the bell-pattern. Not so the African. He hears the resultant as *ending* on the first beat of the gong-gong and therefore as starting on the gong-gong's second note. The rhythm of what he hears together with its nonsense syllables is the third line in the above example. Surely this is a remarkable insight into the African musical mind. Here is the instinctive tendency to think in terms of polyrhythms and here also is a prime example of a feature noted in Chapter 2, namely the tendency for a second pattern (or song) to regard the first note of the background pattern as the place to end on rather than to start on. The nonsense syllables indicate both patterns. It can be seen from the example that the syllable *-dzi* is used for the four hand-claps, and the syllable *GO-* for the bell. Where the bell and the clap coincide, the syllable used is that of the clap. The jingle when spoken by itself is always said in the rhythm we have allotted to it.

This use of a metal bell to lay a foundation-rhythm is wide-spread in West Africa: it is absent from Rhodesia[1] and, as far as our experience goes, from South Africa: a useful piece of research for someone would be to map out its incidence.

From this consideration of the exact plotting of the bell-pattern there emerges a valuable lesson for students. Some people try to arrive at the answer to an irregular pattern by tapping out on the table, while it is played, a continuous succession of small units of time which they imagine are the basis of the time-values of the

---

[1] But the Bemba in N. Rhodesia sometimes chink iron axe-blades together instead of hand-clapping.

pattern. They get a positive answer all right, though almost always it is the wrong one. If you already know the basic time-unit of a pattern, this technique may be useful in clearing up minor difficulties within it: but it is useless to try to discover the basis of an irregular pattern by a series of guesses which, in the nature of the case, are derived from Western ideas of music. When faced with a new rhythm-pattern, the way to find out exactly what it is, is to ask the African to play a steady regular counter-rhythm with it. He can usually do this with his foot. Once we have the two rhythms going simultaneously, it is possible to count the total number of quavers in the irregular pattern and to determine its exact time-values. Without such help one is almost certain to go astray.

The *Gankogui* is usually accompanied by the *Axatse*, which is a rattle. The rattle-patterns are always coterminus with and derived from those of the gong-gong, though they are not usually identical. This slight dissimilarity arises from the technique of playing. In the *Husago* dance the bell and rattle are the same: in the *Sovu* dance they are nearly the same: in the *Nyayito* dance there is more apparent dissimilarity. The *Axatse*, with its method of playing, is seen in Plate 4. It consists of a calabash which, through a small hole in the stem, has been cleaned of its contents. A net of about 1-inch mesh, made of a beautifully flexible and green-coloured native string is woven loosely over the calabash:[1] in doing this, short lengths of bamboo about $\frac{1}{2}$ inch in diameter and $\frac{3}{4}$ inch long, or cylindrical beads of European origin are threaded on the strings of either the left diagonals of the net or the right, but not on both. If the rattle is shaken it gives an intense clattering sound of high pitch. The method of playing is this: the player though not always, is usually seated, and we shall take this posture as the standard. He hooks the first finger of his right hand in the net so as to gather up sufficient slack to make the rattle give a clear, crisp response when in use. He holds his left hand about 18 inches above the left side of his lap. The rattle is played by hitting it either downwards on to the leg, or upwards against the left hand which co-operates by descending slightly to meet the rising rattle. The downward stroke produces a low slightly muffled sound: the upstroke sounds crisp and high. The apparent difference in pitch is at least a fifth, which is the arbitrary

[1] The dye is made from the leaves of the *Detifu Ti* (cotton tree) or the cactus.

interval used on the music-score. A glance at the music-score of the *Sogba* dance, where the standard *Gankogui* and *Axatse* patterns are used, will show what the rattle really does. The rattle-player duplicates the bell-pattern by his downstrokes, and fills in the pattern with a number of upstrokes played in between. When both are played together it is a delightful combination. Both instruments having a tonal quality so different from drums can be heard distinctly when the whole orchestra is playing, even when the big drum is *fortissimo*: they are also tonally quite distinct from the sounds of the claps and the vocal music. Their timbre is excellently chosen for the part they play of giving out their background rhythms.

We should end our description of the background-rhythm section at this point because these are the only two instruments normally used for it. There is, however, another gong-like instrument called *Atoke*, shown at the foot of Plate 2 and, as held in play, on Plate 5, which might as well be dealt with here, though it is actually used, not with the full orchestra, but as a background rhythm to the *Hatsyiatsya* songs which precede the main drumming in some club dances. The *Atoke* is a small boat-shaped instrument made of iron beaten to shape and the length of one's hand and wrist. It is couched on the hand, which is slightly hollowed to hold it steady and yet so as not to let the fingers touch the sides. If this happened, the vibrations would be damped. The desired sound is a very high rather thin and slightly metallic ringing note. This is produced by striking one of the top edges of the *Atoke* with a metal rod some 6 inches long and a ¼ inch in diameter, held lightly between the thumb and first finger of the other hand. This rod has an eye at its upper end to which is fastened a piece of string, which in turn is tied on to the *Atoke* (see Plate 5) so as to guard against loss. Like the *Gankogui*, the *Atoke* is not tuned to a definite note and when several are used together they must be of differing pitch so that the pattern of each may be clearly heard. The notes of the two *Atokewo* we used in research were:

1st Atoke   2nd Atoke

The notes in brackets are also heard: in both cases they are nearly as powerful as the note we give for the fundamental. In an ensemble the higher *Atoke* is usually the one which plays the standard pattern, whatever that may be, and the lower one plays a contrasted variant.

The drums

The drums are the most important section of the orchestra: they form its main body. Plate 2 shows five drums: the drum on the extreme left called *Klodzie* or *Kloboto* is used for special dances and does not immediately concern us. The other four are the normal drum section for a dance, and their playing figures in all the dance-scores we have given. Their names from left to right are *Sogo*, *Atsimevu*, *Kidi*, and *Kagaŋ*. *Atsimevu* is the master drum: the other and lesser drums are collectively called *Asiwui*. It is probable that all these drums were at one time carved (as *Klodzie* and *Kagaŋ* still are) from a solid tree-trunk. In the *Yeve* cult, the *Atsimevu* drum is still always carved from the solid: the barrel type is used in the *Adzida* dance and can be used for *Nyayito* (funeral dance), though for the latter a carved one is usually employed. The southern Ewe living on the edge of a lagoon have doubtless learned the art of the cooper through their contact perhaps for several centuries with Western shipping. They have made ingenious use of their skill for it is easier to make a drum from planks than to carve from the solid tree. The joints in these barrel drums are well made, and must be if the drum is to have any resonance. The iron hoops are not welded, but lapped over. *Sogo* and *Kidi* are closed at the bottom with a wooden floor just as with European barrels. *Atsimevu* is open at the bottom and so are *Kagaŋ* and *Klodzie*. The bottom of *Sogo* is covered with wood but it may have a hole and a cork through which to wet the inside as described below. *Atsimevu* is about 5 feet high and 1 ft. 9 in. in maximum diameter: the sizes of the others can be judged from this by reference to Plate 2. The drums are painted in bright colours: ours are blue with transverse red bands. In all cases the drum-skin is fixed in the same way. It is made from the hide of the *Avugbe* or *Adzoki*, the former being the Red-flanked Duiker: the skin has to be thin but tough. The edge of the skin is rolled over a hoop of wood, circular in section and of a diameter just larger than the top of the drum. The skin is fixed to the hoop by sewing with thick home-made twine: European twine is not strong enough. This twine also serves to fix the skin to the drum and therefore it has a series of double loops hanging down all round. Through these loops pass the drum-pegs which have a notch near their head to catch the string. They sit in holes bored in the side of the drum and are held by friction only. As the method of tuning is similar for all drums we give the details for tuning *Atsimevu* only.

There are two stages in tuning—wetting, and the tuning proper.

(a) Wetting

Stand the drum upside down and pour in about two tumblers of water and leave for two minutes to soak the under side of the drum-skin. Then put the drum on its side and roll it about to wet the peg-holes and swell the joints tight. Now stand the drum upright and wet the top of the drum-skin and leave for three or four minutes as one cannot start tuning straight away.

This wetting is only done before a performance. If, during play, the drum needs retuning, you omit the wetting process.

(b) Tuning

First you hit the rim of the drum-skin gently and with a pressing motion, using an axe-handle or suitable stick, exercising great care to avoid hitting the skin itself. The object is to bed the skin firmly down. The best way is to keep turning the drum towards you so as to impart equal force every time you hit. With the same stick you now tap the heads of the pegs in order, testing the pitch of the drum-skin and its ability to produce the various notes required. This tuning is done with meticulous care and judgement.

The order of tuning the drums is this: first tune *Atsimevu* the master drum: then tune *Sogo* from *Atsimevu*: then *Kidi* from *Sogo*, and finally tune *Kagaŋ* from all the previous three. *Atsimevu* is the deepest drum: *Sogo* must sound fairly low but it must be higher than the master: to test it you play a pattern on the master drum and then its reply on *Sogo* and judge if the reply 'sounds right'. *Kidi* is about a fifth above the master, *Kagaŋ* is the highest of all. Mr. Tay says if it is too high and in play 'covers' the other drums it is bad and must be lowered: but if it is too low it is bad—it must be 'just medium'.

What the exact factors are which determine the tuning is a difficult matter to find out. What exactly is the African listening to? Certainly it is not a case of absolute pitch. We made four attacks on this problem over an interval of nine months and, while we cannot claim to have got to the bottom of the whole matter, the general features are these. On each occasion Mr Tay tuned *Atsimevu* entirely *in vacuo* to within less than a tone of C = 128. On two occasions his tuning was identical. So there appears to be a fairly fixed idea for the best pitch for a particular master drum. He said that when *Atsimevu* is used it *must* be the lowest drum, overshadowing all the others by its fullness and volume and by its rise and fall. If you tune it too high 'it sounds like hitting a packing-case' and loses its characteristic timbre. He was insistent that it must be tuned so that its notes rise and fall very clearly. He was also fairly consistent with *Kidi*. Each time, he tuned it about a fifth higher than the master. He actually ranged between a fourth and a fifth. The tunings were recorded on one occasion by oscillograms and on the others on our Tonometer, so what we have said is not based on guess-work. His tuning of *Sogo* varied: at no time was it higher than *Kidi* but it seemed that he wanted it to lie between the master and the latter. *Kagaŋ* was consistently tuned higher than the others but varied in pitch from about a minor sixth to a minor seventh above *Atsimevu*. Taking into consideration the difficulty of hearing a definite pitch on a drum, the scheme of tuning is consistent.

In some dances *Atsimevu* is not used, its place as master drum being taken by *Sogo*. The only dance in the music-score book in which this happens is *Agbadza*. When *Sogo* is used as master, the orchestra has to be retuned. *Sogo* itself has to be lowered in pitch, but not so low as *Atsimevu* normally is. *Kidi* is tuned lower in agreement with *Sogo*. *Kagaŋ* may remain as it was unless at that pitch it overshadows the others: in which case its pitch must be lowered.

The length, thickness, and hardness of the sticks is most important. Mention has already been made of the particular trees used.[1] The choice is made because the branches of these trees are hard and solid, and have no hole running up the centre. The sticks for *Kagaŋ* are about 22 inches long and $\frac{1}{4}$ inch in diameter, and have a slight whip. Those for the other drums are about half this length and their thickness varies from about $\frac{3}{8}$ inch for *Kidi* to about $\frac{3}{4}$ inch for *Atsimevu*. The *Atsimevu* sticks cannot be used on

[1] p. 52.

Sogo nor vice versa: they would give the wrong quality of note. Similarly *Sogo*'s sticks cannot be used on *Kagaŋ*. Mr. Tay demonstrated this: the *Kagaŋ* notes were not free and full-toned when it was played with *Sogo* sticks, and the same was true of *Sogo* played with *Kagaŋ* sticks. These sticks, rough as they appear, are nevertheless most carefully chosen. Unlike some tribes, the Ewe use perfectly straight ones. On one occasion we noticed Mr. Tay when playing on *Kidi*, reverse his stick. He explained that one of the *Kidi* sticks was broken and he was obliged to use a *Sogo* stick and was experimenting to find the lightest end so as to get *Kidi* to 'speak properly'.

The 'hold' of the stick is important. Plate 6 shows Mr. Tay holding an *Atsimevu* stick: the hold for the others is similar. This hold is dictated by two factors: first, that the stick while able to bounce, must be under delicate and instantaneous control: and second, that as drumming is rapid, the arms must be spared unnecessary action to avoid fatigue. The stick is grasped by the thumb and first finger which act as pivots on which it can swing. The remaining fingers are bent round towards, but not closed on, the palm. For free beats, they remain in this position, but for muting or at any time when pressure is needed, they close in and press the stick to the palm. They are constantly at work controlling the stick during play.

During a dance all the drummers except the *Atsimevu* player, are seated on stools or forms. In the case of *Sogo* and *Kidi* (see Plate 8) the legs are parted and the drum is placed between and in front of them. It has no hole at the bottom and therefore stands upright on the ground. *Kagaŋ* has a hole at the bottom and therefore needs to be tipped up to let the vibrations out. This is done by gripping it with the knees as in Plate 7 (note the long thin *Kagaŋ* sticks, and the characteristic stick-hold of the left hand. A good player plays from the wrist and not from the elbow: it is much more subtle). The *Atsimevu* drum needs a special stand. As it is open at the bottom and also owing to its length it must be canted. This is done by means of a simple and functional stand called *Uudetsi*. It is made of wood and looks something like the figure on page 61. It can be placed at any convenient angle to bring the head of the drum to a convenient height for playing.

This is a good place to mention the *Klodzie* drum (on the left in Plate 2). It is used in the *Atsiagbeko* dance (a figure dance) and is hooked by two loops of skin protruding from the drum-skin, on to one of the horns of the forked *Atsimevu* stand: the player sits to play it. Alternately, in the absence of a stand, *Klodzie* may be played in the same way as *Kagaŋ*.

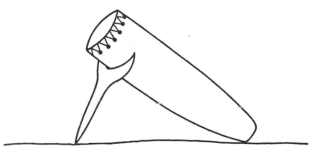

Returning to *Atsimevu*, we see the method of playing in Plate 9. For the purpose of the photo we used a makeshift stand. *Atsimevu* is played either with a stick in both hands or with a stick in the right hand and with the bare left hand (this for a right-handed player), according to the quality and pitch of the notes required.

The notes of the drums

It might be thought by the onlooker, when the drums are in full play, that apart from the master drum which is manifestly a special case, the other drummers are sounding their patterns by just hitting the drum-skin. They are not. They are producing rhythmic *tunes* on their drums. Let us take the drums in order starting with *Kagaŋ*, the treble drum. You can do three things with your drum-sticks. You can hit either stick on the drum so that it bounces off at once. This we shall call a *Free* beat. You can strike the skin (with either stick) and hold the stick down thereby muting the note, making what we shall call a *Muted* beat. With *Kagaŋ* this sounds a minor third above the free beat. Or you can place one stick on the drum without striking it, so as to mute it and while doing this, strike a free beat with the other stick. We shall call this a *Secondary muted* beat. On *Kagaŋ* this sounds about a fourth higher than a free beat.

Though *Kidi* is also played with two sticks it has a more extended range of notes. Essentially the player has the same three choices, free, muted, or secondary muted beats. But he can produce other notes by the amount of pressure exerted in muting or secondary muting. This is fundamental to drum technique: variations in pressure and striking force, variations in the actual manner of striking, all enlarge the drum's vocabulary. Thus *Kidi* has two muted notes. One is for playing *Waiting beats* which are unessential beats inserted in his pattern or between the repeats of it. This note sounds a minor third below the free beat. Yet in most cases, during pattern playing, *Kidi*'s muted beat sounds a major third higher than the free beat. Like *Kagaŋ*, his secondary muted beat is a fourth above the free beat. In between the free and the upper muted beats is a slightly muted one, about a tone above the free beat, which is identified by the nonsense syllable *Kriŋ*. He has, further, two special beats. One called *Dza*, is made by hitting a firmly pressed muted beat simultaneously with both sticks: it sounds about a fifth lower than the free beat. The other is a 'trick' note, a little lower than *Dza* and is used for imitating *Atsimevu*. *Sogo* when it is played with two sticks has a somewhat similar range to *Kidi*. What happens when *Sogo* is used as master will be dealt with later.

We come now to the master drum, *Atsimevu*. The master drummer has the distinguished and distinctive title of *Azaguno*, which denotes that he is publicly recognized as a pre-eminent artist. He has by far the largest vocabulary for it is he who plays the extended patterns and variations: he has moreover, the advantage of playing with both stick and hand. But he has another advantage. All the previous drums make their beats in the centre of the drum-skin. The *Atsimevu* player exploits the possibility of producing different notes by hitting or muting different areas of the drum-skin. In fact, though we think unconsciously, he divides the drum-skin into three zones thus:

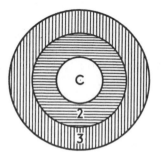

We shall call them the *Centre zone*, *Zone 2*, and *Zone 3*. All his stick-beats are usually made (like the other drums) in the centre zone. But his left-hand beats, and his muting may occur in any zone thus giving him a large number of possible sounds, each different position making a sound of different quality and nearly always also of pitch. Further, it is impossible to pin down his possible beats completely to definite relative pitches, because in any given pattern he may mute a bit harder or beat a bit softer in order to produce the exact quality and pitch of a particular note which suits that pattern. Nevertheless, having said this, one adds that normally he does work to standards. The notes for *Atsimevu* set out below, are approximately those which he uses for the appropriate nonsense syllable. The *Atsimevu* player can hit a free centre beat with the whole of his left hand, or he can make a muted centre beat with it. He can make a free centre beat with his stick or a muted centre beat, or a secondary muted centre beat, the muting being done by the left hand in any of the three zones making three separate notes. He can play free or muted beats with his left hand in zones 2 or 3, each of which actions again makes a note of different pitch or quality. There is one other technique which must be noted. This is called *Uukɔgo*. It consists in hitting the side wall of the drum with the stick making a muted beat and at the same time making a centre beat with the left hand. If the latter is muted, the nonsense syllable describing the note is *Dza* spoken on a very low tone: if the hand makes a free beat, the same word *Dza* is spoken on a high-low falling tone, descriptive of what the African feels the drum is saying.

If *Atsimevu* is not used, and the proper drum to play as master for a particular dance is *Sogo*, it is played in the style of *Atsimevu* with this difference, that no stick is used and both hands are free to make the various combinations of muting, secondary muting, and so on.

The *Sogo* player when *Sogo* is used as the master drum has several additional ways of making beats which are not included in the notes given below as they lie outside his ordinary vocabulary, being more or less 'trick' beats. He can produce the sounds *Ga-* or *Ga-da*, by hitting a centre beat with one or both of the butts of his hand instead of the normal full-palm beat. He also produces a brushing sound represented by the syllables *Ka-tsa* in either of two ways. He brings the hands down one after the other towards

the centre of the drum and outwards in a curved swooping movement, the left hand sweeping over the skin to the left and the
right hand to the right. At the moment of impact the hand strikes
the drum at an angle of 45 degrees so that instead of the flat
of the hand, it is the fleshy outside edge of the hand which makes
the strike and prolongs it by brushing the drum in the course of the
sweeping motion. Alternately he can sweep the left hand over to
the right and the right hand to the left, the paths of the hands
crossing each other. In both cases the sound is the same. Then
there is the elbow-mute beat. Either elbow can be used though
normally a right-handed player will use his left elbow and vice
versa. The point of the elbow is pressed on the drum-skin in the
appropriate zone and a beat made with the other hand. This is,
of course, a secondary muted beat. It is always preceded by one
or more free beats in zone 3 by the other hand. The elbow-muting
makes a very high note not obtainable otherwise and bears the
nonsense syllable *ŋ*. It occurs in such passages as:

$$\frac{3}{8}\ \flat\ |\ \sqcap\ \ |\ \sqcap\ \ |\ \&c.$$

ga ŋ ga - ga, ŋ ga - ga - - -

There is also a special secondary muting in the centre zone
where, contrary to more usual practice, it is the muting and not
the strike which occurs in the centre of the drum-skin. There are
three ways of doing this. The idea is to make a fleshy contact for
the muting. This can be done by pressing the fleshy base of the
hand on the drum, or by tilting the hand at an angle of 45 degrees
so that the fleshy outside edge of the hand mutes the drum. The
third way is to raise a leg and place the calf of the leg on the drum
to mute it. This is not a proper beat and is just 'showing off'.

We may now profitably look at the plates illustrating the playing
of some of these beats. Plate 7 shows free beats being played on
Kagaŋ: the sticks hit the centre of the drum-skin. In Plate 8 a
secondary muted beat is being played on *Kidi*. The left-hand stick
is pressed on the drum-skin to mute it, and the right-hand stick
is about to make a free beat. The result will be the highest note
that *Kidi* can produce, the exact pitch depending on how hard the
left stick is depressed. There are five pictures showing the technique of playing *Atsimevu* the master drum. In Plate 9, the drummer
is playing free beats using two sticks. He is hitting the centre of
the drum-skin and often, when playing with two sticks, uses con-

siderable force producing a very loud noise. Plate 10 shows a
secondary muted stick-beat, played during a pattern where two
sticks are used. The left-hand stick which is not required for this
beat is lifted free by the thumb and forefinger, while the second
and third fingers mute the drum-skin by touching it, or pressing
it (if a higher note is needed) in zone 2. The right-hand stick is
about to strike a free beat in the centre as usual. We call the whole
operation a secondary muted stick-beat. As the basic unit of time
is usually about seven beats to a second, the various movements
required to accomplish these different beats have to be made with
lightning rapidity. Plate 11 shows the same secondary muted stick-
beat on *Atsimevu* when the drummer is playing with the bare left
hand and a stick in his right. The left-hand stick has been tucked
away in the belt of the drummer: it can just be seen at the top
of the photo above the right hand. It is so placed as to be instantly
available to the left hand when needed again. In the picture, the
left hand is muting in zone 2 and the right-hand stick is about to
play, as before, a free centre beat, the combination producing a
fairly high note. If a still higher note is needed, the left hand mutes
in the centre zone just off-centre and the pitch of the note depends
on how hard the drummer presses this hand, and not on the actual
beat made by the right hand. Plate 12 shows *Uukogo* played on
Atsimevu, producing the sound represented by the nonsense syllable *Dza*. The left hand is playing a muted centre beat—note
that the hand is fairly relaxed to produce a low dull sound.
Simultaneously, the right hand beats a muted stick-beat on the
wall of the drum. Note how this hand is pressing the stick firmly
on to the drum as it makes the beat to prevent the stick bouncing
and so striking twice, and to make a clean sharp beat.

The remaining illustrations show how *Sogo* is played when it is
used as the master drum. Plate 13 shows the right hand at the
moment of striking a free beat in zone 3, i.e. near the edge of the
drum. It is not possible to guess what sort of beat the left hand
is going to make next. Plate 14 shows a muted centre beat: the
whole hand strikes the drum and remains momentarily on it to
damp the vibrations, thus producing *Sogo*'s lowest note. In Plate
15 the drummer is making a secondary muted zone 3 beat. This
is an example to show how many different beats are possible. In
this case the drum is muted by the left hand, not in zone 3 or
zone 2 but in the centre zone. He could have done either of the

others but the resulting note would have been different. While the left hand mutes at the centre, the actual beat is made with the right hand by a free beat not quite in zone 3 and not in zone 2 but just on the border between them. To produce the note he needed he had of necessity to strike the drum at this point. Plate 16 shows a muted beat on *Sogo* in zone 2. The hand strikes and momentarily rests on the drum. Note that normally, while playing, the fingers are closed. Compare the fingers in Plate 17. In both left and right hand the fingers are now opened apart. The reason is that the drummer is producing the characteristic mixture of the round drum-tone together with the sharp exaggerated sound of the fingers hitting the drum-skin which is denoted by the nonsense syllables *Ga-tsya*. The syllable *-tsya* with its strong sibilant is onomatopoeic: it says just what the drum produces. The beats being made in this picture are free beats in zone 2 with open fingers.

All these photos show the drum technique of the Ewe people in Ghana. Some 2,500 miles away to the south-east are the Lala tribe in Northern Rhodesia. The Ewe and the Lala are held to be in different language groups : yet a comparison between the plates we have just studied and the pictures and notes in '*The Icila Dance*'[1] show a technique which is identical except that the Lala never use sticks. What the Lala do is what all the tribes known to the author in Northern Rhodesia also do. This technique of drumming is part and parcel of the cultus of African music.

The preceding paragraphs are intended merely to give the general idea of what is happening. It remains to set out the more usual notes used by each drum in musical form. These are the notes used in the transcriptions except where the drummer makes an alteration in the pitch of a given nonsense syllable to suit the pattern-context better. The reader will observe that occasionally the same nonsense syllable is used for different notes : in this case it will be spoken on a different pitch of voice.

KEY
    F = Free beat
    M = Muted beat
    SM = Secondary muted beat
    SMC = Secondary muting made in the centre zone.

[1] A. M. Jones, *The Icila Dance*, published by the African Music Society, P.O. Box 138, Roodepoort, Johannesburg, S. Africa.

The starred notes indicate the basic tuning of the drums and represent a free beat.

TUNING AND NOTES OF DRUMS

1. WHEN *Atsimevu* IS MASTER DRUM

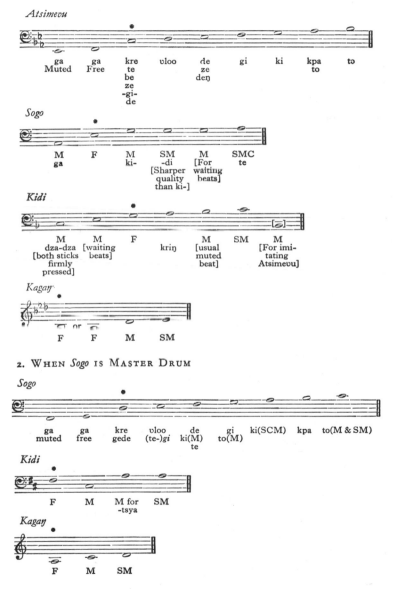

Atsimevu

ga	ga	kre	vloo	de	gi	ki	kpa	tɔ
Muted	Free	te		ze			to	
		be		deŋ				
		ze						
		-gi-						
		de						

Sogo

M	F	M	SM	M	SMC
ga		ki-	-di	[For	te
			[Sharper	waiting	
			quality	beats]	
			than ki-]		

Kidi

M	M	F		M	SM	M
dza-dza	[waiting		kriŋ	[usual		[For imi-
[both sticks	beats]			muted		tating
firmly				beat]		Atsimevu]
pressed]						

Kagaŋ

F	F	M	SM

2. WHEN *Sogo* IS MASTER DRUM

Sogo

ga	ga	kre	vloo	de	gi	ki(SCM)	kpa	to(M & SM)
muted	free	gede	(te-)gi	ki(M)	to(M)			
				te				

Kidi

F	M	M for	SM
		-tsya	

Kagaŋ

F	M	SM

No more should be read into these notes than what is claimed for them : they are the result of considering the pitch of the notes produced in drumming as revealed in various tests combined with the necessity of making a readable score, of using a series of notes which will allow of allotting a different note on the score to each significantly different pitch of drum-beat as represented by the nonsense syllables. The matter is complicated by the fact, already mentioned, that the tuning of drums is relative and not fixed. Therefore any scheme of representation must to some extent be a compromise. The actual range of notes given for the master drum is probably a little too great. The oscillogram appears to give 207 v.p.s. for the highest syllable *To*, which would make it lie not on B♭ but between G♯ and A. Even here we are not certain : for *To* is a syllable whose pitch varies at least a tone according to the context of the pattern played. It is possible that when making the oscillogram Mr. Tay played the lower *To*. If the list of notes errs, we think it can only err within fairly narrow limits.

One curious and interesting reflection arises from these drum-notes. They all fall within the range of the adult male's *speaking* voice. The Tonometer we built for registering speech-tones of men's voices—covering all voices from tenor to bass—and whose tuning was arrived at empirically, has almost exactly the same range. It is tuned from just below DD = 72 v.p.s. in the bass to d' = 287 v.p.s. in the tenor. From this fact there follow two considerations. First, the nonsense syllables are seen to be spoken on the actual pitch of the drum-beats themselves, so this is not a case of *imitating* in the category of speech-tones, a different pitch-category of sounds made on the drum. Second, it sheds light on the subject of Talking Drums. This is not our concern in the present book and as a subject is quite separate from drumming for dances, i.e. from drumming regarded as music. It looks as if one factor involved in the recognition by a receiver of drum messages is the fact that the drum is probably playing a message in the actual range of tone, musical intervals, and pitch of a living speaking voice. This particular point is not dealt with by Carrington in his *Talking Drums of Africa*.[1]

There remains the question as to how this list can be made use of in putting down on paper the musical pitch of the drum-patterns played. The process is in three stages. First our drum-recorder is used. One person plays the *Gankogui* pattern while the master drummer plays his drum-pattern. This is not done on drums but is tapped with brass pencils on the playing-plates of the recorder (see Plate 18). The result is a length of paper on which all the beats are marked and from which it is easy to see the exact time-value of each beat. Appropriate conventional music notes are now written under these marks which show the *rhythm* of the drum-pattern. So now we know the rhythm but not the tune of the pattern. The next step is to write under each note its nonsense syllable, this information being supplied by the master drummer. We now take the actual drum and the master drummer beats out the first few notes of the pattern. On the record paper we write in diacritical signs the kind of beat made for each note and the position of the beat on the drum. We work right through the pattern in this way. Then, using our list of notes together with this information, we can write on the stave not only the time-value of the note but also its approximate pitch. The last stage is to revise this score to see if any modifications of the pitch are required for that particular pattern. Each drum of the ensemble is treated in the same way, using the *Gankogui* pattern as a standard to measure not only its rhythm but also the particular place where the rhythm enters *vis-à-vis* the *Gankogui*. This gives us the way the drum-rhythms are played in relation to each other, thus show-ing their cross-rhythms. We are now well on the way to being able to write out the full score, but not quite, as we have yet to correlate all this with the song and the claps.

The third section of the orchestra is the song and its attendant hand-clapping. The hand-clap is the rhythmic link between the song and the other instruments. It takes its time from the *Gan-kogui*. In the case of complicated clap-patterns these may not be coterminous with the *Gankogui* phrases, they may overlap, but in no case will their total length be greater than that of one *Gankogui* phrase so that however many times they are repeated, the clap-phrases and the *Gankogui* phrases are always in the same phase one with the other. The songs are in apparently free rhythm though this is illusory. The same principles apply to them as those we studied in Chapter 2. The total number of claps to a given song, in-cluding the rests between repeats, will bear a definite mathematical relationship with the number of *Gankogui* phrases covered during the singing, so that when the song is repeated its syllables and claps will fall in exactly the same equivalent places in the *Gankogui* pattern. The length of the song is also related to the length of the master-drum patterns. Here again, when the master drum repeats his pattern, usually his beats will fall either in the same relative places *vis-à-vis* the song words, or at a constant distance of six quavers from them if the standard *Gankogui* pattern is used. Six quavers is half a *Gankogui* pattern. Ewe musicians do not seem to mind if the *Gankogui* pattern and some other contributing pattern overlap in this way on repeat provided—and this is the point—that the overlap is at half-way and neither more nor less than this.

We imagine now that the song is to be transcribed. The melody and words are written on music paper, and the places where the claps occur in relation to the melody are marked in. The claps themselves are played with *Gankogui* and their exact time-value determined. This having been done we know just how the song notes fall in relation to the *Gankogui* pattern and therefore to the drums. One last investigation has to be made. We must find out at what point in the song the master drummer enters with each of his standard patterns. There are only certain points in the song which are suitable for the purpose. When all this has been ascertained we can write out a full score of African dance music.

When this has been done it must be checked. Key points are selected as critical tests: for example, we can say to the master drummer, 'When the melody gets to such and such a note, what beat is *Atsimevu* or *Kidi* making?' It is not difficult to select such key points as to leave no doubt that the score is essentially accurate.

Before we pass on to consider the actual music of the dances, it might be of interest to know how people learn to drum.

It is not everyone among the Ewe who can drum, in fact there are not many who can. The art tends to go in families. There is no direct teaching or school of instruction: it all happens spontaneously. You start as a boy and if you are seen to be musical, your father or musical relations will unostentatiously encourage you. In fact the art is acquired to start with through play, during which one graduates through the mastery of two play-drums.

The first step is the Bottle Drum. To make this you fill an

ordinary European wine bottle with sand and invert it, preferably in a hole in the ground. With one corner of the blade of a chisel, chip away in the centre of the bottom till you have made a hole right through: continue chipping till the whole of the bottom is removed; then smooth the rough edges with the same chisel. Now make a ring of creeper bound with twine, and of a diameter slightly smaller than that of the bottle. Soak a piece of hide in water, place it over the bottom of the bottle and force the ring over. When dry it will never come off. To play the bottle drum, place it between the legs, and play with one finger of the left hand and a little stick in the right hand.

The second step is the Acorn Drum, called *Alagbagovu*. In West Africa these 'acorns' are about 1 foot long and 9 inches in maximum diameter. Make a big hole in the larger end which will be the drumhead, and a small hole in the small end. Dig out the vegetable matter inside. Bore holes round the sides of the large end, a short distance from the top. Fix a drum-skin on in the same way as for a proper drum. This *Alagbagovu* is then used to practise master-drum patterns.[1]

Boys form gangs for practice and, quite contrary to adult custom where each different drumming belongs to some separate and particular occasion or ceremony, they have a shot at playing any drumming which they fancy. Interested and musical adults will from time to time call a promising boy and show him a new drum-pattern—perhaps as a promised reward for, say, running an errand. In this way are the principles and practice mastered till a lad at last has an opportunity to take part in a real drumming. He will still be only a beginner. It takes years of practice and experience to attain the expertize demanded of a master drummer. Most drummers never reach this stage and continue to play the lesser instruments. The whole process is an example of learning within the framework of a society. There are no set proficiency bars: but the system ensures that those who get to the top are true musicians. One would go further: in our experience a good African master drummer is a consummate musician judged by any standards, African or Western.

[1] Compare the boys' Calabash Drum in Northern Rhodesia, described in A. M. Jones, op. cit., p. 49. The custom is identical.

4

THE *NYAYITO* DANCE

THE SOCIAL SETTING

NYAYITO is the Funeral Dance of the Ewe people. The
dance or its songs are also known as *Tɔbaha*, *Leafelegbe*,
Ðekɔlenyaɲu, or *Akpaluvu*. The last word means 'Akpalu's
Drumming' so named because Akpalu is the greatest living composer of mourning songs. His songs are mostly about mishaps,
sudden death, and such serious topics, and are very compassionate.
The song we use is one of his early compositions and is not so
sympathetic as his words usually are.

The dance is in the hands of, and is organized by, the *Nyayito*
society whose senior members are the patrons of the dance. Unlike the societies and clubs we shall study later, the *Nyayito* society
is loosely organized and has no definite rules for admission or
membership. It is formed of elderly or middle-aged people and
though there is nothing to prevent young people from joining it,
they will usually find it too dull and serious. Any elderly person
considers himself a member of the *Nyayito* club and if, say, new
drums are to be bought, all elderly persons in the town will feel
bound to make a contribution. It is a loose federation of elderly
people centred round the patrons, the *Hesinɔ* (song-composer) and
the *Azaguɔ* (master drummer). In all societies and clubs for
drumming and dancing, the *Azaguɔ* and the *Hesinɔ* occupy leading positions as the whole performance largely depends on their
skill, creativeness, and musicianship. In the case of *Nyayito* where
the songs are very important, the *Hesinɔ* ranks above the *Azaguɔ*.
With other societies and clubs, their drum-patterns, their songs,
and their dances are their own property and can only be performed
by the members of the particular society. *Nyayito* is unrestricted
in this way, and anyone can take part. For example, when a person
dies the women mourners may go on singing *Nyayito* songs for

days without reference to the society. So also, when the mourners arrive at the dead man's house, they are at liberty not only to sing the *Nyayito* songs but also to play the *Gankogui* and even the *Atsimevu* (master drum), though they may not use the other drums. This, however, is not the main dance. When a person dies his family will want to have the funeral dance performed, so they send word to call and invite the *Nyayito* club to come. On their arrival they will dance the official *Nyayito*, though anyone who wishes may join in the dancing.

THE WORDS OF THE SONGS

There are many *Nyayito* songs, and new ones are continually being composed. We give the words of two of them to show the sort of sentiment expressed. The first of them is the one used on the music-score.

Song 1

> (Ʊuaviawo) Beble tsitsie menye
> Nye la geɖeawo domee maku ɖo
> Halé ya hee
> Miawo tɔbaha zu make make
> Ʊedzia ɖe dza ɖe 'nyi me ʋenu
> Anyakoawo yi adza wu ge na akpalu-ee
> Mado alɔewo gbe na mi dzro
> Megblɔe na mi be medzi ge na mi
> Ʊu yawo ha medzi ge na mi
> Tɔnye ga ku(a) medze axɔ ɖo gbe loho
> Adevu nava lé, medze axɔ ɖo gbe sati nava tsɔ.

I am an only child with no one to stand up for me, (*lit. A trapped bird am I,*)
I will die alone in the crowd (*sc. I have no brothers or sisters to protect and sustain me*)
Oh! this is the song:
Our '*tɔbaha*' song is never-ending—
It is just like unceasing rain falling in Nyima quarry, (*a big hole made for mud mortar when building*)
The people of Anyako have gone to praise Akpalu (*name of the composer of this song*)
I (*sc. Akpalu*) will sing unceasingly to you like a sparrow
I have told you I will sing it to you
The song of this drumming (*sc. this '*tɔbaha*'*), I will sing it to you.

My father died and I wandered distractedly
  for a hunting-dog to come and snatch, or a leopard to devour.

Song 2

(The words of this song better reflect the usual type used in *Nyayito*.)

Ketɔle yelɔ lawo kue ye gbɔ
'Vinɔkɔ-le mo nye dzakae,
Kpɔto wò deka de futɔwo dome
'Kpɔ kple agbaĩ -wo yi tɔsige
Be ayedzie ayedzie lo ho
Numatae mede afɔ duame nawo.
'Mebena tɔnyea wɔ nublanui
'Vinɔkɔ tɔnyea wɔ nublanui :
Tɔnye le dɔbadzie fekonyi,
Vinɔkɔle nye me agbe nɔ geo.
Kpɔto wò deka nanye zɔzɔe
Nanye afɔ dofe lo ho :
Amekatã me dzeamɔ gbedeka o.

Oh Ketɔ, those who are fond of me, I am bereft of,
    (*Ketɔ: name of a present member of the Nyayito Club*)
Oh Vinɔkɔ, I am ill at ease,
    (*Vinɔkɔ: another living member of the Club*)
You are now left alone·among enemies.
    (*'You' is the bereaved person for whom the song was composed*)
A leopard and a wild cat have met at fishing—
Yes, I said it must be a matter of a truce between enemies,
    (*The leopard and wild cat are mutually hostile: the real meaning is 'I have
    lost my friends and all other people seem to be enemies.'*)
So, as a result, I have left the town.
I say I am in pitiful case
Vinɔkɔ, I am in pitiful case :
My father is pining on a bed of sickness
Oh Vinɔkɔ, I shall not survive.
You are left alone, you must watch your step
    (*'You' is the bereaved person*)
And be careful where you place your feet :
Everyone does not start journeying on the same day.
    (*sc. We do not* all *die on the same day.*)

THE MUSIC

The music is made by the *Gankogui* (bell), *Axatse* (rattle),
Atsimevu (master drum), *Sogo* or *Agblo* drum, and the smaller

drums *Kidi* and *Kagay*. There will also be hand-clapping, the song, and the dancers. The *Sogo* drum does not really belong to this dance at all. The proper drum is *Agblo* which, unlike *Sogo*, is carved out of a solid tree-trunk. It is played with sticks cut from a forked branch so as to leave a small hammer-head with which to hit the drum. *Agblo* is difficult to procure nowadays especially in the towns in the south like Accra, as its real home is some 300 miles to the north. Moreover in towns, drumming customs are not so strictly observed and people do not bother to get the right drums.

Let us look at the score. The whole performance starts like this. A cantor alone and unaccompanied sings the whole song right through, very *rubato*, and in rather dramatic fashion, without the chorus joining in. Maybe the *Gankogui* starts playing during this: if so the cantor pays no attention to its time and makes no attempt to align the song with it. This preliminary singing is a very general practice in dances and not only in Ghana. Mr. Hugh Tracey has recorded the same thing in East Africa. It gives an opportunity for people to know what the words and tune of the chorus are, so that they are ready to join in, and by the histrionic manner of singing it rouses people to an enthusiasm for the dance. We shall call it 'Lining the Song'. When the first cantor reaches the end of the verse, another cantor, preferably with a voice of contrasting timbre starts the song again, strictly *a tempo*: this is the point at which our transcription starts (bar 1). Immediately the chorus, i.e. everybody taking part except the cantor, joins in, and the song proceeds with alternation of cantor and chorus as shown on the score. For the repeat of the song and all subsequent repeats, the whole chorus begins the song from the word *Vuaviawo*. As soon as the second cantor has initiated the song, i.e. in bar 1, people start clapping—anyone may join in—and the *Gankogui* and *Axatse* start playing (bar 2). When the song has reached a suitable place of entry (bar 5) the master drummer enters with his first standard pattern. *Sogo* and *Kidi* immediately come in with the appropriate response to this pattern, while *Kagay*, as soon as he hears them start, joins in with his simple pattern which he goes on playing without a pause, and with no change whatever the other drums are doing, till the ending pattern which brings the dance to a close.

We must now study the music in detail taking each instrument or voice separately, and we will start with the metronome mark ♩ = 113. There is, in the writer's experience, a *tempo giusto* in African drumming which is about ♩. = 140. This means that the quaver, the basic time-unit, is going at ♪ = 420, which is seven beats per second. It is interesting to note that this is just about the speed of the quavers in the tune 'The Irish Washerwoman' when played to accompany an old English sword dance. In the *tempo giusto* crotchets go at 210 to the minute which may be compared with the speed of this *Nyayito* dance. The latter goes at about half the normal speed and that is one of the main features of this drumming. It is a very slow dance befitting the occasion.

GANKOGUI AND AXATSE

The *Gankogui* pattern is a special one for this dance: it is a modification of the standard pattern given in the last chapter, which has the effect of changing an irregularly divided 12/8 time into straightforward triple time. The modification is arrived at thus: imagine that *Gankogui* plays his normal pattern and that at the same time someone claps four times to each 12/8 bar. Now imagine that every time a clap is made, *Gankogui* plays his low bell. The result will be the *Nyayito Gankogui* pattern:

(Underlined notes are the low bell)

Gankogui plays this pattern unceasingly right through the dance no matter what the other instruments are doing.

The phrasing of this pattern in the score looks peculiar. It is Mr. Tay's own choice. He says that the first low bell is 'by itself'; the middle sub-phrase means that these notes 'go together': the final quaver belongs to the first low note of the next bar. In spite of this, the whole bar is one overall phrase, separate from the next bar. Here again we are presented with that feature of African music whereby the *beginning* note of a phrase is considered by Africans to be also the *end* note of the previous phrase.

The rattle (*Axatse*) has also a modification of its standard pattern which, however, is a very slight one giving, perhaps, an added solemnity. *Axatse's* normal pattern is:

In *Nyayito*, the middle note of the first triple group is omitted.

Before going any farther, there is one point about all the music-scores which must be made clear. When an African bell or a rattle is played, or when one makes a hand-clap, obviously the sound produced has hardly any duration in time. Strictly speaking one should therefore write the notes for these patterns as, shall we say, demi-semiquavers. But the effect of this in a score which consists mostly of irregular bars is to make it virtually unreadable. We thought it much more sensible to leave this factor to the imagination of the reader, and to fill out the values of the notes, so that the overall shape of the various patterns shall be made clear. The same thing applies to the drumming.

THE HAND-CLAPS AND THE SONG

From the African point of view we should now discuss the master drum and then the other drums, and finally the claps and song. But as the entry of the master drum is governed by the song, it is easier if we leave the drums till later, and as the song is regulated by the hand-clap, we will take the latter first. There are three possible clap-patterns. The first one (bars 1–19) is used as a general clap for the whole dance but particularly during the first verse. When the other clap-patterns come in, this first pattern may be continued or not at discretion. There is no set clap-party responsible for it. Anyone who is not in the orchestra or dancing will clap. Similarly the variant clap-patterns are introduced at will by some of the people and may continue as long as is desired The fact that the variant patterns occur on the score where they do, is not to indicate necessarily that that is the precise place where they would be used. We have just written them in at random to show how they fit into the score. However, the second clap does have a proper place for entry (see bars 19–28). After the song has been sung once, and as it is repeated, the second clap comes in. This is also the point where the dancers start dancing, hence the quicker clap to give spirit to the dance. It is, of course, in the same rhythm as the first clap with the addition of two intermediate claps.

Note how the clap-phrases are integrated with *Gankogui*. The clap-phrase goes '*clap, clap, clap, rest*', and not '*clap, rest, clap, clap*'. This means that the clap-phrases are staggered with *Gankogui*, each clap-phrase starting right in the middle of the *Gankogui* phrase. This applies to both the first and the second clap-patterns.

The third clap is illustrated in bars 29–39. It is used when they want to get more life into the dance. Clap 2 has been going on and then all of a sudden there is a bout of clap 3 which by its contrasted rhythm and quicker beat gives fire to the proceedings. After a short while they will lapse back into clap 2. This is precisely the same technique as that used by the Lala in Northern Rhodesia.

Claps 1 and 3 are standard forms of clapping in these Ewe dances, so for convenience in future, we will assign names to them. Clap 1, four dotted crotchets to the *Gankogui* phrase, will be called the 4-clap, and clap 3, six crotchets to the phrase, the 6-clap. Another clap consisting of three minims to the *Gankogui* phrase is used in some dances but not in this. We shall call it the 3-clap.

We now turn to the song, which is a good example of additive melody-making. To capture the rhythm—and in spite of its irregular barring it is strongly rhythmical—it is a good plan to tap continuously on the table at quaver speed and then to sing the tune. As it is a tune for dancing it has to be strictly *a tempo*. In spite of this it has an apparently easy freedom which exactly fits the swing of the words. The melody is a long one, extending as far as bar 13 without any repeats. It feels diatonic, with the pivotal points at the tonic and the dominant, but it starts on the dominant and ends on the dominant. This is typically African: the use of these resting points might suggest that the melody has affinities with one or other of the Gregorian modes—the fifth possibly: but the whole ethos of these African melodies is different. In this case the scale used appears to be a diatonic major scale whose final (to borrow a modal word) is not the tonic but the dominant. The song is in the call and response form and, including the repeats, is exactly eighteen *Gankogui* phrases in length. Its melodic form is this: section A extends from bar 1 to bar 8: section B from bar 9 to bar 13 and this section is repeated from bar 14 to bar 18. This is not the real end of the song. If you want to stop singing (see bar 83) you start to repeat it till reaching the word '*midzro*' in bar 8, thus repeating section A. When the song is continuously repeated this is not done, and the real end of the song only becomes apparent right at the end of the dance. In giving the song-analysis here we shall take the full version. When we consider the drumming we shall have to reckon the length of the song as extending no further than the beginning of bar 19 where it starts to repeat because the drumming is regulated by this truncated version. So the form is: $A+B+B+A$.

The metrical form is interesting. Its total length of twenty-four bars is distributed thus: (*a*) bars 1–4; (*b*) 5–8; (*c*) 9, and 10–13; (*d*) 14, and 15–18; (*e*) repeat 1–4; (*f*) repeat 5–8. That is,

$$4+4+(1+4)+(1+4)+4+4 = 26 \; Gankogui \; bars$$

Note that had we not remembered to include the repeat of section B as an essential part of the song, the total length would have been twenty-one bars, which in our experience is un-African. The correct total of bars follows our rule although it is arrived at by the ingenious device of singing (1 | 4) twice, a further indication of the African's fertility of rhythmic invention.

Before transferring this song to the full score, we want to know on which syllables the low bell sounds. We only need to find one such occurrence because we have already aligned the song with the clap, and the clap with the *Gankogui*. The check of our accuracy will be, having written it all out, to notice another syllable on which in our script the low bell occurs and then to ask the singer to perform together with *Gankogui* to see that this is so. At bar 5 we see a familiar feature again. The words '*make make*' form the end of a phrase and coincide with a low bell note: the song-phrase leans towards the first note of the *Gankogui* phrase. The same happens at bars 8, 10, 11, 14, 15, 16, and 19, and so on throughout the score.

Reviewing the melody musically, we would say that while it is not distinguished, it is shapely, well-knit, and quite strong: nothing, in fact, to be ashamed of as a piece of popular music. It is a unison tune but in bar 5 there is an alternative ending to the phrase which can be sung at will, giving rise to parallel fourths.

THE DRUMS

The Africans would treat the drums in this order—*Atsimevu*

(master), *Kidi*, *Sogo*, and *Kagaŋ*. For Europeans, it is clearer and more logical to take *Kagaŋ* first. This small drum is nearly always used to establish a perpetual cross-rhythm with the *Gankogui*. In the present case he does this by placing all his main beats one beat ahead of those of the *Gankogui*. In bar 5 to make clear on the score, the relative positions of the rhythms of the instruments, we have drawn dotted lines down it, from the *Gankogui* bars. These dotted lines have no musical significance whatever. They do not show that in spite of the cross-rhythms, African music falls into line with European music. Returning to *Kagaŋ*, on the score we see that he has the first beat of his bar immediately preceding the dotted line: he goes on like this, consistently staggering his main beats with those of *Gankogui* right through the dance. This is why we have dealt with him first. He sets up a steady undercurrent of polyrhythm *vis-à-vis Gankogui*. He has a proper place to start: he waits till the master drum enters, and the other drums have started replying to the master, and at once joins in on an appropriate beat. Note how he strengthens the main beat of his bar by the semiquaver. The main beat thus becomes a sort of little roll. We have inverted the tail of the semiquaver to indicate that this note is not an essential note of the pattern. We shall use this plan in all dances for all the lesser drums, i.e. for all except the master drum.

The master drummer, playing *Atsimevu*, has a number of standard patterns at his disposal, all of which belong to *Nyayito* alone. He can use each of them any number of times though he must not play the plain unadorned standard pattern more than say six times straight off as he would be accused of dullness and lack of skill. What he does, having first established the pattern, is to play variations on it. But this subject we shall leave to the later dances. In *Nyayito* there seems to be much restraint in the use of variations. Here we are only concerned to study the standard patterns. Besides being able to repeat the patterns at will, he can also play them in any order and he need not use them all. Mr. Tay says he could invent many more patterns suitable for *Nyayito*, but the ones we give are the chief traditional ones. The master drummer can also revert, later on in the dance, to patterns he has already played. It all depends on the aesthetic sense of the drummer and the fitness of the pattern to adorn the dancing of any particular dancer who happens to be dancing.

Let us study the patterns in the score-book. Pattern A runs from bar 5 to bar 10, i.e. it has a duration of six *Gankogui* phrases. The rule of 2 and 3 obviously applies here; also as the song covers eighteen phrases, after playing his pattern three times, the master will enter on the next repeat at the same place in the song as he started from. If the reader will mentally perform this pattern, keeping strict time and mentally counting the value in quavers of the longer notes, marking also where the accents occur as shown by the bar-lines on the *Atsimevu* stave, he will be bound, we think, to admit that this is a strongly rhythmic piece of music. It is manifestly additive in structure. The first 2 bars contain 5 quaver-units each, the third bar only 2, then 2 more bars of 5 units followed by a bar of only 1, leading to 4 bars of 6 units. It is strictly organized. Look, for example, at the nonsense syllable '*ki*'. Whenever it occurs near the end of a *Gankogui* phrase, it invariably falls on the very last note: see bars 5, 6, 7, 8, 9, and 10, and of course on the repeats. So also, the syllable '*ya*' invariably occurs on an accented beat of the *Gankogui*: bars 5, 7 (twice), 8 (three times), 9 (twice), 10 (three times). We can see also that *Atsimevu* is not merely playing a rhythm, he is playing a tune. We further observe how, except for the syllable '*ya*', the master drummer avoids as far as possible making his accented beats coincide with accents in the bell-pattern. This is no theory of our own: a master drummer will freely agree that this is most desirable. It produces the clash of cross-rhythms which is what he is seeking to attain.

Now let us look at the lesser drums *Sogo* and *Kidi*. Their function is to make the correct and appropriate 'replies' to the patterns played by the master. Each standard master pattern has standard replies from *Sogo* and *Kidi*. So, at the start of the dance, as soon as they hear the master start to play his first pattern, if they are good players, a note or two is sufficient to show them which pattern it is and they immediately come in with the correct reply. *Kidi* actually is the chief replier and we will take this drum first. In *Nyayito*, which uses the fairly low-toned *Sogo* drum, *Kidi* imitates these low sounds and the two drums more or less work in concert. To see *Kidi*'s pattern we must look not at bar 5 but in the middle of bar 6, where his repetitive pattern really starts. At his first entry he has to play two extra '*kiyas*' (bar 5). His pattern is '*Kiya . . . kiya . . . kiya, kiya, kiya . . .*'. This he repeats till the master changes his pattern. On the score, in between the words '*kiya*', there are notes with inverted tails. These are waiting beats or filling beats. No one would wish to hear *Kidi* play merely the essential outline of his pattern. *Kidi* is expected to fill out his pattern and he does this by playing all vacant quavers with quiet muted beats. His time being 6/8, shows he has a simple relationship with the 12/8 of *Gankogui*. But the score shows that he anticipates, as *Kagaŋ* does, the main beats of *Gankogui*, and so the bar-lines of *Kidi* are always one quaver ahead of those of *Gankogui*. We can see that he is really playing in step with *Kagaŋ*. When we say that they are crossed with *Gankogui*, we include both the rattle and the clapping, both of which are more nearly in step with the latter. *Sogo*, in Pattern A, needs no comment. He is playing virtually the same rhythm as *Kidi*, though his pattern becomes distinct in the mêlée of sounds when, as is his custom, he plays the words '*WOYE KPE DAGA NA ABUYA*' *sforzando*. That is his special contribution.

When the master drummer decides that he wants to leave Pattern A and go on to another one, he has to give the other drummers warning. This is done by a technique we have called 'Changing Signals'. Each different sort of dance has its own changing signals: it may have one, it may have several. *Nyayito* has three. What the master drummer does is to produce a lull by the repetition of some simple motif. Even here he often produces a cross-rhythm as in the first changing signal on the score (bars 19–21). Here his main beat is continuously a semiquaver ahead of the main beats of *Gankogui*. During these changing signals only the drums are concerned and even then not the smallest one, *Kagaŋ*. When the master starts the changing signal, very likely *Sogo* and *Kidi* will be in the middle of making their response to the previous master pattern. What they do is this: they go on playing that response until the first opportunity, i.e. the correct place in the *Gankogui* pattern, occurs for them to make the proper reply to the changing pattern. This may entail slipping a beat or so, or curtailing the response. In bars 19 to 20 we can see both these processes. *Kidi*, for example, omits the final '*kiya*' of his pattern, then slips a quaver and then plays his response. Note that by so doing *Kidi* and *Sogo* move their main beat of the bar one beat back, so that during this particular signal they are in step with *Gankogui*, and *ipso facto* are now permanently crossed with the main beats of *Kagaŋ*. Like *Atsimevu*, for changing signals,

Sogo and *Kidi* play something extremely simple and rhythmically non-committal, which cannot be called a pattern.

The changing signals must not be confused with another technique called *Uuyoyro*. This is the name given to Waiting Patterns, played by the master drummer when he feels like it, in between the repetition of a standard pattern, at times when he does not want to change this pattern. He is giving a slight relief from the continued repetition of the particular standard pattern but is, at the same time, letting the other drummers know that he is not quitting it and that having finished the *Uuyoyro*, he will repeat it again. It is in the nature of a variant of a changing signal, but it manages to convey the impression that 'He is not going to change his pattern'. The word *Uuyoyro* also is the name given to the beating on the drum made by the master drummer when he is tuning up his drum before a dance is due to start.

Now the master wants to move from the changing signal to a fresh pattern (bars 22 and 23). He does this by making a short pause (it must never be a long silence as this would show his lack of ideas), which is arranged to come just before he is due to make the correct entry for the next standard pattern, and then coming in on the right note *vis-à-vis Gankogui*.

This is a suitable place to deal with another question. It is not any phrase of *Gankogui* which will serve for an entry of the master drum. The correct entry of the master drum is derived from the song. For any given song, and for any particular dance and for any given master-drum pattern there are only a very few syllables in that song on which the master drum can enter his pattern. In the case of Pattern A, there is only one, and that is on the words '*make make*' (bar 5). With Pattern B, this will not be suitable: he must enter while the chorus is singing '*hee*' (bar 22), and nowhere else in the song is suitable. We would naturally like to know why this is and what are the factors governing his choice. Unfortunately we can give no firm answer. To watch an African choosing a suitable place is to realize that his aesthetic sense is keenly discriminative but we have failed to elicit exactly what is the basis of his selection other than the remark that 'it is not suitable' or vice versa. Mr. Tay did, however, say that it is most important that the master-drum pattern must not burst into bustling prominence during a quiet or sustained passage in the song and that this suitability of entry is bound up with the way the master-drum pattern falls *vis-à-vis* the melody. They must both suit each other. That is as far as we can get. We should add that once the master drummer has made his correct entry by reference to the song, he then chiefly follows the *Gankogui* and the song occupies a place of less importance in his mind. He must not neglect it, and he must be careful not to play anything which spoils it, but nevertheless it ceases to be crucial.

Master Pattern B (bars 22–25, which include a repeat) occupies two *Gankogui* phrases and thus will keep in phase with the song. Though so short, it has several interesting features. It avoids entering on the main beat of the *Gankogui* by starting with a rest: and while it ends on the low bell-note, its last beat is the second unaccented beat of a group of two, thus making a cross-rhythm here. Its very first bar, consisting of a dotted quaver rest and a dotted quaver is typical African practice: it is, of course, playing 2 against 3, which is a feature often present in drumming. The most interesting point is in the middle of bar 23 at the words '*gaze kre kre ki-*'. Here is an ingenious way of introducing triple time—for that is what it is—while still employing the quaver as the basic unit of time. In essence it is another way of playing 2 against 3 : it consists of six semiquavers grouped in two sets of three, which are played against three quavers of the song. Note how cleverly the pattern is constructed. The word '*kito*' occurs each time on the second and fourth accent of *Gankogui*, and the whole pattern is an expansion, and a play on, the initial motif '*Ga kito*'.

We pass on to the other possible changing signals for *Nyayito* (bars 27 and 28). On the score they are introduced on the very last word of the song: this is not caprice, for this is the place where they would most likely start. In both signals the master drummer is doing essentially the same as he did in the first signal, namely, playing six beats to the *Gankogui* phrase: this would seem to be the underlying structure of the *Nyayito* changing signals. The response of the *Asiwui* (lesser drums) is the same for all three signals. *Kagaŋ* is still permanently crossed with the rest, but though the master is, in a way, crossed with *Gankogui*, his first beat of the group of six coincides with the beginning of the *Gankogui* phrase— a different state of affairs from his performance in a standard pattern. It must be understood that he can go on playing a changing signal as long as he likes but he would not merely repeat any of those given in the score as that would be considered dull. He would introduce slight variations without altering their basic structure. Again, a changing signal must occupy at least one full *Gankogui* phrase: it cannot be less and normally is more. Any changing signal can be used after and before any pattern according to the whim of the player.

Before going on to the next pattern there are two other matters to mention. From time to time the master drummer, whose playing obviously overshadows everyone else, wants to give a chance to the *Asiwui* to display themselves. He does this by ceasing to drum for a short period. This can never take place at a changing signal. For instance in Pattern A, a good place for the master to stop would be at the beginning of bar 7 after the word '*kiya*'. Having stopped here he could wait as long as till the end of the song in bar 14, before starting to play again. During this time the *Asiwui* would play very brightly to display their drumming and their patterns. This pause may be due also to the desire of the master drummer, who is responsible for the playing of the whole orchestra, to see if the *Asiwui* are playing correctly. He will start a new pattern, play it several times and if need be, incorporate with his pattern the essential beats of the *Asiwui* patterns to help them to get on to their proper response. When he thinks they have got it, he may stop playing for a while to see if all is well. Then he resumes the pattern.

A good *Kidi* or *Sogo* player may be a great help to the master drummer. The performance of the latter is a piece of continuous creation within the prescribed limits of the standard patterns and free improvised variations on them. A man cannot be at his most inspired all the time and may, during a dance, run short of ideas. If a good *Kidi* player senses this he will come to the rescue. During a changing signal he will think of a good pattern for the master to play next and will start playing his response to it. As soon as he hears this, the grateful master drummer will launch into the appropriate pattern. In good drumming there is this unspoken co-operation going on all the time between all the leading performers.

Let us now examine Master Pattern C (bars 29–34). On the score, in bars 29 and 30, we have left the drum-staves blank until the time of their respective drum's entry for this pattern. Strictly speaking we should have filled these in with the latter part of the changing signal, because the drums go on playing all the time. However, as we gave in Pattern A, an example of how it all joins up, there is no need to go on doing so. It is clearer to view the patterns in isolation. The master, in Pattern C, enters at the same point in the song as he did in the previous one. This new pattern is four *Gankogui* phrases in length. This means that as the song covers eighteen phrases, when the song repeats, the master pattern will not lie in the same relation—it will be two *Gankogui* phrases out of phase. This is not important: it is an example of what we said before, namely, that provided the right point of entry *vis-à-vis* the song is made, the master drummer thereafter treats its time-relation to his playing as of secondary importance. Anyhow, matters will right themselves on the next repeat of the song, when the master pattern will once more enter on the word '*hee*' (see bar 30). The time of this pattern is a mixture of 3/8 and 5/8, though not altogether in alternate bars. Despite this it has a strong swinging rhythm. Once again the master avoids entering on *Gankogui*'s main beat, in fact his first main beat is on one of the least accented of those of *Gankogui*; also, as before, he ends his pattern on the main beat of *Gankogui*. A pattern of this irregular nature is bound to be well crossed with everything else: and so it is except for the notes in brackets.

Kidi makes the main reply, with *Sogo* more or less duplicating it. These two drums are in phase with the first beat of the *Gankogui* phrase, though as they play a duple rhythm against the bell's triple time, they are otherwise well crossed: and likewise they are crossed with *Kagaŋ*. In this Pattern C, of the eight rhythms being played simultaneously, no less than seven are crossed with each other.

The score shows plainly that the notes in brackets on the master's stave, are a duplication of *Sogo* and *Kidi*. At these points, if he wishes, the master may remain silent. One might wonder what the African thinks of the coincidence of the rhythms of all three drums here. Mr. Tay says it is quite all right because, though they play the same pattern, as they each play it on a different pitch, they can be heard separately and therefore it sounds well. As a matter of fact it is part of the pattern to emphasize strongly the *Sogo* and *Kidi* beats, and in accompanying them the master is merely reinforcing this feature.

By this time the reader may be inclined to say, 'I do not see how anyone could play such a series of conflicting rhythms'. We sympathize, but nevertheless we make three observations. Firstly, in actual performance this sort of music makes a glorious sound: it is all intensely rhythmic and vital, though not in the European sense. Secondly, the African seeks precisely what is on the score, the multiplicity of conflicting rhythm-patterns which he hears as distinct and yet contributory elements. If he is a skilled dancer he can follow one drum with his arms or shoulder-blades and another with his feet, though usually he will select one drum to dance to. Thirdly, the complexity of Pattern C is only by way of introduction. It is child's play compared with what we shall later encounter.

Master Pattern D (bars 35–39) covers three *Gankogui* phrases and therefore having been played six times it will enter, at the seventh time, in the same place in the song at which it started. Once again the suitable entry for this pattern is on the word '*hee*' (bar 36). It avoids, as usual, entering on a strong *Gankogui* beat, and this time it ends by straddling the low bell-note. The notes given to the nonsense syllables '*kiŋ-kiŋ*' (end of bars 37 and 38) are not always played. They are introduced from time to time: when not played, there is a rest at these places. The reason for this is that these two notes really duplicate the *Sogo* and *Kidi* patterns: note that *Kidi* is emphatic at these points in his pattern. Further confirmation is that *Sogo* does not start playing when the master introduces this pattern until these words '*kiŋ-kiŋ*'. We see once again that *Kidi* is the chief replier and that *Sogo* duplicates his pattern in simpler form. Mr. Tay says that when *Sogo* and *Kidi* play together (though at different pitch) as in *Nyayito*, it makes a very good sound. *Sogo* and *Kidi* both play in 3/4 time but their main beats are permanently crossed. One might have shifted *Sogo*'s bars to agree with those of *Kidi*. But the African must have the final judgement: Mr. Tay indicates, on request, by a nod of his head, where he feels the stress in any pattern to fall. *Sogo* and *Kagaŋ* are in phase, though one plays 3/4 and the other 3/8 so there is still a slight conflict. *Kidi* is permanently crossed with *Kagaŋ*. Both *Sogo* and *Kidi* are crossed with *Gankogui*. The master drum being in irregular time, crosses everybody at one point or another. *Kidi* has two possible replies to this pattern. He can go on playing as in bar 36, or he can go on playing the full version given in bar 37. It will be noticed that both are in 3/4 time and in both the bars have the same relationship with *Gankogui*, the main beat of the bar being a quaver late on *Gankogui*'s main beat.

Master Pattern E (bars 41–49) introduces a new technique in patterns. As usual for the master drum its barring is irregular: it avoids starting on the main *Gankogui* beat and its last beat falls right between the bell-beats. But its chief characteristic is indicated by the star marked in bar 43. The section of the master pattern from the star to the end of bar 46 may be repeated as many times as desired before repeating the whole pattern. On the other hand there is no need to do this at all, and the pattern may repeat as marked on the score. The pattern as it stands has a length of six *Gankogui* phrases and therefore will, in this form, keep in phase with the song. The starred section is four *Gankogui* phrases long, and therefore if it is repeated the total pattern will now be ten phrases which number does not look promising. If, however, the drummer repeats it twice more, the overall length will now be eighteen *Gankogui* phrases which will cause the full pattern, if it is now repeated, to start at the right place in the song. The pattern is in the form of a duet between the master and *Sogo* and *Kidi*, the latter two working in concert. The master beats loudly '*kpa kpo*' and is answered *forte*, '*hive*'; this is all repeated piano: the master beats a strongly duple short piece, which is echoed in the same rhythm but in contrasting melody by *Sogo* and *Kidi*, while the master waits in silence. It gives the *Asiwui* a real chance to come to the fore.

This Pattern E *can* be used for this particular song but Mr. Tay says it does not 'make it interesting'. Anyhow, Pattern E is chiefly used for a humourous interlude in the dance. All the drums except the master stop playing and there is some fooling. Perhaps some man will rush out and carry a drum to the edge of the dancing circle—and so forth. Meanwhile in the absence of the *Asiwui*, as the master is still playing, the onlookers will shout *Sogo*'s and *Kidi*'s nonsense syllables at the correct times for their response to the master. The author has seen Mr. Tay get a European audience to make a response like this, in nonsense syllables. It is very effective and gives one quite a thrill to answer his drum in this way.

We now come to the last pattern for *Nyayito*, Pattern F (bars 48–51). This pattern has a peculiarity in that it has five alternate forms. These are not master-drum variations such as we shall later have to deal with. Each one in fact can be used as the basis on which the drummer would build such variations. Therefore each of them has to be reckoned as the standard pattern. On the other hand they are not five separate standard patterns : they contain common features which proclaim that they are really modifications of one and the same pattern. The various alternative forms of Pattern F can be seen on the score in bars 53 to 56. We have printed at the top of the score, the *Gankogui* pattern to show the master pattern's relations with it and also, on the second line, an imaginary 3-clap which does not occur in practice. The other drums are omitted as they are the same as in bars 48 to 51. Now at the start of bar 49 and also at bar 53 we see that Pattern F has a special characteristic in that it is the one and only *Nyayito* pattern which actually starts on the low bell. This happens in all its five forms. Again, in bars 53 to 55, we have underlined in the first three versions of the pattern the nonsense syllables *kito*, in version 4 the word *gaga* which takes their place, and in version 5, the corresponding word *tote*. We can at once see why the African considers all these versions still to be the same Pattern F. They start at the same place *vis-à-vis* the *Gankogui*, and they have *kito* or its equivalent occurring three times in every *Gankogui* phrase, and at the same points in the phrase: in other words, these syllables *kito* are based on the 3-clap. Even in Alternative 1, where the pattern is extended to cover three *Gankogui* phrases, the word *kito* occurs consistently.

Whichever form of Pattern F is used, it will fit into the whole drumming in the manner shown in bars 48 to 52. The pattern starts in the now-familiar place in the song and, counting the rests in bar 51 as part of the pattern, extends for three *Gankogui* phrases. It is for once, in divisive and not additive rhythm, being consistently in 4/8 time. *Sogo* and *Kidi* virtually duplicate each other and are also in 4/8 time which, however, is staggered at half a bar's distance in relation to the master drum. The result is a ding-dong : every time the master plays *kito* the *Asiwui* answer *kede* or *krebe* which are both in the same rhythm. We tidy-minded Europeans would doubtless like the bar-lines of the three drums to coincide but they cannot. If they did, you would either have to shift the master's bar-line one quaver to the right in which case he would be saying '*kiTO*' which he does not: or you would find that *Sogo* and *Kidi* would have to say '*KEde*' and '*KREbe*' respectively, which again they do not. To get over the difficulty by using accentuation marks is only to confuse the basic issue. Contrasting with the strongly duple nature of this pattern, *Kagaŋ* pursues his staggered triple way. In spite of the cross-barring the pattern feels much more 'European' than anything else we have so far met.

Looking now at bars 53 to 56, we notice that all the versions save for Alternative 3, have a length (including rests, if any) of three *Gankogui* phrases. The latter is only one *Gankogui* phrase in length. So they will all be in phase with the song. Incidentally, Alternative 1 is a further proof that the rests are a part of the pattern, for this version fills out the rests with notes. It has two further points of interest. At the end of bar 55, at the word '*tagide*', it uses the same triple device that we encountered in Pattern B (bar 23). Without our saying it is triple one might, from the score, conclude that it is a simple syncopation. It is not and it never is: always it appears as a little piece of triple time played just twice as fast as the normal triple time built on the basic time-unit of a quaver. The same triple motif is seen in reverse in bar 54 to the syllables '*-toki*'. What is to happen when Alternative 1 is repeated? There are two courses. You can wait for one or two *Gankogui* phrases and then start again: a master drummer would know by the context of the dance and song, how long to wait. Or you may repeat the pattern immediately. In this case, as the pattern starts on the low bell-note, the final *kito* (bar 56) becomes the first *kito* of the repeat. This is what we mean by saying that the African has a tendency to consider the end to be also the beginning.

In Alternative 4 we find the whole of the first half of the pattern constructed in the condensed triple time mentioned before. Here it is unmistakable though in true African fashion each little triple piece is preceded by a quaver (on the syllable *to*) which does not share the tripleness.

There remains only to study the ending pattern (bars 57–59). In Northern Rhodesia we found no such organized way of bringing a piece of drumming to a close. As the drum-rhythms were crossed, the only way to end was what in fact happened: one man would get tired of playing, and throw down his drum, thereby breaking the cross-rhythms. The dance would, as a result, collapse. The Ewe have a special ending technique for every form of dance and the pattern varies according to the dance. When the master drummer decides to close the drumming (and *ipso facto* the dance) he may, in this dance, take either of two courses. He may drop into one of the changing signals to alert the other drummers and then play the ending pattern: or he may finish the pattern he was playing and without any interlude, round off with the ending pattern. In the score we imagine he is doing the former. Now the master drummer cannot stop anywhere: he must pay strict regard to the song and end in a suitable place. The idea is to choose a suitable place fairly early in the song, so that when the orchestra stops, the song and the claps will go on for some time by themselves till they reach the end of the verse. They cannot stop till they reach that point, and the whole idea is to stop the orchestra sufficiently soon to allow the song to show its beauty by itself. Thus, in the song we have chosen for the score, a good place to play the end pattern is just after the chorus have sung 'Beble' (bar 58). Let us go back for a moment to the beginning of the score, where the song is set out in full, and look at bar 8. The word *midzro* is the real end of the song and is followed by a rest. Had the master drummer chosen this word (which is on a low bell and therefore theoretically eligible) to start playing his end pattern, the singers would have to stop as it is the end of the song, and everything would cease at the final note of the orchestra. By starting just after 'Beble' in bar 58, he secures that his final beat coincides with the end of one of the sections of the song. Nothing could be more suitable. The song goes on till it finally comes to rest on the word *midzro* in bar 83.

The master-drum pattern is in two halves, both incorporating the special triple motif. During the first half of this, the *Asiwui* go on playing their response to the changing signal: but the playing of it is ample warning that they are at last going to abandon their cross-rhythms and bring the dance to an end by a short and peremptory *coda* in synchrony. That is what happens at the words 'Tevlo tega'. Everyone curtails his bar so as to come into line with the master. They all imitate the pitches of his drum, falling on the final note. *Gankogui* and *Axatse* also finish here. They all play *fortissimo* and it is a dramatic climax performed with hair-splitting accuracy.

We shall see, as we study the other scores, that on the surface they look very much alike in build and in spirit, so far as the European student is concerned. Yet to the Ewe people the *Nyayito* is just as solemn and mournful as our own funeral music is to us in the West. Mr. Tay gives the answer. He says that even if the song is not slow or sad in its melody, yet the spirit of mourning is conveyed in three ways. First, the conduct of the people; they will not dress in style (compare some of the later dances) and they will sit very patiently. Second, the slow speed of the drumming; and third, the meaning of the words of the song. The whole dance thus produces an ethos of mourning.

5

YEVE CULT MUSIC

EWE TRIBE: GHANA

SOCIAL SETTING

THERE are among the Ewe people a number of religious cults. They have been described by others,[1] but some account must be given of the cult whose music we are to study in order to place it in its setting. The *Yeve* or *Tɔhono* cult is the Cult of the God of Thunder. It belongs to the Ewe alone, which in this context embraces the Ewe, Fɔ̃, Dahomey, and Toŋgo peoples. Many cults are by the impact of modern change more or less in process of disintegration, but *Yeve* preserves to the full the old-time influence and cohesion. It is a secret society and all joining it have to undergo a period of instruction during which they learn the special cult language, the cult songs and dances, and the cult customs. During this time they are clad in a white sheet, have their heads shaven, and walk with head and eyes downcast to show humility, and they live in the cult house. The cult regalia, which will be used for dancing is expensive, and during the training period one has to work hard to accumulate the necessary funds. For example, men wear voluminous knee-length skirts containing many yards of different coloured material so plentiful that they can rest their elbows on the waist when dancing. They learn to sway it and twirl it in dancing to display the colours which make a brave show. They are bare above the waist but wear beads—gold or silver if one has them—on the chest. Anyone may witness their dances, though without taking part. In the case of the *Adavu* dance, during which the cult objects are brought out and borne round, all spectators have to be bare from the waist up. This does not apply to their other dances.

---

[1] A. B. Ellis, *The Ewe Speaking Peoples of the Slave Coast of West Africa*; M. Manoukian, *The Ewe-speaking People of Togoland and the Gold Coast*; Pierre Verger, *Dieux d'Afrique*, Paul Hartmann, Paris, 1954, has excellent photographs of cult customs; J. Spieth, *Die Religion der Eweer in Sud-Togo*, pp. 172–88.

Members of a cult are sworn brothers and will help each other even if they come from different lodges.

The focal point of the Yeve cult (as of other cults) is the cult house. This consists of a series of outer fences with staggered entrances so as to ensure secrecy, in the middle of which are various rooms and buildings including a very secret room where the sacred objects of the cult are kept. There is also a special cult tree planted here, and in this central enclosure lives a male keeper. The outside of the cult house is painted with patterns to warn everyone of its nature. Should anyone make unauthorized entry within the fence, the caretaker will beat a drum and all members will rush to the cult house where the culprit, sitting bare-backed in the entrance to the fence will be tried and maybe fined (to the tune of about £25 nowadays). Everyone realizes this obligation, though perhaps the worst offence a non-member can commit is to insult a member of the cult. The sanction behind these disciplinary customs is the generally held belief that if you refuse, the cult has powers to cause your house to be struck by lightning.

Dancing is a very important activity of the cults, and every priest of the Yeve cult wants his members to be able to dance better than those of any other Yeve branch. This spirit of emulation should be noted. We believe it is quite an important element in African dancing as a whole: in fact 'showing off' seems to be one of the vitalizing factors in good dancing. Normally a cult dance takes place in a special dancing area outside the main entrance in the cult-house fence. The whole arrangements and layout for the dance are organized on traditional lines and so, in order to be able to picture such a dance we need to know its general dispositions. The diagram of the cult buildings and fences is merely schematic: the actual disposition is a secret of the cult.

On the stools at X and Y near the cult trees, sit the priest and the priestess: it does not matter on which side. The priestess is the leader of the women members of the cult, or maybe the priest's wife. In front of the stools are three benches or forms. On these are sitting those members of the cult (of both sexes) who are not dancing that day, either because they are too old, or are not full members, or just do not feel like dancing. These people do the singing and the clapping. They are dressed in their ordinary clothes. Across the arc-shaped line of forms, are placed a line of stools or forms for the orchestra who also sit, except for the

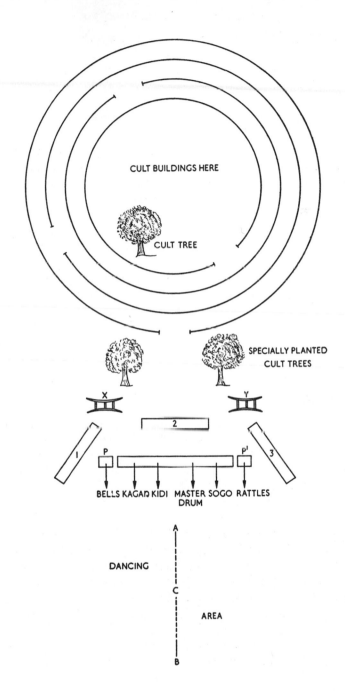

CULT BUILDINGS HERE

CULT TREE

SPECIALLY PLANTED
CULT TREES

X   Y

2

P   P'

1   3

BELLS KAGAN KIDI   MASTER SOGO RATTLES
                    DRUM

A

DANCING

C

AREA

B

master drummer if he uses the *Atsimevu* drum. At *P* or *P'* sits
the *Gankogui* player. If there are two *Gankogui* bells being used,
both players must sit together. This also applies to the rattle,
Axatse. The rattle player sits at *P'* or *P*, i.e. on the side opposite
to *Gankogui*. The drummers sit on the forms in the order shown
in the sketch. In the Yeve cult the cantors for the songs will be
one or other of the spare people sitting on the forms behind the
drums. The exception to this is that if there is a dancer who also
has a good voice and who wants a special song he can introduce
it by acting as cantor himself. He walks into the dance area from
the cult house playing on the *Adodo*. This is a native-smelted iron
hand-rattle. It consists of a short iron tube at each end of which
are welded several small conical bells each having a clapper. In
front of the drummers is the dance area, and all the people present
are facing towards it.

When the dancing starts, those who are going to dance—and
they will be the majority—are inside the cult-house fence dressed
in their cult regalia. When the drumming and the singing and the
clapping get going, they come by ones or twos, usually the latter,
into the dance area. They start dancing at *A* and dance forward
either to *B* or perhaps only as far as *C*. Having reached either
point, the dancers wait and have a rest, and then dance back, or
if tired they may merely use a shuffling dance-step for the retiring
movement. Meanwhile another pair will come in to dance. Ewe
dancing is strenuous especially for the men who use their chest
and shoulder muscles to move their shoulder-blades to and fro
with considerable force, in addition to the muscular actions of
their arms, and of course the foot movements. They therefore do
not keep up the drumming for long at a stretch. Individual dancers
only perform for about a minute or two at a time, and the drummers will not go on for more than about a quarter of an hour
without a break. In contrast with Northern Rhodesian custom,
a complete Ewe drumming, except for a 'Wakes' drumming
which may go on from 8 p.m. right through the night till sunrise, will usually last only for an afternoon, say 2–6 p.m. or occasionally in the morning from sunrise to say 11 a.m.

THE MUSIC

As the cults are religious societies they abound in customs and
ceremonies: music is part of the ceremonial. Indeed it is more

than this, for it is interwoven into the very fibre of the society. We shall, therefore, expect it to share that conservatism which is a feature of religious observance. Here, if anywhere, we shall find the true unadulterated traditional music of the Ewe people. The influence of modern American dance music or of Western part-singing learnt in school has not penetrated the traditionalism of the Yeve cult. Moreover, as the cult is a closed society and much care is taken in the training of neophytes, and as the members can be, and are, readily summoned for practice, their music and dancing is on a different level from ordinary folk-music performed by villagers as their normal recreation. As spectators do not take part in the performances, these are in the category of professional productions by highly trained devotees.

The Yeve cult has seven dances: the word 'dance' includes not only the actual choreography, but the corpus of songs that belong to it in particular, together with its special drumming and orchestral accompaniment. Each dance is clearly distinguished by these features from any other dance. In order to differentiate these we shall have to anticipate our detailed study by making reference to the *Gankogui* patterns. The seven dances are these:

1. *Husago*

It has a special *Gankogui* pattern which for the present we will represent as:

2. *Sovu*

Two *Gankogui* styles are used. The first, called *Gankogui fofo*, gives the characteristic pattern for the dance which is:

The tied notes produce, of course, only one sound and so this pattern is a syncopated one.

The second *Gankogui* style is called *Gankogui mamla*. This is a set of free bell-rhythms created on the spur of the moment. The only rule is that the low bell-note *must* coincide with its incidence in *Gankogui fofo*.

3. Sogba or Sogo

For this, the usual *Gankogui* pattern is used but it is played quicker than usual. The pattern is:

Sogba is also characterized by having very interesting master-drum patterns.

4. Adavu

Adavu, which is the fastest dance of all, also has interesting master-drum rhythms. It has two *Gankogui* patterns either of which may be used, both being much simpler than usual. They are:

(*a*)   or (*b*)

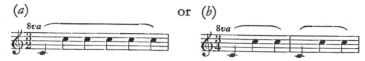

After playing *Adavu* you enter into *Afovu*, of which it is a preliminary.

5. Afovu

This has two possible *Gankogui* patterns:

(*a*) the standard pattern as given for *Sogba* above;

(*b*) you may, if you like, lay the *Gankogui* on its side and beat it in this position. In this case you will play:

Afovu is the next fastest dance to *Adavu*.

6. Agovu

This employs the standard *Gankogui* pattern (see *Sogba*).

7. Avelevu

The standard *Gankogui* pattern is used but it gradually increases its pace as the dance proceeds. In Northern Rhodesia we never came across a single example of *accelerando* : but here, undoubtedly, it is, and this is not the only example of its use by the Ewe. This must not lead the reader to conclude that such changes of speed are as usual in African music as they are in the West. As so much African music is dance music, which obviously for the most part demands a constant tempo, we should not expect to find *gradual* changes of speed to any large extent; more especially, when we reflect that there is no orchestral conductor to keep the instruments together during such a change of time.

Any or all of these seven kinds of dancing may be used at any meeting of the Yeve cult. We propose to take three for detailed study. They are *Husago, Sovu,* and *Sogba.*

All the Yeve cult dances have a special introduction which is in two parts, the first being invariable and the second varying according to the particular dance which follows. Every Yeve dance starts by the playing of the Yeve cult signal. This is played on the master drum alone, with no other instrument and no song and no clap : this is the invariable part of the introduction. After this the master drummer plays the dance signal which indicates the particular dance to be performed. This signal is played as a solo on the master drum but the other instruments come in at the appropriate point. At the end of this signal, the music of the dance itself starts.

THE *HUSAGO* DANCE

Besides the song and clapping, the instruments required are *Gankogui, Axatse,* and the three drums *Kagan, Kidi,* and *Atsimevu.* The latter is not quite like the one in Plate 1. It is as long, but narrower and is carved from a solid tree-trunk hollowed out. Its sound is not as deep as the drum illustrated and corresponds more nearly to that of *Sogo.* In fact, in these days, *Sogo* is often used as the master drum in the absence of the proper drum. The right hand beats with a stick, the left with the bare hand.

1. *The Yeve cult signal*

Mr. Tay is not a member of the Yeve cult, but being a master drummer he knows a lot of their drumming and has had experience of playing for them. While he knows the rhythms, he says he does not know the traditional nonsense syllables used by the members. In our score he has used his own syllables though he says any master drummer would understand them and be able to produce from their use the right sort of beats and the correct rhythms.

Let us study the score at figures 1–8. Here we have a special sort of drumming which is played in a declamatory sort of way, as if the drummer was speaking in words. Each phrase, separated as it is from the next by a prolonged rest, is, as it were, one sentence of the announcement. It is played *rubato* and its metrical structure has nothing whatever to do with the *Gankogui* pattern. It is in absolutely free rhythm: while the drummer feels the innate rhythm of the phrases, he declaims them in a somewhat theatrical fashion, which he emphasizes by the duration of the rests, which are very effective in giving a rather startling pungency to the cult signal, and whose length depends on his sense of musical fitness.

Our scoring of this Yeve cult signal represents Mr. Tay's method of playing. As it is a *rubato* piece, other master drummers might vary the speed in places. Obviously this was a difficult piece to transcribe with accuracy. We did it thus: we found the metronome speed from the crotchet lengths in bar 1: Mr. Tay then played the whole signal on our drum recorder, which gave us a long strip of paper with all the beats marked on it: using the crotchet-lengths in bar 1 as the standard unit, we measured on the paper the lengths between each beat, and the lengths of rests and were thus able to give them their value in musical notes: the bar-lines and phrase marks, which show the rhythmic organization of the piece were arrived at by asking Mr. Tay what he felt when playing. It is, in our opinion, a beautifully balanced piece of music, closely knit, and all germinating from the little motif comprising the first three notes of bar 1, to the nonsense syllables *ga deŋ*. This motif launches each of the phrases from 1–6: numbers 5 and 6 though different in pitch have still the same rhythm. The rhythm begins in silence and the rest at the beginning is part of the pattern. In playing, Mr. Tay showed by a nod of the head that he felt the presence of the rest. The first announcement is made (bar 1) and repeated (bar 2): it starts again in bar 3 but breaks off into a pretty little pattern *toto tevlo tegba*: this is repeated and lengthened in bar 4: in bar 5 the original motif reappears with a change of accent and pitch, in the motif *ga kito kito*, repeated four times: bar 7 is a musical *comma* in the announcement, and bar 8 brings it to a close, using the interesting combination of an *accelerando* with *diminuendo*. We barred this for convenience in reading, but it is actually a continuous unaccented roll.

2. *The* Husago *signal*

After a pause at the end of the Yeve cult signal the master drummer goes on to announce the *Husago* signal which extends in the score from bar 9 to the end of bar 19. First a word about the speed. The change of metronome sign from $\sqcup = 77$ to $\sqcup = 132$ is misleading. It had to be made because the *Husago* signal leads straight into the main dance which is at $\sqcup = 132$. The effect is to make the *Husago* signal appear to be slower than it is. In reality, it is slightly brisker than the cult signal. Thus if we compare the motif '*ga deŋ*' in bar 1 with the notes for the syllables '*ga tegi*' in bar 9 we shall find that the speed of playing both is similar. In the same way, the crotchets for '*ya-ya*' in bar 8 are going at $\sqcup = 231$ and those for the same syllables in bars 12 and 16 at $\sqcup = 264$.

Like the cult signal, this *Husago* signal is in free rhythm and is declamatory. It is also divided into phrases clearly defined by the long rests in between. Its form is this: *A* (bars 9–12)+*A* (bars 13–16)+*B* (bars 17–19) which latter is a bridge leading into the main dance. The *accel e dim.* roll of bar 8 is here embellished by the other instruments (bars 12 and 16). At bar 17 the feeling of free rhythm is abruptly broken by the sudden and strident announcement of *kide kide* made purposely by the master drummer to signal his entry into strict time for the dance. He emphasizes this in the two following bars, bar 19 being specially designed to show the other instruments the exact speed at which he wants the dance to go.

So far all has been plain sailing: we now plunge into something we have not met with before, and for which bars 18 and 19 were a studied preparation.

Hitherto in this book we have been at pains to emphasize that African music is built up from a small basic time-unit whose speed is constant right through a piece, and in polyrhythm is constant for all instruments. Our motive was to discountenance any idea that because of its apparent complexity of accent the music must be composed of such irregular elements as 5 against 4, 9 against 7, or any other combination of this sort. To suggest this sort of thing may be intriguing by its novelty and may appeal to our romantic sense but it has, so far as our experience goes, no basis

whatever in real fact. But we have to reckon with another fundamental characteristic of African music which is the principle of
three against two. We have to grasp the fact that if from childhood
you are brought up to regard beating 3 against 2 as being just as
normal as beating in synchrony, then you develop a two-dimen-
sional attitude to rhythm which we in the West do not share.
This bi-podal conception is so much part of the African's nature
that he can with ease not only play a broken pattern in duple time,
containing notes and rests of various values against a similarly
broken pattern in the time-relation of 3 against 2, but he can also
do this when the bar-lines of his short triplets are staggered permanently with the duple bars and, still further, he has no need to
regard these short triplets as triple at all and can perfectly well
play a duple pattern at the speed of the individual notes of these
short triplets. It may seem incredible but it will all be illustrated
in this *Husago* dance.

In monorhythm, the African's use of short triplets is very
sparing. As far as our experience goes, no African singer or
drummer during the course of his own monorhythmic line of
music will break into an extended series of short triplets or use
any other such device which upsets, except for a passing moment,
his consistent use of his own basic unit of time.

When the African plays 3 against 2 in polyrhythm what he
sometimes does is to set up this relationship permanently right
through a piece of music or a main section of it. This is apparently
a denial of our insistence on the constancy of the basic unit of
time. For if you play permanently two rhythms 3 against 2 what
you are really doing is employing two basic time-units. For example:

To anticipate our studies, let us say that *Husago* is going to fall
into this class: at the same time we shall show that it is exceptional.

But this is not the only way to exploit 3 against 2. There is another way, and it is this which the African usually employs:

Both voices are still in the relationship of 3 to 2 (3 bars of the top line to 2 of the bottom), but this time it is the top line which is going quicker. Now if, as before, the top line represents the basic time-units, the bottom line is going *slower*. When this happens, the basic time-unit is not *apparently* forsaken by any instrument, for in this case the slower time is a definite compound of the basic time-units: whereas the top line takes them two at a time, the bottom line takes three at a time. This makes an enormous difference to the sound of a piece of music, for 3 against 2 played in this form by Africans produces no audible clash of basic time at all. If the lower voice sings in dotted crotchets or dotted minims, all the notes coincide with multiples of the basic beats: the same holds good if this voice sings triplets, which of course will be composed of crotchets or quavers, &c. Only if this voice sings dotted quavers or semiquavers, &c., will the notes fall *between* the incidence of the basic time beats. A good example of this technique comes from Northern Rhodesia.[1] In the *Mganda* dance the song for the most part preserves just this relationship with the drums. What one hears is that the song seems to move in a steady *legato* surrounded by the drumming: there is no suggestion of what to us in the west is the typical 3 against 2 pattern, and one would never know of its existence in this *Mganda* without careful analysis.

We may now resume the study of *Husago* and we look at bars 20 and 21, noting first the master-drum pattern. The master drummer continues in the common time he established in bars 18 and 19. We notice that Master Pattern 1 (bars 20–50) is all the same. Where is all the usual interest and varied rhythm? The answer is that he is establishing an unusual relationship with the

[1] A. M. Jones, 'The Mganda Dance' in *African Studies* (Journal of the University of the Witwatersrand, Johannesburg, S. Africa), Dec. 1945.

Gankogui and uses a simple pattern which will help everybody to get the clash of time. *Gankogui* is playing a perfectly simple duple pattern

The master is playing 3 against 2 to this which, one might expect, would result in his playing a triple pattern. But, and here is the subtlety, that is just what he is not doing. Though he plays 3 against 2, he yet plays a perfectly simple duple pattern

He is playing 3 against 2, taking *four* beats to a bar. He starts in bar 20 synchronously with *Gankogui*: and a little reflection and a study of the score will show that he will be in phase with *Gankogui* again after every twelve beats. To show this on the score we have drawn a bar-line down to the *Atsimevu* stave at bar 22, and so on after every twelve beats of the master. If now one looks at bars 20–22 as a whole, one can see that two patterns of *Gankogui* fit three patterns of the master. How simple in structure but how difficult to perform! This is an example where the 3 against 2 is set up by taking the 2 as the basic time and then playing 3 (i.e. quicker) against it. This is not apparent from our score where it looks as if we have slowed up the *Gankogui* beats. The reason for using dotted quavers instead of quavers as the basic time-unit is that the score would be unreadable later on in Pattern 2 if we did not do so. Mr. Tay told us that *Husago* is tricky, and that not very many people can either dance or play it. It is considered a very interesting drumming (and no wonder!) but it needs good players. Even the *Gankogui* player must be a good man as the *Gankogui* changes its rhythm in the changing signals, which is unusual. As to the dancers, he said that while many people may have been dancing the previous dance, as soon as *Husago* is started only about 10 to 20 per cent. of them will remain to dance it. The following professional tip shows the difficulties. Mr. Tay says that when the *Gankogui* player enters at bar 20, he says to himself, 'I must beat my main beats (i.e. his dotted crotchets) on every third beat of the master drum, and then "pop in" my quick notes (dotted quavers) in between'.

Let us now pass on to bars 22–24 in order to see what the

other drums do. *Kagaŋ* at first surprises us : his function usually is to set up a cross-rhythm with *Gankogui* : here he merely doubles *Gankogui*'s pattern. It would probably have been too difficult for him to do otherwise. Kidi replies to the master. We have in *Nyayito* pointed out *Kidi*'s dependence on the master drum. Here is confirmation indeed, for while *Kagaŋ* follows the bell in his basic time-units, *Kidi* follows the master. So we get the overall division that *Gankogui* and *Kagaŋ* are playing 2 against 3 of the master and *Kidi*, with the added complication that *Kidi* staggers his bars with those of the master, his pattern lying exactly athwart that of *Atsimevu*. See how the master plays two low notes each time *Kidi* plays his pattern *ti-gi-diŋ* so as to let that pattern stand out. Incredible as it may seem, especially in view of the fast speed ($\downarrow = 264$), this is how *Husago* is played.

3. *The song*

> Gbedzia do loo gbedzia do
> Adza maxenua, adza nado gbe vɔ
> Gbedzia do loo gbedzia do
> Adza maxenu adza nado gbe vɔa?
> Ka xoxowo nu wogbea ka yeyeawo ɖo
> Dzadza do adza nado gbe vɔ
> Ka xoxowo nu wogbea ka yeyeawo ɖo
> Dzadza do adza nado gbe vɔ loo
> Dzadza do loo dzadza do
> Adza maxenu adza nado gbe vɔ.

We cannot give a translation of this song as it is in the cult language.[1] The only straightforward piece of Ewe is the fifth line *Ka xoxowo* . . . which is an Ewe proverb, 'New ropes are twisted in the same way as old'.

The melody of this song, which from the Western point of view is in a diatonic minor key, is an extraordinarily long one for an African tune, extending over twenty-three *Gankogui* phrases (bars 26–48). In spite of its length, it has no clear-cut repeats within itself except for the last five bars (44–48) which even then contain slight variations. Nevertheless its construction is very compact and it consists of the subtle exploitation of only three

---

[1] There is a text on the Yeve cult which gives specimens of the secret language in D. Westermann, *A Study of the Ewe Language*, translated by A. L. Bickford Smith, O.U.P., 1930, pp. 211–15.

musical ideas. The first idea is in bars 26 and 27, finishing on the
first note of bar 28 : the second goes from bar 28 to bar 31 : and
the third from bar 36 to the first note of bar 40. The whole song
is a broad and dignified and closely interrelated melody. We may
analyse its form thus :

$$
\begin{array}{lll}
\text{Bars } 26\text{--}31 & (A+B) = 2+4 & \textit{Gankogui} \text{ patterns} \\
\phantom{\text{Bars }} 32\text{--}35 & (A'+C) = 2+2 & \text{,,} \qquad \text{,,} \\
\phantom{\text{Bars }} 36\text{--}39 & D = 4 & \text{,,} \qquad \text{,,} \\
\phantom{\text{Bars }} 40\text{--}43 & D' = 4 & \text{,,} \qquad \text{,,} \\
\phantom{\text{Bars }} 44\text{--}48 & (A+B) = 2+3 & \text{,,} \qquad \text{,,} \\
& \text{Total} \quad \overline{23}
\end{array}
$$

The song follows the rule of 2 and 3 except that we should have
expected one more *Gankogui* phrase at the end before repeating it,
so as to bring the total to twenty-four and not twenty-three
Gankogui patterns. This seemingly trivial point is a serious one
because it means that with an odd number like twenty-three, when
the song repeats, its notes are not likely to fall in the same place
vis-à-vis the master drum. There is one and only one place where
the song is allowed to start at first singing and that is during the
Gankogui phrase whose first note coincides with the main beat of
the master's pattern. This can be seen in bar 26. When we come
to the repeat in bar 49, this is no longer the case. Several new
facts come to light here, and they will recur in other dances. In
the first place we believe that the 'ideal' form of the song consists
of twenty-four *Gankogui* phrases. All our experience prompts this
conclusion : and it is reinforced by the fact that were this the case,
i.e. if the repeat started in bar 50, the song would start again in
the correct relation to the master pattern. What seems to have
happened is that the last bar (bar 49), which would either prolong
the final note of the tune or would be a rest, has been telescoped
with the first bar of the repeat. This is not surprising : Africans
do not appear to like a long drawn-out interval in music. For
instance, in singing a European Iambic hymn-tune set in common
time, at the end of the second line where we wait for three beats,
they have a tendency to shorten this to two, making an incomplete
bar of only three beats. In this *Husago* song it so happened that
the last syllable falls on the very first note of the *Gankogui* pattern, and the repeat does not start till near the end of the pattern.
Thus if you wait to make the song total twenty-four patterns,

there would be a long pause from the beginning of bar 48 to nearly the end of bar 50 with 'nothing happening' as the Africans say. The remedy is to *overlap* the end and beginning bars of the song. Another factor is this: if, as is evident, the song marches by the *Gankogui* phrases, from the point of view of the singers only, there is no reason why they should not start the repeat in any phrase, provided they start at the right point within it, which is what they do in bar 49. Thirdly, Mr. Tay on numerous occasions when this sort of point crops up, says that while the master drummer is careful to pay strict attention to the song on his first entry, so as to come in at a suitable point, thereafter he does not worry very much about where the song has got to, except that he keeps one ear on it so as to avoid spoiling it by unsuitable beating. If the melody soars up in a piquant melodic phrase, the master must not kill this by a clatter of beats: similarly, if the melody descends and rests or moves quietly on or round a low note, he must follow the spirit of the tune at this point. In practice if he is playing a standard pattern, this may mean nothing more than a slight variation in the zones of the drum on which he plays or the sort of beats he makes. The standard pattern remains recognizable but may be toned down in such contexts. The point we are really making, however, is that normally, having entered at the right place in the song, the master goes on playing more by reference to the *Gankogui* than to the latter. The song is really controlled by the cantor; if he likes to pause before a repeat, he may do so. On the other hand, it could be the master who waits before repeating his pattern, filling in the intervening space with waiting beats. The genius of African music is partly its fluidity, and a successful performance depends on the unspoken but nevertheless real co-operation between the cantor and the master drummer, and indeed everybody.

A word must now be said about the entry of the song. There are two ways of doing this: the version given in the score is the more usual one. The key to this method is that the cantor waits till he hears the master start playing his main pattern, i.e. *tete gaga*. He can then enter the song after the master has played this once (i.e. in bar 20), or four times (i.e. in bar 22) or seven times, &c., his aim being to enter in any bell-phrase whose first note coincides with the master drum's main beat. In the score we show how the cantor may allow a little time for the drums to get settled before his entry. There is another quite different way of starting. Suppose before the drumming starts the people have already decided to dance *Husago*. In this case the master plays the Yeve cult signal and then stops: he omits the *Husago* signal. The first cantor then lines the song *rubato* as we described in *Nyayito*. A second cantor starts the song again *a tempo*, and when he reaches the right place, i.e. the syllable '*do*' at the end of the cantor's first line, he turns to the orchestra, and the *Gankogui* starts and the other instruments come in as in our score at bars 20 to 22, the people taking up the chorus. This business of starting draws attention once again to the elasticity of African musical procedure. It is all so well organized and yet at the same time so delightfully informal. Within the prescribed limits of custom, no one quite knows what is going to happen: it depends quite a lot on the inspiration of the leading performers. These men are not making music which is crystallized on a music-score. They are moved by the spirit of the occasion. The result is a feshness and spontaneity and an element of surprise that we in the West may well envy.

4. *The drumming (continued)*

Returning to the drumming we examine Master Pattern 2 (bars 51 ff.). Of the four master patterns we give, all are short with the exception of this one. The shortness is no doubt due to the difficulty of drumming in *Husago* though we do not remember Mr. Tay having said so. The master's basic time is still 3 against 2 of *Gankogui*. The pattern itself enters at the sign :ς: in bar 54 and extends for 6½ *Gankogui* patterns to about the middle of bar 60. It is preceded by a short introduction (bar 53) which need not be played again during repeats, and seems to be designed to help him to enter his pattern at the right spot: but it can be repeated if desired. In mood it is sharply contrasted with Pattern 1 which was fairly quick and rather bumpy. Here the essence is the slow steady phrase *to to tegi* (bar 54) which appears in various guises right through the pattern. There is a pretty play on the accentuation of *tegi*. In bars 55, 56, 57, 59, and 60 the accent is on the first syllable: in bar 58 we suddenly have a piece of triple time with the accent shifted to the second syllable. In bar 59, though he is already playing 3 against 2 to the bell, the master uses, by way of variation on bar 55, a short triplet. This, and indeed the whole pattern, shows that the master is not thinking of his playing as being merely an exercise in 3 against 2 to the bell. He thinks of his pattern as existing in its own right and he plays about with it just as he would if his basic time-units were the same as for *Gankogui*.

The master pattern enters at a very peculiar place. In bar 54 we can see that his basic idea is to divide the 12 quavers of which the *Gankogui* phrase consists into 3 sets of 4, as contrasted with *Gankogui*'s 4 sets of 3. In consequence, he has to enter between, but not in the middle of, the two quick dotted quaver bell-beats. Probably the introduction in bar 53 was designed to help him to achieve this. We have already said that his pattern extends for $6\frac{1}{2}$ *Gankogui* phrases (to bar 60): this means that on his repeat he will displace his relationship by exactly half a bell-phrase so that, on repeating the second time, he will enter at his original point. This can be seen at bar 67. One more point: although this seems to be an extended pattern, in reality it is not. It is a succession of variations on one phrase of twelve quavers length, with one exception at bars 57 and 58 where the phrase is exactly half as long again. Twelve quavers is also the length of the *Gankogui* phrase, but the master places his phrases athwart those of the bell, making his main beat fall on the fourth quaver of the latter, at a point which is right off and between its rhythm. It is a remarkable example of cross-rhythm playing: 3/2 against 12/8[6/8] staggered by a minim.

A surprise awaits us when we look at *Kidi*'s playing. *Kidi* always hunts with the master and acts as a foil, making suitable replies to his patterns. In Pattern 1, *Kidi* and the master use the same basic unit of time. But here in Pattern 2 *Kidi* forsakes him and, adopting the basic time-unit of the bell, plays 2 against 3 to the master. But, and this is most remarkable, in spite of having changed his time, what *Kidi* plays in Pattern 2 is virtually the same as what he played in Pattern 1. In both it is a duple rhythm: in both he starts off beating *ti-gi-diŋ*: in both he ends his pattern with some muted filling beats. The only change is that he plays fewer filling beats in Pattern 2 and lengthens his initial phrase (compare bars 49 and 53–54). Yet, while the patterns are almost the same, *Kidi* stretches the basic time-unit in Pattern 2 and so takes half as long again to play it.

It is obvious by his time-units that he is going by the bell, but the mutual relationship of their main beats is rather obscured by the unfortunately necessary use of dotted notes on the score. If we rewrite the two patterns more simply, yet in the exact time as on the score, we get:

Both instruments have the same length of phrase—one bar of common time, but *Kidi*'s bars are staggered with the bell by the astonishing amount of one and a half beats. We can see how this comes about. *Kidi*'s nonsense syllable -*yi*- has to fall on the main beat of the *Gankogui* phrase: therefore his pattern must start three quavers back. Anyone who can do such a thing must get a tremendous rhythmic thrill in the doing. Small wonder that *Husago* players have to be competent.

This *Kidi* response in Pattern 2 is *Kidi*'s foundation-pattern for the whole *Husago* dance. At any time when the master plays a prolonged changing signal, *Kidi* will move on to this pattern and stay on it till the master announces his next pattern, having first answered the changing signal itself with the correct reply. For example, if the master, after playing bar 80, instead of at once moving on to a new pattern, goes on playing *to to to*, &c., *Kidi* after the four *to*'s in bar 80, will fall back on to his foundation-pattern till the master announces a new pattern.

Kagaɲ needs no comment: he goes on as before, doubling the bell-pattern. This completes the review of the drums except to point out the proper place of entry for the master pattern in relation to the song. In Pattern 1, the song depended on the master for its entry and that is exceptional. Here, as is usual, the master depends on the song. The proper place for his entry is the syllable '*do*' at the end of the cantor's first line (bar 53). Note once again how the cantor's melody leans forward to the end of the line, where his last note coincides with the beginning of the bell-phrase, making a natural focal point for the entry of the master. This is the same syllable as is used by the *Gankogui* in the alternative method of starting the dance described above in section 3.

We pass on to Master Pattern 3 (bars 68–73). The master enters on the same note of the song as in the previous pattern (bar 69).

His pattern is exactly two *Gankogui* phrases long and he is still playing against it at 3 : 2. Note how, though he starts exactly with the *Gankogui* phrase, the master secures an additional cross-rhythm and breaks the even flow of his own pattern at the beginning of bar 70. He is still playing in 3/4 time but, by introducing the crotchet rest, he makes a jerk in the flow, and the three syllables *to to to* which follow, being all of equal accent, feel like a bar of 3/2 time cut short at the end by the *reprise* of the pattern in bar 71.

Kidi, in this pattern, returns to his allegiance and uses the same time-unit as the master. Here is a good example of the 'call and response' between the master and *Kidi*. The master says, '*tsimano mano, gbevu na vuto*' and *Kidi* at once replies '*alelelele*', during which the master, so as not to smother him, merely plays three even beats.

Suppose at the moment the master starts this pattern, *Kidi* is playing his foundation-pattern because of the changing signal. How does he move from this to his response in Pattern 3 ? He goes on playing his foundation-pattern during bars 68 and 69 and the first crotchet of bar 70, and then, at whatever point in that pattern he finds himself, he leaves it and at once plays '*alelelele*' at the proper place (bar 70).

Master Pattern 4 (bars 74–77) is the simplest of all. Here the master is playing a straightforward 3 against 2 to the bell with no cross-rhythm, and with his bars in phase with those of the bell. *Kuguy* goes on as usual and it is left to *Kidi* to provide what little cross-accent there is. All *Kidi* is really doing is to strengthen the last beat of *Atsimevu*'s phrase by playing *kriy*, and then play-ing muted filling beats in between.

We have left the changing signal till now because it figures also in the ending pattern. Let us look at bars 78 to 82. In bar 78 we are imagining that the previous pattern is just ending. The master wants to change to a new pattern. The first thing he does (bar 79) is to give a warning. But note what he does! He suddenly leaves his 3 against 2 and for this one *Gankogui* phrase, he uses *Gankogui*'s basic time-units, playing with him in 6/8 time. During this, *Kidi* is still playing his response to the previous pattern whatever that happened to be: so he may or may not be still playing 3 against 2. Now in bar 80 the full changing signal operates. Again it is remarkable. This time it is *Gankogui* and *Axatse* who make the jump. They suddenly, and for just one bar, leave their own basic time-unit and adopt that of the master. They switch from 12/8[6/8] to 12/8[3/4]. *Atsimevu* reverts to his own basic time-unit but plays in duple time. Both *Kidi* and *Kagaŋ* double, or partly double the bell-notes. So bar 80 is the big 'All Change' played in synchrony. At bar 81 *Kagaŋ* signifies the end of this departure by producing a special note—'*gaŋ*'—and relaxes into his usual rhythm. *Kidi* falls back on his foundation-pattern until he knows what the master is going to do. *Gankogui* and *Axatse* resume their usual pattern, and the master will fill in with waiting beats of some sort or other till the song reaches the right word for him to introduce the next pattern.

The ending pattern (bars 84–88) starts with the changing signal. The master decides to bring the whole dance to a close. He first plays the changing signal (bars 85 and 86, which are identical with bars 79 and 80). But having played '*to*' four times on G he plays three more on B♭ (bar 87). He then plays his final phrases '*azagi toto, kpodo*', the last two notes being strongly accented in a manner which clearly indicates to everybody that this is the end. The other instruments distribute their allegiance. *Gankogui* reverts to his usual pattern until the two final notes where he plays synchronously with the master. *Axatse*, the rattle, strangely enough forsakes *Gankogui*, and doubles the rhythm of the master (bars 87 and 88). *Kidi*, after the changing signal, reverts to his foundation-pattern until the final two beats where he doubles the master. *Kagaŋ* does the same. Right at the end therefore, the dance is rounded off by two quavers played simultaneously by all instruments. As in *Nyayito*, the song now goes on with its hand-claps till it reaches the end of the verse and thus all comes to a close.

Husago surely is an astonishing display of rhythmic virtuosity. We shall meet in this book other examples of considerable complexity but it will be a complexity of patterns rather than that produced by the interweaving, in a full orchestra, of simpler patterns based on two different units of time. It is this which makes *Husago* so difficult and yet so thrilling. Having studied this ingenious and masterly interplay of rhythms, we salute the consummate musicianship of those who enjoy playing them.

THE *SOVU* DANCE

Sovu is another of the Yeve cult dances. It is a general dance which can be performed at any time when the members meet. It will be profitable for us to discuss first the *Gankogui* pattern which differs from any we have so far encountered. When Mr. Tay played this bell-pattern it was fairly obvious that he was playing a modification of the standard *Gankogui* pattern by omitting one of the crotchets in the second half thus:

Gankogui: Standard Pattern

„ Sovu (apparently)

But was it this? There is a *prima facie* case both for and against it. It is similar to the standard pattern and is partly additive in structure and feels 'African'. On the other hand it adds up to ten quavers, a fact which puts us on our guard. We played this to Mr. Tay and he said, 'Yes, but you are just off it.' We asked him to tap with his foot. It was then clear what he was doing: it was this:

Gankogui 4/4

Foot-beats 4/4

Had we followed our first inclination, our answer would have been utterly wrong. But there is more to be extracted from this matter. Though the two versions look so different when written, by how much in actual fact do they differ? The best way is to use a graph. Obviously each version must take the same time to play, which we can represent by spreading both patterns over forty squares, thus:

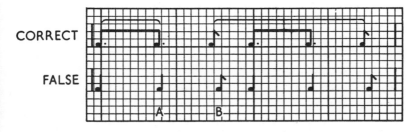

If the metronome speed for the crotchets in the top line is

$\downarrow$ = 100, then as a crotchet occupies 10 squares, and as 100 crotchets take 60 seconds, each square represents

$$\frac{60}{100 \times 10} \text{ secs.} = \tfrac{3}{50} \text{ secs.} = \text{just less than } \tfrac{1}{16} \text{ sec.}$$

The graph shows that at point B we were $\tfrac{1}{16}$ sec. off time and at point A, only $\tfrac{1}{32}$ sec. wrong. In short, our first version is almost exactly right, and yet when we find out what the African is really doing we discover that it is totally wrong for it is based essentially on the wrong underlying conception. It was worthwhile explaining this matter for it shows how fatally easy it is for us to think we have found out an African rhythm, when all the time we are wrong, and it shows how necessary it is to check all these patterns by seeking an African counter-rhythm, so that we can find out how he himself regards the pattern. In the last resort that is the thing which really matters. Whatever the pattern sounds like to us, we must always find out what he *intends* the rhythm to be. There is always present the human factor. However much we intend to beat at a certain rate, there is bound to be some slight inaccuracy due to human frailty, an inaccuracy which would perhaps be quite enough to lead an investigator to a false conclusion if he relied solely on his ears or his instruments.

Having correctly analysed the *Gankogui* pattern what else do we find? Counting in semiquavers, the phrase is $3+3+2:3+3+2$, and so on. It is nothing other than the Samba rhythm (or as the Ewe call this American dance, the La Conga). Students of jazz should take note of this. Everyone realizes nowadays that jazz has its roots via New Orleans, in Africa, and more especially in West Africa. There is a tendency for people to go to West Africa, hear a typical jazz rhythm and declare they have traced its origin. Usually the opposite is the truth. Africans have taken to jazz like ducks to water, and certainly in parts of West Africa the modern African town dance-bands are nowadays 'swinging' their own folk-music and thereby totally distorting it, substituting for its essential basis of cross-rhythms, the typical reiterative bass of jazz which in essence is completely Western. We must be very much on our guard when we hear what appears to be an African dance before we accept it as in the genuine tradition. But *Sovu* is completely African. So here is a first-class example for the jazz research worker. Samba definitely has its roots in Africa in the conservative

Yeve cult. Or at any rate, *Sovu* has the identical rhythm in its bell-pattern.

The score shows how the African thinks of this *Gankogui* pattern: the phrasing is not ours, it is Mr. Tay's: the first two notes form one phrase, and the remainder form another, but both together form, in his mind, one complete pattern. Incidentally, Mr. Tay says that this *Sovu* pattern is considered to be the easiest of all the *Gankogui* patterns. If we now look on the score at the *Axatse* pattern, which as usual is a partner of the bell-rhythm, we see quite a different phrasing. Mr. Tay is firm about this: he says the rattle-player feels and knows that his grouping of beats is different from that of the bell. The first and the fourth notes of the pattern seem to him to be 'by themselves', though he also said that other Africans might feel differently about this phrasing.

The Sovu *song*

> Wlui nado loo, adoe nya hɔ̃
> Ahɔwɔ vodua wlui nado,
> Wlui nado hee, adoe nya hɔ̃
> Ahɔwɔ vodua wlui nado, adoe nya hɔ̃.

The meaning of this song would be known to the Yeve cult members, but we ourselves cannot translate it.

From the score we see that the song is a very short one and is in the straightforward form $A+B+C+D$, there being no repeats. Including the rest at the end, which Mr. Tay says is what he wants in order to feel that the repeat comes right, it occupies eight *Gankogui* patterns. It has several points of rhythmic interest. Its first stressed syllable *loo* (bar 6) and its counterpart *hee* (bar 9) avoid coinciding with the main beat of the *Gankogui* and produce a cross-accent. But the end syllable of the first, second, and third lines (bars 7, 8, and 10) and the syllable *-do* in bar 11, which is the last syllable of the repeat of line 2, all fall on the accented bell-note. In several cases the song closely follows the syncopated bell-pattern: this can be seen in bar 6 at the words '*adoe nya hɔ̃*' and again for the same words at the end of bar 9; while the second half of the first line of the song almost exactly duplicates the bell-rhythm (bar 11).

Reviewing the tune we notice it is pentatonic. This is not an invitation to conclude that a pentatonic scale is a widespread feature of African music. After all, anyone of us can write a pentatonic tune on the basis of our Western diatonic scales; and nearly all the African music we have studied in various parts of Africa is undoubtedly not pentatonic. Nevertheless there does seem to be a tendency among the Ewe people to avoid the subdominant in melody, while at the same time admitting the leading note which they sing as a neutral note, flatter than we do. The *Nyayito* song is an example of this: so also is the song for the *Sogba* dance.

There is an imposing array of hand-claps in this dance. Either Clap 1 or Clap 2 will be used by the cantor to get the song going, but the use of all the five claps by the people is a matter of choice, and all five claps can be, and are, played simultaneously if so desired. This particular score, incorporating so many clap-patterns, brings into prominence the point we have remarked on before, namely, that however the African himself regards the division of the voices in his orchestra, in actual performance, the claps are always closely associated with the *Gankogui* pattern both in their accents and in their length of phrase.

The drumming

The *Sovu* dance starts like this: the master drummer first plays the Yeve cult signal (see *Husago* score): then he plays the *Sovu* signal, during which the *Gankogui* and *Axatse* come in, followed by *Kidi* and *Kagaŋ*, and when everybody has got going nicely, the cantor starts the song. The song can enter at any time after the *Gankogui* has started, whether the master drum has started his first main dance-pattern or not. If the song comes in quickly, the master drummer prolongs the end of the *Sovu* signal by repeating the beats for the syllable *dza* (see the opening bars in the score) until a suitable place in the song is reached on which to enter his main pattern. Some cantors are rather sluggish in starting the song: in this case the master can, if he likes, start a main pattern before the song starts.

The *Sovu* signal, as can be seen from the opening of the score to bar 7, is extremely simple and obviously designed to get the *Gankogui* player on his correct time and beat. Rhythmically the master's pattern is the same as that of *Gankogui* but he phrases it differently and it thereby becomes virtually a different pattern. When *Kagaŋ* enters he duplicates the master's rhythm, using his phrasing, and thus continues right through the dance. In *Sovu* therefore, *Kagaŋ* departs from his usual role of setting up a cross-

rhythm with *Gankogui*. The *Kidi* drum supplies the most interesting pattern. Like the master he is playing in 4/8 time, but his
pattern is not syncopated and is, accordingly, in strong contrast
with everyone else. The last three beats of his pattern (middle of
bar 3) being inverted, are muted beats, but in this particular
pattern 'they must be heard' as Mr. Tay puts it, which means that
they are not in this case waiting beats but an essential part of the
pattern. *Kidi* enters at an interesting place *vis-à-vis* the master, just
before the latter's syncopated beat.

We pass on to Master Pattern A. This occupies exactly eight
Gankogui bars (bars 7–14). Normally, in *Sovu* the *Atsimevu* patterns are very long—one pattern would, says Mr. Tay, fill a page
with nonsense syllables. For the purpose of our study he gives
examples only of short ones. As soon as he starts Pattern A, the
master leaves his regular divisive rhythm and makes an additive
pattern of irregular bars and accents, thereby establishing cross-
rhythms, but at the same time he does something rather unusual
in that, in spite of the changes in bar-length, he contrives that his
phrases keep more or less in step with *Gankogui* (see what he does
at the beginning of bars 7, 8, 10, 11, 12, and 13). He is playing
athwart *Gankogui* at the beginning of bar 9 and in bar 14. If we
compare the master and *Kidi* staves we see also that in spite of
his additive pattern the master so arranges his beats that *Kidi*'s
pattern is a highly suitable reply to him. In the middle of bar 12
the master provides an instructive example of toying with the
basic time-unit for the sake of variety. Look at the words '*azegi
degi*' : he starts off-beat on *a-*, plays the next and unaccented syllable
-ze- on an accented *Gankogui* beat and then uses the *Gankogui*
syncopation as a little triple motif, pulling himself into phase with
the underlying *Gankogui* 4/4 time at the word *degi*, whose second
syllable is accented. It is very ingenious and a rather charming
rhythmic interplay.

There are only two possible places in the song where the master
can enter his Pattern A. Both are equally suitable. One is that
adopted in the score, namely at the end of the cantor's first line,
on the word *hɔ̃* (bar 7) : the other is exactly one *Gankogui* bar later,
on the syllable *-do* of the chorus (bar 8). We do not know why
either entry is suitable, nor do we know how it comes about
that if you shift the whole master pattern one *Gankogui* bar to
the right it is still as suitable over its whole length, as it was

before: and why it would not be suitable if you shifted it to any other position. Yet there is no doubt that Mr. Tay feels with sure conviction, what is and what is not suitable.

In Pattern B, *Kagaŋ* goes on as before: *Kidi* has the same response as he had in Pattern A. The points in the song at which the master can enter Pattern B are the same as for Pattern A. Master Pattern B has, in addition to its irregularity, which here is not very pronounced, two other features which it shares with Pattern A. First, it begins and ends with the nonsense syllable *vlo* (bars 18 and 29, cf. bars 7 and 14): second, it manages to keep in step with *Gankogui* to the extent that it has an accented beat on every one of *Gankogui*'s low notes. Perhaps this is a special characteristic of *Sovu* drumming. We shall see it again in Pattern C though less consistently applied. From bar 21 to bar 26, the master introduces a pleasant clash of rhythms with the other instruments, bringing himself into agreement with them again in bar 27. The pattern occupies twelve *Gankogui* bars.

Master Pattern C is, like Pattern A, of eight *Gankogui* bars length. It has two possible entry points one of which differs essentially from those we have previously considered. Mr. Tay prefers the one we have shown on the score in bar 32, namely to come in during the cantor's first line, three quavers before the end word *hɔ̃*. The second entry takes place in bar 33: this time the master pattern is moved only half a *Gankogui* bar to the right. As *Gankogui*'s bars each contain the syncopated motif twice, we can see that this is a possible move as far as *Gankogui* is concerned but it still leaves us guessing as to why the master pattern will still suit the song. Our own guess is that this master pattern happens to be a subdued one: it has only one high note (bar 34) which if moved four quavers to the right *vis-à-vis* the song would coincide with an accented melody note, which would not, we think, be a real clash.

Kidi has a new response. In bar 33, *Kidi* ends his pattern with *kriŋ* which is a nice foil to the master's *kide* which extends beyond it by one quaver. The same happens in bars 34, 35, and 36. The master then adopts *kree* as the final of his phrases (bars 38 and 39) which is a short abrupt end, and now the roles are reversed, as *Kidi* ends his phrases after and not before the master. So in the whole pattern there is a ding-dong: first the master finishes after *Kidi*, and then *Kidi* finishes after the master. In this Pattern C

Kidi staggers his pattern with the *Gankogui*. He is still in 4/4 time, as he was in the other two patterns, but now his main beat of the bar falls consistently one beat ahead of that of the bell.

We pass on to the changing signal, bars 42 43. It preserves the characteristic prevalence in *Sovu*, of the syllable *vlo*, which syllable is played *sforzando* to bring the change in (bar 43), and again in bar 44. Bar 45 is just a gentle roll on the drum played piano, which continues till the master strikes up the next pattern. *Kidi* has a special response. It is still in 4/4 time and still off-beat with *Gankogui*, but *Kidi*'s main beat now falls a quaver late on *Gankogui* instead of, as in Pattern C, a crotchet early. We asked Mr. Tay if *Kidi* could play the response to Pattern A for the changing signal. He said you cannot do so: it would not suit.

Lastly, the ending pattern. Let us take *Atsimevu* first. There is in this pattern a new feature and that is the deliberate *accelerando* which starts in bar 51 and continues to the end of the music. This *accelerando* is part of the pattern. With no separate orchestral conductor to control such a move, these African musicians have their own special way of dealing with it. First of all, the master drummer warns everybody that he wants to embark on the *accelerando* by playing the *accelerando* signal. In the *Sovu* dance this signal carries the nonsense syllables *tegade* (bars 50 and 51). He plays it three times, and thus alerts all the instruments. Their business henceforth is to follow his quickening pace. This is achieved by a sort of communal feeling. Instead of playing this signal the master may play one or other form of waiting beats, but for the ending they *must* have an *accelerando*. For instance he could play either (*a*) or (*b*) below:

Whichever he uses, he quickens the pace and then moves into the ending proper, still quickening. He plays *vlo dede* six times, *togato* three times, and then the two final arresting phrases played strongly and almost defiantly, making a very fine closure. To return to the *accelerando* signal, *Gankogui* and the rattle go on with their normal pattern right to the end but adjust their time by the master. So does *Kagaŋ* except that he has two special final beats played synchronously with the master. *Kidi*, as soon as he hears the *accelerando* signal, at once makes the proper response, *kriŋ kriŋ* (bar 50) and continues this until the master's final phrase. Here, as in other ending phrases, *Kidi* plays in synchrony with the master (bar 57) and indeed imitates the rise and fall of the master's playing.

When the *accelerando* starts, the song and claps follow the master's quickening time. If the song verse ends at or just about the final beat of the orchestra, it is not repeated: this is the situation in our score (bars 56 and 57). If, however, the song has not ended when the orchestra stops, both the claps and the song must continue till they reach the end of the verse, just as we have seen in the previous dances. But there is the added complication of the *accelerando*. What happens is that when the orchestra stops, the song continues at the pace which it had attained at that point.

THE *SOGBA* OR *SOGO* DANCE

This is the last example we give of Yeve cult drumming. *Sogba* can be used at any time when the cult members meet. The instruments required are the same as for *Husago* and *Sovu*. As in the other Yeve dances, the master drummer starts the dance by playing the Yeve cult signal: then he plays the *Sogba* signal: after this there is a slight deviation in procedure as we shall see in a moment, and then he starts playing his first standard pattern of the dance.

The *Sogba* signal is a short one, occupying only four *Gankogui* patterns, but is not so free as the other signals we have studied because, though played as a solo by the *Atsimevu* drummer, it is metrical, being based on the *Gankogui* phrase. The *Gankogui* is not played during the signal but the master drummer keeps its pattern in mind while playing (bars 1–4). Yet although he is playing with an imaginary *Gankogui* and despite the fact that for once the master is playing an almost consistent divisive rhythm in 2/4 time, as we see from bars 1 to 3, he deliberately crosses his main beats with those of *Gankogui* so that only one accented beat of his pattern falls on an accented bell-beat. Thus what one hears the drum playing is only half as interesting as what the African conceives himself. The *Sogba* signal ends on the seventh playing of the syllable *de*. On this seventh beat *Gankogui* and the rattle start playing, both of them using their normal standard pattern (bars 5 ff.). As soon as these two instruments start, the hand-claps may come in. In *Sogba*, these are the 4-clap and the 6-clap and they are usually performed simultaneously (bars 5 ff.).

Another feature in *Sogba* is the entry of the *Asiwui* (lesser drums): both *Kidi* and *Kagaŋ* come in immediately after *Gankogui* starts. *Kagaŋ* uses his normal rhythm, which is, as always, crossed with the bell by moving his triple bar one quaver to the left (e.g. see the beginning of bar 6 and compare *Gankogui* and *Kagaŋ*): *Kidi* plays a form of waiting pattern which is in 3/4 time, whose main beats are staggered not only with *Gankogui* but also with *Kagaŋ*, *Kidi*'s main beat being two quavers early on *Gankogui*'s. Now in *Sogba* people do not like to hear everything starting at once, and so while all these instruments are making their entry, the master drummer just 'doodles', playing some form of simple waiting beats of which bars 6 and 7 are one actual example. Strictly speaking there should be no bar-lines here as his waiting beats have no accent. When he hears that all the orchestra is going nicely, the master drummer plunges into Pattern A. There we must leave him while we look at the song.

The song

> Sovi Agbade-a ɖu ɲyanya-tɛ
> Mawɔ dza, maku dza.
> Ayee-he, vodu aye-hɛ,
> Mawɔ dza, maku dza.

Note. *Sovi Agbade* is the name of a small sub-cult of the Yeve cult.

So = Thunder, *-vi* = small: so, 'Little Thunder God'.

The melody of the song is unusually regular, being triple, and mostly in 3/8 time with three bars of 3/4 time interspersed in it. The regularity of the song is further emphasized by its relation with *Gankogui*, for its accents are in phase with the bell-pattern all the way through. It is a short song covering six *Gankogui* patterns whose grouping may be analysed as $(1+1)+(1+3)$ (bars 7–13). Now here is a difficulty: theoretically the song should start repeating in the middle of bar 13 but Mr. Tay says it does not do so. One waits for a complete *Gankogui* pattern and then repeats (bar 14). This would give us seven *Gankogui* patterns for the song and appears to break our rule of multiples of 2 and 3, but does it? Mr. Tay has, on other occasions, been loth to start a song-repeat immediately after the last verse. He says it is breathless, and so it is if there are many repeats. Coupled with this is the fact already noted that once the master drummer has entered at the right place in the song, he does not worry about it much, so that the insertion of an extra *Gankogui* phrase for a breather, will not worry him unduly. On the whole we regard the matter thus: we still think the song consists of six *Gankogui* patterns and that bar 13 is an extra bar which in this case is not counted in the song length.

The tune is a good strong serious melody with no internal repeats except that the first reply of the chorus forms also the end of the longer chorus section, where it breaks into harmony which includes a fourth, and rather surprisingly for the Ewe, also a third. The whole melody is closely knit. Thus the first phrase (bar 7 and part of 8) is inverted at bar 9 and part of 10. The chorus in bar 8 is imitated a fourth higher at bar 10, and then cunningly extended, the tune ending with a repeat of bar 8.

Just before the repeat the cantor sings the word in brackets— [*Voduwo*] (bar 14). This word, extracted from the song text, is by way of an embellishment to the repeat. It is not really a part of the song and is just an interjection by the cantor. The Ewe people do this quite a lot. We had an example in *Nyayito*, where the bracketed word [*Vuavyawo*] means 'The Orchestra', as much as to say, 'Come on orchestra!'

The main drumming

We now pick up the story of the drumming at the point where we left the master 'doodling' before entering on his first Standard Pattern A (bars 8–17). He has two possible points of entry in the song. He may enter as on the score, on the first syllable of the word *nyanya-te* (bar 8), or he may come in at the end of the repeat of the first chorus words, i.e. on the word *dza* in bar 11, though this entry is not so suitable. The reason is that the master must be careful not to intrude on the rise and fall of the song melody at the chorus-words *aye-he* (bar 11) for if he does this will, says Mr. Tay, spoil the song. But the *Kidi* pattern will sound well with this part of the song and should be allowed to predominate. Mr. Tay says also that the master cannot enter suitably in any of the later words of the song from *aye-he* onwards. When we look on the score at the entry he himself chose, we see that this allows the chorus-words *aye-he* to be sung while the master is completely silent, which shows what foresight is needed on the part of the master drummer in choosing where to enter his pattern.

The whole pattern is a play on the nonsense syllables *gaga*. This word occurs nine times and is at the end of a phrase which differs each time, and forms a varied preliminary to it. There is also a clever play on the position of *gaga* vis-à-vis the bell. Five times it falls on the low bell-note (bars 9, 11, 12, 14, and 16), and four times it is off-beat, being one quaver late on the bell, though this word *gaga* is always accented strongly on the first syllable (bars 10, 13, 15, and 17). We asked Mr. Tay how he felt this pattern was phrased. He divided it into nine sections as represented by the phrasing on the score. We then said, 'Suppose these sections are grouped, how would you group them?' Without hesitation he grouped them into four major sections thus:

vlo vlo vlo vlo gaga	= 1 *Gankogui* pattern	
to gaga, gategide gaga	= 2	,, ,,
vlo vlo vlo vlo gaga, ga gaga, gazegree tete gaga	= 3	,, ,,
ga gaga, dzadzadzadza gaga, ga gaga (which		
with the rest before the repeat)	= 4	,, ,,
Total	10	,, ,,

This sort of inquiry we regard not only as interesting but as vital to the full comprehension of African music. We want to know not only what the African plays but also how he feels about it, in other words its internal musical organization as he sees it.

One further point about Pattern A. Though it lends itself to a consistent 3/4 barring and therefore looks as if it is in divisive rhythm, this is deceptive, and is brought about because the word *gaga* falls on each low bell-note. The pattern really consists of short phrases, not all of the same length, each separated by a rest, in fact little bursts of drumming all ending on *gaga*.

During this pattern *Kagaŋ* goes on as usual. *Kidi*'s response (bar 8) is a variant of his waiting beats in the preceding section. He plays the response with marked emphasis, especially the last two syllables *tiŋ-tiŋ*. While he, like the master, is in 3/4 time, *Kidi*'s main beat of the bar occurs a crotchet in advance of the latter.

This has two results: it makes him have a permanent cross-rhythm with *Atsimevu*, and also with *Gankogui*: it further secures that the last accented note of *Kidi*'s pattern falls on a low bell-note (e.g. see bar 9). How often have we remarked this tendency to lean towards the first note of the *Gankogui* pattern! Yet though *Kidi* is crossed with *Gankogui*, and so also is *Kagaŋ*, they cross it by different amounts, *Kidi*'s bar-line being one quaver ahead of *Kagaŋ*'s.

We pass on to the waiting beats (bar 19). These are also the changing signal, and are used not only to change from one pattern to another, but at any time during the repeats of one pattern, so as to keep in step with the song. We recall that the song covers six *Gankogui* patterns. Master Pattern A has ten bell-patterns, Master Pattern B has eleven. A good drummer may play these waiting beats between repeats till the song reaches the right point of entry for his pattern. The master drummer merely duplicates the 4-clap in an embellished form. The nonsense syllable *-deŋ* is difficult to reproduce in musical notation. It is a short rising scoop and is made by first hitting a free stick-beat and immediately after muting the skin with the left hand in zone 2, causing the pitch to rise before it dies away.

Kagaŋ goes on as usual. *Kidi* is playing the 4-clap rhythm consistently one quaver late thus producing a cross-rhythm both with *Gankogui* and with *Kagaŋ*, and incidentally with the master and the claps. In fact the whole orchestra is well crossed.

Master Pattern B has two possible entries in the song. It can come in as did Pattern A, during the word *nyanya-te* (bar 22): or it can enter just after the final word *dza* of the first chorus-phrase, i.e. in bar 23. It could *not* enter in bar 26, after the song-word *ayehe* because Mr. Tay says the song tune for this word would be disturbed by the opening master-drum beats which contain some fairly high notes and you need more subdued beats here. The whole pattern extends over eleven *Gankogui* phrases (bars 22–32) and this seems irregular; but though a poor master drummer might go straight on to repeat without reference to the song, Mr. Tay says that a good man will either keep silence or play waiting beats in bars 33–35, and then repeat. This brings the full total for the pattern to fourteen *Gankogui* phrases. We used no pressure on Mr. Tay to elicit this conclusion. When he was playing *Kidi*'s pattern on our recorder he played just what is on the score quite instinctively, filling in these bars with waiting beats before repeating his pattern.

Certain of the notes on the *Atsimevu* stave are in brackets. They do not belong to the master pattern, but are duplicates of the essential rhythm of *Kidi*'s playing, and the master drummer may play them quietly to help *Kidi*: alternately he may keep silence. Here we have a rather interrupted playing by the master, consisting of short peremptory-sounding phrases interspersed with replies by *Kidi* who, as he plays not with the master but between his phrases, shares with him the honours of the pattern.

The master's pattern is irregular in time and he seems studiously to avoid placing an accented beat on the low *Gankogui* note (see the beginning of bars 22, 23, 24, 25, &c.). He does so only once (bar 29) and even then he is in the middle of a phrase.

Kidi has to follow the master carefully in this pattern. Unlike his usual custom he does not merely play one simple response. He has two distinct patterns to be introduced at appropriate places. Whenever the master plays what is written in bars 22, 23, and 24, *Kidi* responds with the nonsense word *kidi*. For the rest of the master pattern, *Kidi* inserts in the gaps the reply *kidigidiɲ*, played in sets of three with a rest between each set. Then when the master has ended, and before he repeats, *Kidi* continues with this, and goes on with it while the master starts to repeat his pattern. This causes *Kidi* to arrive comfortably at the right spot to make once more his correct reply to the first part of the master pattern (see bar 36). Yet in spite of this apparent freedom arising out of his duty to reply at the proper moment to *Atsimevu*, if we look along the *Kidi* stave on the score we find his pattern is most symmetrically organized. He plays his first response three times: then his second response which consists of a little motif thrice repeated, he plays six times. If A is the first reply and B is the little motif in the second reply, the analysis is:

$$3A+(2\times3B)+(2\times3B)+(2\times3B).$$

We now look at Master Pattern C which covers seven *Gankogui* phrases (bars 39–47). It has two possible entries in the song, one of them different from any used in the previous patterns. The first is similar to one of the entries of Pattern B: it is that used in the score (bar 29) where the master comes in just after the first chorus-phrase. The other entry is in bar 42: the master may come in on the first high bell-note, i.e. just after the song-word *ayehe*. This, it will be noted, is just three *Gankogui* patterns later than the first entry. It lends support to the view that the song is really of six *Gankogui* phrases length for the Ewe people not infrequently play a pattern, if it is of twelve-quaver length, either in phase with *Gankogui*, or starting exactly half-way through its phrase. They seem to think it is more or less one and the same whichever they do.

There are two alternative ways of repeating the pattern in addition to that given in the score (bar 46). In the form we have written it, the master pattern and the song keep in step as each cover seven *Gankogui* patterns. But the master may put in waiting beats after he ends his pattern at the beginning of bar 46 and go on till the song arrives at his alternate entry point after *ayehe* : this adds three *Gankogui* phrases to the overall length between repeats of the pattern thus bringing its total up to ten *Gankogui* phrases. Or, the master may continue the waiting beats right through the remaining part of the song-verse and into the repeat till he reaches the ordinary starting place, which would give a total of fourteen *Gankogui* phrases between repeats.

Just as Pattern A was a play on the nonsense word *gaga*, so Pattern C revolves round the accented syllable *ga*. When it is stressed, *ga* occurs in this pattern either on the half-way quaver of the *Gankogui* bar, or on the low bell-note (see bars 39, 40, 41, 42, 43, and 44). Inspection shows the master pattern to divide in this way :

bars 39 and 40: 41 and 42: 43, 44, and 45, i.e. its form is 2+2+3.

All the master's bars are staggered with *Kagaŋ*. With *Kidi* he is in phase all the time and for at least half the pattern these drums duplicate the same rhythm-pattern. On the whole this makes it a dull pattern though it has a sprightly opening.

Lastly we look at the ending pattern (bars 48–51). When the master wants to end the dance he moves on to the beginning of the ending pattern, playing *de degi* as in bar 49. When the *Asiwui* hear this they quickly change to the appropriate accompaniment. For *Kidi* this is merely his waiting-beat pattern: *Kagaŋ*, who all through this dance has been playing with one stick only, seizes his second stick which is necessary if he is to play the pattern on the score. As soon as the master hears that these drummers have responded he plays the final ending, *azegede kito, azegegi*. For the first half of this *Kidi* goes on as before, and then joins in synchrony for the end phrase. Note how the African orchestral playing is organized so as to secure correct changes without a conductor being present. There is always some form of warning given by the master. Here it is twofold: first to get the *Asiwui* on to the ending pattern, and second, when the master wants the synchronous playing for the final phrase, he prefaces this with a short phrase which warns *Kidi* who, still beating his previous rhythm, has thus time to prepare himself. *Kagaŋ* keeps on right to the end with his ending rhythm but his very last note is highly stressed and in consequence raised in pitch. All the instruments, as usual, come to an abrupt end with the master drummer. The song and its hand-claps go on, also as usual, till the end of the verse is reached, and that is the end of the dance.

We conclude our study of the Yeve cult music with one cautionary remark. All the music on the scores is what one master drummer played on one particular occasion when we recorded him. Other master drummers might play these patterns in a slightly different way, though *essentially* it would all be the same. This underlines the cardinal thesis that African music is 'spontaneity within limits'. There is room for the personal contribution and for the inspiration of the moment. When we crystallize it on a music-score, by that very act we make it un-African. No two African performances are identical. What we have done is to take, as it were, a series of snapshots of African dance-music: and this, in fact, is the only possible way to study it in detail.

6

CLUB DANCES—THE *ADZIDA* DANCE

DANCING in Ghana is more organized than in many other parts of Africa. In Northern Rhodesia, for example, there are no societies connected with the art: drumming and dancing happen spontaneously either on occasions which by custom demand it, such as a wedding or a funeral or for a very sick person, or at any time when people feel like it. Among the Ewe people the nearest equivalent to this communal approach to dancing is the *Agbadza* dance which we shall study later. Apart from that, dancing is controlled by organized groups of people. The religious cults are groups of this sort and they preserve the oldest and most traditional and perhaps the most *virtuoso* music. But quite outside the cults there is another musical social grouping which both originates and fosters the growth of nearly all the non-cult dancing, and this is the dance clubs. Any artistic person who is keen on singing, dancing, or orchestral playing will join a dance club: in fact he (or she, as the sexes are mixed in these clubs) may belong to several. Every village of any size will have a club and towns will have many. Each town is divided into four *To*'s (a military division) and each *To* will vie with the others in being able to put up a good dance show: the members of a *To* are proud to have many different dances in their *To*, and this means having many clubs, because each club is the purveyor of one kind of dance only.

The whole corpus of club dancing is called *Ahiãvui* (*Ahiã-* = men and women: *-vui* = drums). The atmosphere of club dancing contrasts strongly with the serious, ritualistic, religious spirit of the cults. In *Ahiãvui* there is a lot of laughter and fun-making and a general spirit of jollity. The clubs are very popular and indeed there are more club dances than cult dances. Each has its own style: the *Gankogui* rhythms are of differing speeds and patterns:

the drumming differs: there are different songs for each kind, though a common feature of *Ahiāvui* songs is that they are long. To mention just some of these club dances, they include:

Adzida, Takara, Kpɔmegbe, Britannia, Man of War, English, Kpele, Kedzanyi, Atsia, Adzro, Kete, Woleke, and Abuteni.

Of these, we shall choose *Adzida* as a representative specimen of club dancing for detailed study. Meanwhile there is a good deal more to say about club dances in general.

Each of the names in the list above is the name of a dance club: you have the *Adzida* club, *Takara* club, and so on, and each style of dance (and *ipso facto* each club) has a definite conscious origin. It happens like this. A song-composer and a master drummer will get together and if they succeed in creating a good dance they will form a club for it. Then as it becomes popular, people from elsewhere will come to the composer to ask if he will help them to start a similar style in their own town. If he agrees, the composer will go to their town and show the group the lines on which he composes, and the patterns of the dancing and so on, and their own local composer will carry on in the new style. The new club thus formed will feel itself to be the son of the first club. It will sing, besides its own locally composed songs, some of the songs of the parent club and their master drummer will go to it to learn the proper drum-patterns. When all this is mastered the new branch will be ready to appear in public, and at the first performance some members of the parent club will go to help them with the songs and the drumming. If a club applies in this way to a mother club and gets permission to use their style, the new club can only use that style and no other. Even though they are at liberty to vary the style, the basic elements must continue to be those as performed by the mother club. In some cases a man with a good musical memory will just go and listen to the mother club and then go home and start their style without permission. This may well bring a quarrel but on the other hand it may be accepted by the mother club as a tribute of appreciation, and they may be gratified to reflect that, after all, 'they are spreading our style'.

Unlike, say, Central African drumming, for which there is no organized training, the dance clubs put in a great deal of hard work in rehearsing and in building up a repertoire which, under this system, is their own exclusive property unless they give permission for its use by others.

Mr. Tay calls these *Ahiãvui* 'fancy drumming' for several reasons. In contrast with the stylized dress of the cults, you are free (within limits to be described) to appear in fancy clothes of your choice—indeed in your best dancing attire: you are free to dance how you like as there are no restrictions and set patterns like those of the cults: and in contrast to the sombre and sympathetic atmosphere of a mourning dance, the *Ahiãvui* are gay affairs and the whole dance-place is decorated. The club dances are occasions for members freely to enjoy themselves with bright colours, music, and that freedom of creative dancing so beloved of the African.

Each club chooses a uniform colour and style of dress though the men in particular have a costume whose main features are common to all clubs. They wear a sort of specially made collarless double-breasted polo shirt, adorned if possible with silver buttons: and special shorts called *Atsaka* which are very full round the waist, and have a long waistband which gathers them in and is knotted in front. Incorporated in the back of the shorts is a piece of contrasted material, while on the lower back edge of each leg are sewn spurs of material—Mr. Tay calls them 'peaks'—which stick out behind. Over the shorts, but not so as to cover the peaks, you wrap a cloth and over this various coloured scarves, the whole making a colourful display which is very effective when it wreathes and sways in dancing. Usually men wear no hats but they may if they like make a fancy one of cloth. Women wear on their heads the usual African kerchief (in Ewe —*taku*) and of course their clothes are brightly coloured but not of any set design.

There is undoubtedly a strong vein of exhibitionism in this dancing. When we ask, 'Why do you put on fancy dress?' the answer is, 'To show to the people'. Similarly, a new club having well rehearsed the dance, the leader will say, 'Now we must show this to the people', and the club will be keen to display what fine dance-steps, drumming, and dresses they have got. One has only to watch drummers in action, especially, we think, if they know they have been spotted, to see how histrionic and exhibitionist they can be. They appear to be utterly abandoned to the music but candour compels us to state that quite a lot of this activity is personal display. As to the dancers, it is one criterion of a good dancer that he can give a spirited and interesting performance. When he dances he is not merely being motivated by the music or the spirit of the dance, though this is a very important element. Coupled with it, is an undoubted intention to display.

When a new club is formed they *must* start their public appearance with a ceremony called *vuloho*. An established club can also do it on any day when they are going to dance, but they need not, and we think, usually do not do so. This *vuloho* is a procession into the town, a ceremony which takes about an hour and a half and which is done in this way. Before dawn, say at 4 a.m., all the members, taking the drums and other instruments, assemble right outside the town, using the windward side so that when they start playing the sound will carry right over the town. This assembling outside the town is called *Gbedzidede* or *Gbedziyiyi*, and its purpose is a religious one, for the pouring of libations and the solemn declaration of the name and aims of the club and prayers for blessing. The leader of the club will say something like this, 'We want all the spirits of the land to help us. By the head of Abraham, no one is to quarrel or to do *so and so* (stating the rules of the new club).' He then pours a libation to confirm these words. The leader addresses the spirit of a departed master drummer saying, 'We want you to be with us and your skill to be with us, so that our dancing may appeal to the people'. Then, as is usual in concluding a libation, all the members exchange greetings.

It is interesting to inquire what sort of rules are made and to see how beneficent and moral an influence a well-run club can be. There can be no age restriction in these clubs so the conduct of older members will have a powerfully moulding influence on the younger ones. Among the aims will be, for example:

No quarrelling

No abusing of other clubs

Restrictions on the relations of the sexes (as these clubs inevitably bring folk close together)

Restrictions on immoral dancing or dances which might bring bad spirits to the town.

Abusing is quite a common failing of these people. Young folk in a club sometimes think their drumming so superior to that of other clubs that they start what Mr. Tay calls 'political drumming' which is frankly abusive and derisory and is intended so to be. For this purpose they usually play not their own drumming but that of another club. The name 'political' implies that it is an outrageous burst of abuse which is just assumed for the moment, at the end of which the leaders of both parties, as in politics, will drink and talk as friends. However, the custom is that the abused club will invite the abusers to a dance, having prepared some specially potent abuse which they calculate will surpass what they received. This mutual abuse is designed primarily to make people laugh (note the exhibitionism again) but of course it may go too far and cause offence. It is this sort of thing that the club rules try to suppress, though it should be noted that such abuse never takes place between clubs who live in the same *To*.

The Ewe nowadays adopt a puritanical attitude to posture in dancing. An instance was cited to us of a club which introduced a style where the dancers put their hands on their *own* hips. This offended the social sense of the whole community who threatened drastic action.

As to bringing bad spirits to the town, this might happen if, for example, a club were to play *Fiasiɖi* drumming out of season. *Fiasiɖi* being a cult of the earthly gods of the seasons, whose ceremonial drumming is done at specified times, it would be socially very bad indeed to use their drumming for club purposes, and it would bring very bad fortune to the town.

Let us return to the new club who have just finished the libations and Naming Ceremony outside the town. They wait for the sun to come up (about 6 a.m.) and then start to dance and sing special *vuloho* songs in procession to the town, with dance-steps designed to show off their foot and leg and also their arm movements. Everyone in a club possesses a rattle (*Axatse*) which has been specially made for him and all, except the drummers or anyone else who has to use his hands, will be playing their rattles in the procession. The bigger drums are each carried on the head of a young man. He puts a thick coiled cloth on his head to take the weight: he puts a handkerchief round the drum and holds the ends to steady it. The drumhead is towards his back, and the drummer walks behind him and plays as they go. The procession goes straight from the place of the early morning rites, through the town, to the place where later they will give their display, and on arrival the first thing to do is to pour another libation. Then they may sing one or two of the *vuloho* songs again, but this time *in situ*, and also some *Hatsyiatsya* songs (we shall explain these in a moment), and then generally between 10 and 11 a.m. they break off and go home for a bath and for food. This concludes the first preliminary to a new club's first public display.

At about 2 p.m. they all reassemble at the dancing-place whence they broke up, and begin the second preliminary to the main show. Leaving all the drums behind, but taking all their *Gankoguiwo*, *Atokewo* (see Plate 1) and rattles, they go in procession round all the four divisions of the town, playing and singing the special kind of song called *Hatsyiatsya*. This may take up to two hours, which brings them back to the dancing-place at about 4 p.m. where they finish the song they are singing and then pour yet another libation. The following description, while applying to this libation in particular, shows what, in general, takes place at the other libations. Two liquids are needed: (*a*) spirit or home-made wine contained in an ordinary tumbler, a gourd or a calabash, and (*b*) water in a calabash. The leader, who must be bare-footed and bare-headed, and bare-shouldered (you usually pull your top garment off the shoulders and let it drape round the waist), steps forward in front of the assembled club. He faces east and begins the prayer by calling on the gods after this manner:

MAWU GA, DZIFO-MAWUWO, ANYIGBA-MAWUWO . . .
God   great,   heavenly gods,   earthly gods . . . (we call you
. . ., &c.)

Then, by name, he calls on great deceased song composers and drummers. In his prayer he invites the gods to 'come and bless us and be among us: and if one brother steps on another, let there be no quarrel: and we want healthy life in our club, and absence of death. We are calling you. HERE IS A DRINK FOR YOU'—*he holds the glass of spirit and still facing east, pours three times, starting at his right, thus*:

Leader

Then he takes the calabash of water and says, 'HERE IS YOUR WATER *to cool your heart (sc. from the effects of the spirit or wine):* we do not give you the spirit to make you drunk or angry'. *He pours the water three times as above, swishing it out of the calabash in a forward swinging manner.* This having been done, all the club members exchange greetings saying, 'The gods will see that our wishes are accepted'. This is the end of the second preliminary.

Let us now imagine that all this time we have been witnessing the inauguration of the *Adzida* club. All will have taken place as described but now the special *Adzida* music will begin. Having finished the libation, the leader now steps back to his place and a cantor lines the special song by which everyone knows that they are now going to dance *Afãvu*. This *Afãvu* is the introduction to the main *Adzida* dancing, but is quite separate from it. It is only a short extract from the *Afã* cult drumming and dancing. It is played at this point, just before the main dance, in order to get the blessing of the physicians (all members of the *Afã* cult are physicians) and the gods whom they serve. *Afãvu* will be played only for a short while—say three minutes or so—and then, at last, begins the main *Adzida* dancing, for which the club really exists.

We proceed to our analysis. There are three separate musical performances to consider, namely the *Hatsyiatsya* songs and accompaniment, the *Afãvu* music, and the *Adzida* dance itself.

THE *HATSYIATSYA* FOR *ADZIDA*

Before any dance of any *genre* starts, or during the course of a dance while the drumming and dancing has stopped for a breather, everybody will sing one or more *Hatsyiatsya* songs. There is no drumming and no dancing for *Hatsyiatsya*, and surprisingly enough there is never any clapping. There may or may not be a bell or bells—it depends on circumstances and the kind of dance being performed. When people sing without an audible time-background Mr. Tay says they can keep in perfect time because they have a mental time-background: some people may mentally go by a clap, others by the *Gankogui* or some other instrument. *Hatsyiatsya* songs are thus an introduction or an interlude for a dance. But this does not mean that they are of lesser importance than the songs for the main dance. Quite the reverse is the case: the main songs in any dance are the *Hatsyiatsya* which precede it. Each kind of dancing has its own special *Hatsyiatsya*: one might say that the songs for the main dance are subsidiary, for you *could* do without them, but you cannot do without the *Hatsyiatsya* songs. These songs contain the best musicianship as contrasted with the songs of the main dance which are easily composed and learnt, and they express the main idea of the dance to which they belong. Thus in the case of club dances, it is the *Hatsyiatsya* songs which in their words show the general background of a club—its purpose, desires, and principles. Not infrequently the *Hatsyiatsya* will mention the actual name of the dance which is to follow. One common musical feature of these *Hatsyiatsya* is their *tempo*. They always go very slowly (cf. in *Adzida*, ♩. = 93 for the *Hatsyiatsya* as against ♩. = 162 for the main dance). We have given no *Hatsyiatsya* songs for the dances so far studied, but all dances have them. In dealing here with the *Hatsyiatsya* for *Adzida* we indicate the sort of thing which happens in every case, though it should be remembered that the instruments used, if any, may vary with the dance. For instance, *Hatsyiatsya* for *Adzida* use the little gong called *Atoke* (see Plate 1) and so do many club dances such as *Kpete* and *Dunekpoe*. The cults never use it, nor does *Agbadza*.

We have explained how the *Hatsyiatsya* songs would be sung in procession round the divisions of the town. The same or similar songs would be sung when *Hatsyiatsya* are sung *in situ* in the intervals of a dance. To save repetition we shall for the *Adzida Hatsyiatsya*, deal with the latter and for this purpose we must first illustrate the dispositions at the dancing-place for the *Adzida* dance itself.

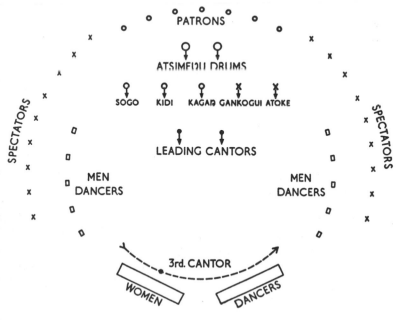

Normally all the members of the club, with the exception of those actually dancing and the cantors, are seated. During the *Hatsyiatsya*, besides the two leading cantors, the men need about six men with good voices who stand at the ends and in the middle of the men's chairs on each side of the dance arena. The idea is to 'impart the song to everybody, including the spectators'. Each of these men is entitled to carry a small fly-switch called *Awudza*. During the main *Adzida* dance these six men will sit down, put away their *Awudzawo* and take their rattles, in fact they just join in what the other men are doing. During the *Hatsyiatsya* only, and not in the main dance, if there are two or three good women singers, they go and stand with the six male cantors: they each carry a *Papa* which is a switch made of ostrich feathers set in a handle. The two leading cantors standing in the dance circle, and with their backs to the drums, each carry two long and very handsome switches called *Sosi*. These are made from horsetails and they cost nearly £3 each as they are imported from afar (e.g. Kano in Nigeria or Nyame in French Togoland).

In the *Hatsyiatsya* for *Adzida*, the instruments used for accompanying the song are two *Atokewo* and two *Gankoguiwo*. The two *Atokewo*—there are always two, neither more nor less—must be of different pitch but there is no standard interval. The ones we used were a semitone apart. Either one of them plays the standard *Gankogui* pattern with which the reader is by now familiar (see the top line in the score), and the other plays variations. Usually it is the higher one which plays the standard pattern. The object of choosing instruments of different pitch is to keep their patterns distinct. One *Gankogui* plays simple patterns, the other does elaborate variations and it is this one which is the senior. Mr. Tay says he himself always chooses the higher pitched one for the variations because he wants them to stand out well: but he says it is really a matter of choice. All four instruments play simultaneously and we must now examine their music.

While the high *Atoke* plays the standard *Gankogui* pattern, the low *Atoke* plays one or more of a set of standard variations. We give two usual ones, but each club can develop its own patterns here. They can be played or changed at will and at any time. The ones we give are, rhythmically, extremely ingenious. We will look at Pattern B first, for that is the simpler one (bars 11 ff.). Against the high *Atoke* who is playing in an irregular 12/8 time, the low *Atoke* plays triple time but at double speed: that is to say his unit of time is not a quaver but a semiquaver. Thus the low *Atoke* keeps in step with his friend so far as the overall phrasing is concerned, but what remarkable cross-rhythms take place during the 12/8 bar. The combination looks impossible to play, but we assure the reader that it is not, and that it makes a bright, cheerful, and altogether charming sound.

Atoke Pattern A (bars 1–10) is still more ingenious: it is a variant of Pattern B which involves a change of time in the middle of each *Gankogui* bar. Let us look at bar 2. The *Atoke*, still using a semiquaver as its time-unit, plays four bars in triple time, and then three bars in duple time. The total again is twenty-four semiquavers. In the duple piece, the score fails to show one musical feature. When the dotted quavers are played, the player does not make, as he generally does, a sharp clean tap, but allows the iron striker, after hitting, to linger on the bell, producing a sort of buzzing roll. Mr. Tay would not allow us to make a clean beat here; obviously the buzzing is part of the pattern. Pattern A really is a delightful rhythm even played by itself, but it gains added piquancy when in combination with *Gankogui*. When the low *Atoke* starts Pattern B he may enter either at the start of a *Gankogui* bar, or (as on the score at bar 1) in the middle of it. In any case he will let *Gankogui* establish himself before coming in. If he chooses the latter course, instead of starting at the appropriate part of his pattern, i.c. at the duple phrase, *Atoke* plays his pattern from the beginning but doubles his first phrase so as to get himself into correct relation with *Gankogui*. This is all set out in bars 1 and 2.

Reviewing both Patterns A and B we may inquire as to whether there is not an underlying rhythm which makes them reasonably easy to play. There is: if one thinks in terms of simple hand-clapping it can be seen from the score that *Atoke*'s triple bars taken two at a time correspond to a 4-clap, and the duple bars, taken singly, to a 6-clap. As usual in African music, the seemingly complex turns out to be based on essentially simple relationships.

We now examine the *Gankogui* playing: as the low *Gankogui*, though playing the simpler pattern, is dependent on the high one, we must take the latter first. The high *Gankogui* has to have a very competent player. He has no set patterns but is playing spontaneously just as the spirit moves him, though he must keep an ear on the other *Gankogui* and adjust his playing so that he does not play anything unsuitable in combination with the latter. For the purpose of transcription we had to be content to take just a few of the kind of patterns he does play. This crystallizes the music far too much and gives only the very slightest account of the continually varied rhythms which the high *Gankogui* produces. This is sheer *virtuoso* playing and is expected to be complicated and much crossed with the low *Gankogui*. Normally, *vis-à-vis* the high *Atoke*, the *Gankogui* players stagger their entry: Mr. Tay says, 'In playing the *Gankogui* we are taking *Atoke* as our leading pattern, therefore the *Gankoguiwo cannot* play the beginning note of their pattern on any *Atoke* note, except in certain patterns which do not spoil *Atoke*'s playing. If you do start on *Atoke*'s first beat you must be very careful what patterns you play.' We shall presently give some examples of such possible patterns and make some attempt to see why they are suitable.

High *Gankogui*'s Pattern 1 (bars 3–6) occupies one *Atoke* phrase, but both its entry and its accents are staggered with it. This is the only example we give of the normal staggered entry: we were interested to seek examples of the other sort so as to try and find out what are the principles underlying the fact that Mr. Tay regarded them as somewhat abnormal.

Pattern 2 (bars 7–10) occupies only half a high *Atoke* phrase and its initial note falls with that of *Atoke*. But we can see what is happening: as *Gankogui* is playing in 3/8 time he could keep in perfect step with *Atoke*'s 12/8 barring, but what does he do? He staggers his bars one quaver to the right. It looks again as if he is deliberately setting up a cross-rhythm with *Atoke*. On the other hand, this cannot be said of Pattern 3 (bars 11–14) which not only starts synchronously with *Atoke* but keeps in step with both high and low *Atoke*. If Patterns 1 and 2, with their cross-rhythms, are suitable to *Atoke*, why is Pattern 3? We simply do not know: perhaps someone else can spot it. Pattern 4 (bars 15–25) confirms our original idea. Here we have a pattern whose length is one complete high *Atoke* phrase, itself divided into two sub-phrases, starting on *Atoke*'s first beat and yet consistently staggered with it by again moving the bar-line one quaver to the right.

Now let us look at the low *Gankogui*. His choice of pattern is guided first by the high *Gankogui*. He keeps always to simple patterns even if he is a good performer, and he will go on playing one pattern for quite a time—say for five minutes. He chooses a pattern which goes well with what the high *Gankogui* is playing, or he may take a nice little piece from the latter and go on playing that. The low *Gankogui* is also guided by the song, for if the song is changed, he can change his pattern.

Bars 2 ff. show his Pattern A. It is duple and as we see by bars 3 ff. it is in step with the other *Gankogui*. It is bound to conflict with the triple part of the low *Atoke*, but it also crosses the accents of the duple part, as its bars are staggered with those of the high *Atoke*. His Pattern B, bars 13 ff. is interesting. In the first place, as his time-unit is a dotted quaver or semiquaver, it does not matter which, his essential relationship with the high *Atoke* is 2 against 3. Secondly, he has staggered his entry *vis-à-vis* that bell. If you imagine the high *Atoke* to be accompanied by a 4-clap, the low *Gankogui* places his principal stress on the second of those claps, and consequently his least accented note (e.g. his first note in bar 14) will fall on the most accented note of the high *Atoke*. His relationship with the low *Atoke* is very close, and his notes coincide with it, though as he is playing duple time the whole spirit of his pattern is different. He is playing 2 against 3 to the high *Gankogui* while the latter is playing his Pattern 3, and is in step with him (see bars 13 and 14), but when the high *Gankogui* goes into his Pattern 4 (bars 15 ff.), the low *Gankogui* is now staggered with him though still playing 2 against 3.

One important consideration remains. In the previous chapters it is evident that the bell and rattle and hand-claps belong to one family of rhythm-making which we call 'clap technique'. All the contributing rhythms start together on the first note of the bell-phrase. The essence of drumming is its cross-rhythm technique. Now where are we to place this multiple bell-playing? We find on inspection that it has a foot in each camp. The two *Atoke* bells obey clap technique: they both lie fair and square within the bar-lines of the high *Atoke*. The two *Gankogui* bells obey drum technique, exhibiting as they do, the principle of the staggered bars. The high *Gankogui* player may be likened to a master drummer in that he has freedom to play what he likes. The low *Gankogui* behaves rather as one of the lesser drums.

We have yet to consider the *Hatsyiatsya* song itself, which with the bells forms the whole musical *ensemble* of the *Hatsyiatsya*.

The Hatsyiatsya *song*

Gokuwo be tohiame miele be ahɔkelia lavasi mia woe?
Fiadzawu be tohiame miele be ahɔḑeli, lavasi mia woe?
Adzidaviawo he, be afiḑe gokua yi ho—o—o?
O Adzida nu viawo
Lãgbelãgbe gokuwo-e do galele vɔ,
Adzidaviawo mido gbeda
Ku metoa nugbe avesewo bla ahɔdzɔ—o
Agbohia miegba na avugbewo ſe tagba he
Ahɔfia gã wo dɔḑe ahɔme ḑe ayo
Tetewo be tohiame miele be ahɔ ḑeli lavasi mia woe?
Adzidaviawo he, afiḑe gokuawo yi ho—o—o?

'In this drum-circle,' says Goku, 'what on earth can possibly defeat us?'
'In this circle,' says Fiadzawu, 'what on earth can possibly defeat us?'
O members of the Adzida club, where is Goku (today)?
O you members of the Adzida club
Goku, *in extremis*, has come to the end of the struggle.
Ye members of the Adzida club, offer prayers.
When death wages war, the Avese Bird can avail nothing.
{ The fortified enclosures in the field of the Red-flanked Duiker which
  are often smashed!
  Real meaning: The difficult times in life, in which with Goku's help
  we were successful!
Great war leaders (*sc.* Goku) have perished in the battle—well! well!
  what a pity!
'In this drum-circle,' says Tete, 'who on earth can possibly defeat us?'
O members of the Adzida club, where has Goku gone—oh?

Notes:

1. Goku, Fiadzawu, and Tete are staunch members of this club.
2. Goku has died, and they are singing to give sympathy to his family.
3. The Avese Bird (line 7). It has a long red feather in its tail, which is used in the cults as a head-dress and used in medicine: it is possibly connected with the belief that the cults can alleviate, though not prevent, death.

We now look at the music-score and are confronted with a pleasing novelty. Two cantors start the song by overlapping the same melody each using different words. At the overlap we find two fifths, a fourth, a major second, and three octaves. But what about the discord? This is not hard to explain. It arises from the tone-pattern of the spoken words. In speech the voice falls in saying '*be tohiame*' (⁻ - - -)—see bar 2, second cantor; therefore the song melody must fall. In order for it to do this, the note on the syllable '*be*' has to be raised: it might have jumped up to E making a unison with the first cantor, but Africans dislike leaps and also dislike the leading note. In any case the discord is an unaccented note in both voices. There is no harmonic significance here.

Like many *Hatsyiatsya* songs, this one is long and occupies no less than twenty-four high *Atoke* bars: it can be analysed thus:

Section A bars 1–6, subdivided at bar 4 $= (4+2)$ *Atoke* bars
„ B „ 7–13, „ „ 8 $= (1+6)$ „
(The second half of this section generates from the opening notes of section A: compare bars 2 and 8.)
„ B′ bars 14–20, subdivided at bar 15 $= (1+6)$ *Atoke* bars
„ A′ „ 21–24 $= 4$ „
Total 24 „

We said before that the high *Gankogui* player has a role similar to that of a master drummer. Though he is playing spontaneous variations on his bell he must watch the song and arrange to play beautiful patterns at suitable places in it, that is, at prolonged notes (e.g. bars 14 and 15) and especially when the melody descends low. Moreover he will invent his own patterns to suit the whole style of the song, and to be a good player he has to be familiar with it. In one respect he departs from master-drum technique, for he makes his entry for his patterns quite irrespective of the song-words, and he may change from one pattern to another at any moment.

So the *Hatsyiatsya* songs go on till people begin to warm up. Then is the time to introduce the main dancing. In the case of *Adzida*, as we have seen, this is preceded by a short bout of the *Afãvu* cult drumming. The special *Hatsyiatsya* cantors put away their switches (*Awudza*), and sit down. The *Gankogui* players cease to act as drummers and the *Gankogui* will resume its normal function. The small *Atoke* bells will not be needed till the main *Adzida*.

THE *AFÃVU* FOR *ADZIDA*

For *Afãvu* three drums will be necessary. *Atsimevu* is not used: its place as master drum is taken by *Sogo* which is therefore played with two bare hands and no stick as is customary in these circumstances. Besides *Sogo* there will be *Kidi* and *Kagan*.

The *Gankogui* plays his standard pattern and for this *Afãvu* uses a fairly quick *tempo*. The rattle may use either his standard pattern (bars 33 ff.) or the one given in bars 48 ff. In *Afãvu* the rattle player is usually the cantor himself.

For the hand-claps there are three choices. The important one is the 6-clap (bars 33 ff.): the reason why this is preferred as the basic clap is that as the *Gankogui* and drumming go fast, a quick clap is felt to be more suitable. To this clap may be added, at choice and anywhere in the performance, either the 4-clap (bars 38 ff.) or the 3-clap (bars 48 ff.). In passing, though this has nothing to do with *Afãvu*, we might mention an interesting variant of the 3-clap which is used in the traditional dance called *Amedzro* and in the *Kete* club dancing. The last of the three claps gets delayed by a quaver rest producing a syncopation:

Now let us look at the song. As this *Afãvu* is an extract from the drumming of the *Afã* cult of physicians and diviners, the words of the song include some technical cult terms.

The Afãvu *song*

Bokɔnɔ menyiba loo
Batsie lelee, awunɔ menyiba-ee
Awunɔ menyiba-ee: batsie lelee
Awunɔ menyiba.

Members of the Afã cult, by your leave!
?   ? , great physicians, by your leave!
Great physicians, by your leave: ?   ?
Great physicians, by your leave!

Notes:
1. Bokɔnɔ: members of the *Afã* cult.
2. Awunɔ: 'gown-owners'. A senior '*bukɔ*' of the *Afãvu* (medicine) cult is called *Awunɔ*. It indicates those who have worked great cures and are senior grade people.
3. Menyiba: If there is, for example, a senior master drummer present and he asks a junior to play the drum, the latter takes the drum sticks, turns and bows to the expert and says, 'Menyiba nami' = 'By your leave'.
4. Batsie lelee: we do not know the meaning: it may be cult language.

Instead of lining the song in the usual way, the cantor uses a variant both of words and melody by way of introduction (bars 26–32). He sings in a dramatic way, rapidly and in free time, drawing out the pauses between the phrases in an arresting manner. Then after a final silence he intones the song proper *a tempo*. At the first syllable of the chorus the cantor starts clapping: this syllable '*Ba-*' is a signal for everyone to join in the song and clapping and for the orchestra to come in also. On repeats the chorus sings the whole song including the cantor's part. The melody is undistinguished, but what is its tonality? We write it in key G but it would not alter the tune if we eliminated the sharp from the key-signature. This would, however, mean that the frequent repetition of the note B in bars 26 to 29 would be a harping on the leading-note, which in our view is un-African. If Africans use the leading-note—so our experience goes—it is either as a passing note or as a final. Even so, it is difficult to decide what to do here, for this note B is actually used as a final (bar 30).

The whole song covers exactly four *Gankogui* patterns (see e.g. bars 37–41): but there is a whole *Gankogui* bar's rest before the repeat, which gives an unusual total of five. We cannot regard this bar as an insertion as Mr. Tay feels that it belongs to the song. So the analysis is:

Section A   bars 37 and 38,   2 *Gankogui* bars subdivided = (1+1)
    „   B   „   39–41,   3   „   „   = (1+2)
                                               Total   5

THE DRUMS FOR *AFÃVU*

The nonsense syllables given here may or may not be the proper ones. Mr. Tay has never heard from an *Afãvu* cult drummer what exact words are used.

Kagaŋ has three possible patterns. The first (bars 33 ff.) is suitable for all three *Sogo* patterns: the second (bars 54 ff.) is suitable for *Sogo* Patterns B and C but not for A. The third is suitable for *Sogo* Pattern A but not for B or C: but it is not suitable for the particular song we have chosen and therefore does not appear on the score. It is this:

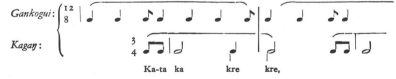

Kagaŋ's entry for *Afãvu* is at the point where the cantor starts the clapping. Though he is free to change to his alternate patterns when he likes, he can only do so at the end of a changing signal and is of course governed by the 'suitability' principle.

We next take the *Sogo* (master drum) patterns and *Kidi*'s replies. When he first enters, he does not start on a main pattern, but plays the first part of the changing signal (cf. bars 34 and 35 with bars 49 and 50). He goes on with this till he gets near the point in the song where his first main pattern will enter. If he is a good drummer he will not just go on repeating the same motif '*gazegi*': he may play anything suitable, and he may play the motif '*gede*' of the latter part of the changing signal (see bar 51) about three times before his main pattern. The little pattern '*gazegi*' is staggered with *Gankogui*, its bar-line occurring one quaver after that of the latter. At the end of this introduction he pauses just a little (bar 38) and then starts on his first main pattern. *Kidi*'s reply during the 'introduction', while suitable here, is not suitable for any other of the master-drum patterns except the changing signal where it could be used in place of the normal one we give. Like *Sogo*, *Kidi* plays in 2/4 time but as he keeps in phase with *Gankogui*, his bars are crossed with those of the master drum. So, looking at the whole score for the introduction we see that all the instruments are in phase except *Sogo*, a simplification which we do not often meet with.

Master Pattern A stretches over eight *Gankogui* bars (39–46). Here for once we have a purely divisive master rhythm which keeps consistently to 2/4 time, though the master secures variety in his relationship with *Gankogui* in an ingenious way. His pattern falls into two equal sections. During the first he arranges that his phrases start *after* the beginning of the *Gankogui* bar and lean towards the low bell-note which stands at the beginning of the following bar (bars 39–42). In the second half (bars 43–46) the master changes his tactics, prefacing the change by a short triplet (end of bar 42): thereafter he keeps perfectly in phase with *Gankogui*, taking his cue from the low bell at the beginning of the bar and no longer leaning over to the following low bell. The proper place in the song for *Sogo* to enter Pattern A is at the beginning of the second half, on the word '*Awuno*' (bar 39).

When the master finishes the introduction *Kidi* goes on playing his response thereto. As soon as *Kidi* recognizes by its first few

beats, what the master's first main pattern is, he starts making the
suitable reply. The reply pattern we give (bars 40 and 41) is
suitable for most *Afāvu* master patterns and certainly for all the
three in the score. This reply is in triple time against *Sogo*'s duple,
but is in phase with *Gankogui*. Note the two words '*kidia*' in bar
40, separated by four waiting beats: we shall have to refer to this
half of his pattern later on. Taking all the orchestra we observe
that in Master Pattern A everyone is in phase, the cross-accents
being obtained by *Sogo*'s phrasing and by *Kidi*'s triple time.

The changing signal (bars 49–53), when our song is being used
—though there are others also—must enter a quaver after the
song-word '*-ba*' which is at the end of the first section (bar 49).
This means that the master may have some time to wait between
the end of his first pattern and the word in question: it all depends
on what his first pattern was. In the score we see he has to wait
for two *Gankogui* bars (47 and 48). Mr. Tay says as the song is
a short one and therefore the waiting cannot be for long, the
master may wait in silence. He can, and otherwise would, fill in
with a few beats. The second half of the signal presents an unusual feature in the *diminuendo* passage (bars 51–53). This can be
played as long as necessary until the song reaches nearly the right
place for the entry of the next pattern. You can go on right up
to the entry, but it is better to make a slight pause, which must
not be much longer than a crotchet (bar 54). The rhythmic form
for the master in the changing signal is the same as in the introduction and need not detain us. *Kidi*'s reply is quite different.
It is in 2/4 time, and *Sogo* is too, but while *Sogo* staggers his bars
with *Gankogui* by moving them one quaver forward, *Kidi* moves
his one quaver back. The result is that *Kidi*'s main beats come
in the middle of *Sogo*'s bars and his strong beat '*kiŋ*' reinforces
Sogo's high note '*gi*'. This relationship is altered by *Sogo* at the end
of bar 49 where he slips a quaver and comes into phase with
Gankogui. Thereafter *Sogo* and *Kidi* are crossed more thoroughly,
their bars having only a quaver displacement.

At the end of the changing signal we show on the score (bar
54) how *Kagaŋ* behaves if he decides to change his pattern. All he
does is to switch over to his new pattern at the right point *vis-à-vis*
Gankogui. This entails, in this instance, omitting the second of
the two notes in his motif. His alternate pattern in triple time,
which is perhaps the most usual pattern *Kagaŋ* plays at any dance,

is as usual crossed with *Gankogui*. Every time the low bell sounds it occurs between, and not on, *Kagaŋ*'s beats.

There is an interesting point arising from what happens in the *Sogo* playing at the end of the changing signal. Suppose a *Sogo* player has to wait a long time before the entry point for his next pattern arrives: we asked Mr. Tay if the master could, having played '*gede gede*' several times, lapse into waiting beats by playing the 4-clap rhythm with one hand. If he did this it would fit nicely the entry for, say, Master Pattern C which would fall on the second beat of this group of four (see bar 69). Mr. Tay said no: if you play the 4-clap pattern, he said, you are introducing another rhythm: you could beat the 6-clap time, but this would be 'just beating time and saying nothing and it does not mark the time for any other instrument, so by doing this you have no control over anybody'. The proper course is to continue playing '*gede*'. We do not pretend to comprehend what is involved in Mr. Tay's remark. We set it down as a pointer to further research.

Master Pattern B enters in the same place in the song as Pattern A (bar 54). It occupies ten *Gankogui* patterns and after a short introductory passage (bars 54 and 55) it becomes a play on the phrase '*kito kito kito*', or its rhythmic equivalent '*to to to*' (bars 56, 57, 59, 60, 61, and 63), which ensures its homogeneity. It is additive in form which produces cross-accents with *Gankogui* but each time the phrase '*kito . . .*' occurs, it starts on a low bell-note. *Kidi*'s response to this is the same as his response to Pattern A: but he has to make an adjustment at his first entry (but not on his repeats). He starts playing one of the long '*kidia*'s' on *Sogo*'s fourth note. Now the three short '*kidia*'s' (bar 56) *must* start on a low bell-note. Therefore to achieve this, when he first enters, *Kidi* has to play not two but three of the long '*kidia*'s' (bars 54 and 55). In all repeats he plays the normal two.

When he has finished with Pattern B, the master plays the changing signal as before (bars 65–68) and moves into Pattern C. At the end of the signal we show on the score (bar 69) how *Kagaŋ* changes back to his original pattern: it is, we recall, a matter of choice.

Master Pattern C is short and only uses six *Gankogui* bars. It has a rather strident and declamatory spirit which is attained partly by the abrupt rests, and partly by the peremptory sound of the descending word '*kidia*' (bars 72 and 74). It enters in the same place in the song as the other patterns and is mostly, but not entirely, a mixture of 3/8 and 3/4 times. The exception, in bar 71, does not in the least break the strongly flowing rhythm of the whole. The master has three focal points, where his accented notes fall on the low bell (bars 72, 73, and 74): otherwise he seems studiously to avoid, as far as he can, any rhythmic correspondence with *Gankogui*. In the first half of *Sogo*'s pattern, *Kidi*, also in triple time, is well staggered with him, but in the second half they join forces and both keep in phase with *Gankogui*. At this point (bars 72–74) we have the rare spectacle of all the orchestra playing in phase with *Gankogui*'s bars. Apart from the song, this is the first time that the score has more or less resembled, in its rhythmic layout, our own Western music.

We must now go back to the rattle-player. In *Afãvu* usually it is the cantor who plays the *Axatse*. He is standing and therefore cannot play it in the normal way and so he plays it obliquely between his left hand and the upper part of his left leg. After the *Afãvu* has been going for about two minutes the cantor, waiting till the last words of the song are being sung, holds the rattle upright and shakes it for a few seconds. This is the signal for the *Afãvu* to end (bars 75 and 76). On hearing the rattle start shaking, *Gankogui* goes on as usual till the final syllable of the song, which falls on a low bell-note, and then plays a special ending pattern of which there are two forms (bars 75–77). In the shorter form he stops playing at the end of bar 76 while the longer form goes on through bar 77. When the singers hear the rattle shake they stop at the end of their verse (bar 76). The drummers, of course, do not know exactly when the rattle player is going to close the dance: in other dances it is the master drummer who decides this. They go on as usual till the end of the song and then break off whatever they happen to be playing, and all individually and with no regard for keeping time with each other, beat a roll of notes of approximately quaver value or less, with a rapid *diminuendo* to *pianissimo*, and in about four seconds the whole dance closes.

That is the end of the analysis, but we must now see how this *Afãvu* fits into the whole performance of the *Adzida* club dance. As we said before, it is a prelude to the main dance and at these club dances it is always played three times. The cantor starts the song, then the drumming comes in and goes on for a short spell of only two or three minutes, and then they bring the whole thing to a close. After a short pause they do all this again, and then again for the third time. Each time while the drumming lasts, several dancers come into the dancing-area and dance, the rest all sitting on chairs or forms as shown in the *Adzida* dance plan. After a short interval at the conclusion of all this, the main *Adzida* dance starts.

THE *ADZIDA* CLUB DANCE

Adzida is very well known and very popular in Ewe-land. It has its own special features which we will now describe, starting with the *Adzida* dancing plan on page 135. Seated round the back and gracing the proceedings are the patrons of the club. In front and with their backs to them are the orchestra, all seated except for the *Atsimevu* players. The orchestra is often accommodated in a big roofless sort of bandstand, with a plank floor, the sides consisting of polished and carved posts like cage-rails, with some small glass windows in the thickened corner posts, and with two doors, one on each side. Alternatively, the drummers may be in the open, in which case the two *Atsimevu* drums are supported on a double *vudetsi*. For *Adzida* there are two *Atsimevuwo*. Normally the two master drummers take turns to play, though they could play certain rhythms together. The other drums needed are *Sogo*, *Kidi*, and *Kagaŋ*. There is a *Gankogui* and, for the first part of the performance, two *Atoke* players. In front of the drums is the dancing-area, surrounded partly by male dancers seated on chairs when not dancing, and by the women dancers seated on forms placed opposite the drums. Spectators may gather round outside the whole set-up. All the male dancers have to come with a rattle and they act as chorus for the main songs, singing and playing their rattles.

The three cantors marked on the plan have important functions, especially the two leading ones. The third cantor, during the dance, wanders about inside the circle to keep things going and to inspire enthusiasm. He carries one of the lesser switches (*Awudza*) and uses it with actions which illustrate and point the meaning of the song, for example, holding it like a gun if hunting is mentioned and so on. The two leading cantors, each carrying two of the magnificent long-tailed switches (*Sɔsi*) stand in front of the orchestra, facing the dancers. They swing the switches in a sort of ceremonious twirl, moving their feet at the same time, and all in time with the *Gankogui*. The movement consists of two swings: (1) swing the *sosiwo* up above the head allowing the tails to hang back behind the shoulders; (2) then swing the *sosiwo* up and forwards in a circle away from the body, keeping the switches close to the outside of the arms as they circle, just as in using Indian clubs. Meanwhile the feet are placed alternately forward and back, the back movement being the important one and carrying in the African mind a definite stress. This is done continuously without shifting one's ground. The cantors can arrange with each other to start either with the left or the right foot, as they must both act the same. The movements in relation to *Gankogui* are as follows:

Gankogui:								
Feet:								
L = Left								
R = Right	L	L		R	R		L	L
B = Back								
F = Forward	F	B		F	B		F	B
Tails:	: up :← circle		→: up :← circle		→: up :← circle →:			

You lift the tails above the head just before the foot moves forward so that at the moment it touches the ground, you start the forward swing. From the musical point of view this is really drum technique because the foot and hand movements are staggered, though the feet are in phase with the *Gankogui*. The main *sosi* movement, which is the circle, starts on the unaccented foot-beat so its rhythm is crossed both with the feet and with the bell.

With the women are two female cantors standing, when at rest, one at each end of the forms. For most of the time they are clapping and while doing so they walk to and fro in front of the women's forms to keep the women going, crossing each other as they do so. The first song and the dance are started off by a male cantor, the male cantors being responsible for the men's singing, and then both men and women join in the chorus. On the repeats the cantors of both sexes join in singing the cantors' part. The clap which the women use for *Adziua* is a modification of the 4-clap (bars 83 ff.). They only clap the first two of each group of four claps: during the intervening rest they roll the forearms over each other, the claps and the roll making a continuous graceful movement.

We now come to a most extraordinary feature of *Adzida* singing. There are in *Adzida* some songs for men—in which case the male cantors start them—and some songs for women, which are likewise started by the women cantors. Now the odd thing is that these songs though quite different in words and tune are sung simultaneously. Mr. Tay says that the tune sung in the higher pitch of the women's voices does not clash with the tune the men are singing. The men may, and sometimes do, sing the women's song if they want to: otherwise they merely sing a few well-known songs. It is the women who sing the special songs belonging to *Adzida*: when we had a recording made of the *Adzida* song used in the score it was a woman, Madame Kpevie, who was the cantor, the chorus being sung by mixed voices. But there is one *caveat* in respect of this superposing of two different songs. The first song of the dance, until the master drummer reaches the crucial nonsense syllable *tegede-DZA* in his drum-pattern (bar 103), *must* be sung by all the men and women together. Thereafter they may sing different songs. Mr. Tay says that the idea behind this practice is to avoid monotony. It is restricted to the *Adzida* dance proper and does not occur in the preceding *Hatsyiatsya* songs. At times the woman cantor in leading off one of the special *Adzida* songs is helped by an extra male cantor, who leaves his place in the men's department and comes and stands in front of the women's forms.

THE *ADZIDA* SONG

> Miele tome ɖe, be tome afiɖe manɔ—ee
> Dada tome miele ɖe, tome manɔ—ee:
> Miele tome ɖe, be tome afiɖe mianɔ—ee
> Dada tome miele ɖe, tome manɔ—ee.
> Adzidaviawo nu de dzɔ,
> Nu wɔ atsivi eka heko ɖe, katogbe lava ɖo.

> Well, we are in a drum-set: in this set I will live,
> In this exalted circle where we are, I will live:
> Well, we are in a drum-set: in this set we will live,
> In this exalted circle where we are, I will live.
> Ye members of the Adzida club, something has happened—
> Let them laugh at us: pride comes before a fall.

Notes:

Line 2: 'Dada' = Field Marshal: you might translate 'brass-hats' but in this context there is no military significance: so, 'exalted circle' (cf. Dada Kundo = Field Marshal Kundo, and Avadada Katsriku = Field Marshal Katsriku).

Line 6: Literally, "The son of a stick has suffered and the rope has jeered, but his turn will come.' There is a hidden meaning. If you cut sticks you have to put a rope round them to carry them home. While the sticks are being cut, the rope may laugh at the sticks' misfortune, but his turn is coming: he will have to coil himself, with trouble, round the sticks. Probably something happened to this *Adzida* club and they are being laughed at: but the singers are saying that the tables will be turned on the laughers.

Adzida is a quick dance and this bright and jolly song suits its spirit admirably. When the claps are integrated with the *Gankogui* (bars 83 ff.) we find that the basic unit of the song time is 2 against 3 of the *Gankogui* time-units, so that the song has to be written in dotted quavers which rather belie its swift and very duple character. As can be seen from bars 84, 88, &c., there is some harmony in parallel fourths. In this case, however, the harmony crosses the melody line, the first three fourths being a descant, and the remainder sung as usual below the melody. The song stretches over eighteen *Gankogui* patterns and its analysis is this:

Section: *A* + *A* + *B* + *B* +*A*
Bell-patterns: [2+2]+[2+2]+[1+2]+[1+2]+4 = 18

Repeats may be made either straight away, preserving the continuous overall length of eighteen patterns, or the cantor *could* wait for one *Gankogui* pattern before coming in again.

THE INTRODUCTION TO *ADZIDA*

The song is started in the usual way, by the cantor announcing it very *rubato*: on this occasion he only sings the first part of it, which he may repeat as many times as he likes (bars 79–81) and then starts *a tempo* from the beginning again and the chorus, which at this point, we recall, includes both men and women, takes it up (bars 82 ff.). When the cantor reaches the word '*ɖe*' (bar 83) the *Atokewo, Gankogui, Axatse*, and the hand-clapping all come in. This is really the introduction to the main drumming. At the right point the *Atsimevu* will play the introduction pattern by himself, with no other drums playing yet. The clap we have already dealt with. *Gankogui* plays his standard pattern though at the necessary quick *tempo*. The rattle pattern is unusual: the rattle is held upright and is hit against the left hand only, producing merely the 4-clap rhythm. This goes on until the end of bar 99 where we must leave it for the moment. The first *Atoke* player duplicates the *Gankogui* rhythm. The second *Atoke* player, if he is a good man, will come in simultaneously with his mate as it is a mark of prowess to be able to demonstrate one's alert readiness: he may, however, wait for one *Atoke* pattern and then come in. He has a fixed repetitive pattern (see e.g. middle of bar 83 to middle of bar 85) which. is very similar to the *Kidi* pattern played in *Afāvu* (e.g. middle of bar 73 to middle of bar 75), though the accentuation is different which results in his bars being staggered with those of *Atoke* 1. As in the *Kidi* pattern, on his first entry the *Atoke* 2 plays the first half of his pattern twice. Anything unusual in African music is interesting so we pursued the matter. The player wants his pattern to end on a low *Gankogui* note and therefore he must start it in the middle of the previous pattern but one: but he also wants the *Atoke*, when it first makes its entry, to start on a low *Gankogui* note. Hence the additional piece of pattern. Mr. Tay said we were right in comparing the *Atoke* with *Kidi*'s playing in *Afāvu*, only in the latter case he says *Kidi*'s aim is to secure that the *beginning* of the second half of his pattern coincides with a low *Gankogui* note.

Reviewing the whole score at the entry of the orchestra we see that everybody including the song is in the same phase with the exception of *Atoke* 2.

Let us now consider the master drummer. He hears the song start and then he hears the orchestral instruments start. He waits for two or three *Gankogui* patterns, or even more if the performers are not dead in time, and then he comes in with his introduction pattern, choosing a suitable place in the song to do so. In the song on the score this will be shortly after the low bell-note at the end of section *A* of the song (bar 86).

We must digress for a moment here. As we have said before, in any dance of any sort, the entry of the master drum for any pattern *must* be made at a suitable point in the song. Another point is this. The master drummer watches the dancer. If the latter's shoulders are going:

$$\frac{3}{4} \quad \text{♩} \quad | \quad \text{♩} \quad - \quad | \quad - \quad \text{♩} \quad | \quad \text{♩} \quad - \quad | \quad \&c.$$

back, back,   back, back,

he will choose a pattern whose salient beats actually fall on all these shoulder-beats: or he may choose a pattern which emphasizes only the second of each pair of shoulder movements but never only the first of the groups, which in African thought are an *arsis* leading to the main stress on the second beat. This means that the master drummer has two principles to follow. As regards the orchestra he deliberately cuts across their rhythms: but he assists and encourages the dancers by including some beats in synchrony with their movements.

To return to the *Adzida* introduction pattern. The actual drum pattern covers only four *Gankogui* patterns and is in phase with them (bars 86–90). The pivotal syllables are the word '*gidega*' which, coming at the end of each phrase, falls on a low bell-note, being supplanted the fourth time by the high syllable '*to*'. This pattern is played three times with a rest between repeats (bars 86–99). This rest may be of any number of *Gankogui* patterns' duration. On the score we give it one pattern (bars 90 and 95), which is what Mr. Tay did when recording. The idea is to call the attention of the drummers and everybody else. At the conclusion of the third repeat (bar 100), the master drummer omits the final note, seizes his second stick (he has been playing with one stick and one bare hand so far), and launches *sforzando* into the phrase 'HLEBE GEDE . . .'. This is the signal for the club yell.

THE CLUB YELL

Each of the many dance clubs has its yell: the one we give on the score is a very common one. The yell for *Adzida* starts after the master has played the nonsense word '*gede*' four times. No matter what point the song has reached, even in the middle of a line, the singers abruptly break off and shout the yell. This is not singing, but the approximate tones of voice are indicated on the score (bars 100–6). The yell is made without any reference to the time or rhythm of the instrumental accompaniment. They just go on with it till they have finished. The approximate time-values on the score were arrived at by letting Mr. Tay perform and observing how many *Gankogui* patterns he covered, noting at the same time the rhythmic swing of the yell.

WHAT HAPPENS AT -*DZA*

During the yell, all the instruments except the rattle and *Atsimevu* continue to play as before. The master drummer, having played '*gede*' five times, changes to duple time for close on two *Gankogui* bars, then after a triplet he beats out the crucial syllable -DZA (bars 101, 102, and first note of 103). To go back to bar 100: when the rattle-players hear by the master pattern in bar 99 that he is about to play the yell signal, they all hold their rattles high and vertical and shake them rapidly and go on doing so till the master reaches -DZA (bar 103) on which exact point they stop. On this syllable also, the *Atoke* players cease to play and will not be heard any more in the dance. The syllable -DZA is therefore the point at which the whole introduction finishes. It is also the point at which the full drum section of the orchestra enters. But there is no break in the music: continuity is preserved by *Gankogui* who goes on beating as if nothing had happened, while the yell straddles the end of the introduction and the beginning of the next section.

We will now regard -DZA retrospectively and see what happens after it. *Gankogui* goes on as before. The rattles having stopped at -DZA, wait for three quavers in silence and then play the ordinary standard pattern, picking it up at the appropriate beat so that it accords with *Gankogui* in the usual way (bar 103). Normally it is the seated male dancers who do this. The cantor, who has been playing standing up, puts his rattle under his chair and takes his switch (*Awudza*). Immediately he has played -DZA, the master drummer tucks the second stick in his belt as he is about to play the main *Adzida* patterns for which he needs one stick and one bare hand. He then plays a short introduction to the main pattern, moving from the former to the waiting signal before actually starting Pattern A. This introduction may enter, as on the score (bar 103), i.e. on the fifth quaver of the *Gankogui* bar, or on the eleventh, just before *Gankogui*'s quaver beat. At whichever point he enters, the *Atsimevu* player plays the introduction without any curtailment in the latter case, where his relationship with *Gankogui* will correct itself at the waiting signal (bars 107 and 108) which may be prolonged *ad lib.* so as to enter the song at the right point. This *Atsimevu* introduction is not a formal one. Its purpose is to get the *Asiwui* going properly and on time before the master brings in his main pattern. Anyway, it is a very jolly little rhythm and the odd thing is that in spite of its function of setting the pace for the other drums it is in 3/8 time while the others are in either 3/4 or 2/4 time. We have before remarked that when the African crosses a rhythm he really thinks he *is* beating time.

Four quavers after *-DZA*, *Kagaŋ* enters (bar 103) in phase with *Gankogui* and continues his simple 2/4 pattern right through the dance irrespective of any change in the master drumming. At the same point *Kidi* enters with a special 3/4 pattern which he goes on playing only until the master drummer starts Pattern A. *Kidi's* bars are staggered with *Gankogui*, his main accent falling two crotchets after the low bell. *Sogo* enters with *Kidi* and keeps in phase with him playing a similar pattern. The phrasing of this is interesting and is Mr. Tay's. One would expect the last two phrases (bar 105 and part of 106) to be taken as one, being an extended version of the two previous ones. Mr. Tay says you cannot, because that is 'too long for one breath'. Is the connexion in the African mind between drumming and speech so close that even the phrases of the drum-patterns are regarded in the light of speech-phrases and therefore subject to the dictates of breathing?

After the yell, the cantor waits for about two *Gankogui* patterns and then starts the singing again. He takes this opportunity to change the song and start a fresh one. On the score we have had to continue the previous song because it is the only proper *Adzida* song we could get. But it does not matter so far as the principles of the music are concerned.

THE MAIN PATTERNS FOR *ADZIDA*

Master Pattern A is irregular in rhythm, and is really longer than it appears to be. The actual playing, starting in bar 109, finishes in bar 118. Then there is a wait for nearly three *Gankogui* bars before the repeat. Mr. Tay said that if he had started the repeat in another place 'probably it would have been on [*sc.* in proper relation with] *Gankogui* but it would not suit'. Counting the rests, the overall pattern as given by Mr. Tay is twelve *Gankogui* bars long. Its chief feature is its studious avoidance of any close rhythmic connexion with *Gankogui*. Not once does an accented beat occur on the low bell, and even with the bell-bars *Atsimevu* seems to place his accented beats 'between the cracks'.

Kidi answers with a triple-time pattern which is crossed with *Gankogui* by a quaver's distance. It is rather a long one for *Kidi* and has a special form for accompanying the first part of *Atsimevu's* pattern both at its first entry and on repeats. During the rest of this pattern and the whole time *Atsimevu* is playing variations on it, *Kidi* plays his response in its normal form which can be seen repeated many times between bars 113 and 121. The special modification referred to above can be seen in bars 110, 111, and the beginning of bar 112. The point is that *Kidi* has to make an audible reply during *Atsimevu*'s rests at the end of his first two phrases. *Kidi* then plays '*gagigiŋ*' in synchrony with the master and after that the second half of his normal pattern. If one looks at bar 121, one can see how this procedure is repeated when *Atsimevu* repeats the standard pattern. *Sogo* hunts with *Kidi* but plays a pattern which feels rhythmically entirely different. The rising and falling sounds in *Sogo*'s pattern on the syllable '*teŋ*' are produced by playing a centre free beat with the right hand and half-muting with the left. If this muting is done at the proper moment the note given by the drum can be controlled so as to give a gliding sound.

When the master repeats Pattern A (bar 121) he does so without reference to the point the song has reached.

Master Pattern B (bars 124–31) starts with a phrase reminiscent of, but subtly different from, the start of Pattern A. The pattern, eight *Gankogui* bars in length, is characterized by its broken nature. Of the 96 quavers in the whole pattern, only 40 are actual beats, and no less than 56 are rests. Yet these rests are not haphazard. The score clearly shows what the master drummer is aiming for. He is giving the *Asiwui* a chance to show themselves. Every time except once (bar 129) that they start their pattern, *Atsimevu* is silent. This is more evident when we realize what their patterns are. *Kidi*'s pattern is '*tigidi kidigi*' only: the remaining notes are waiting or filling beats. Similarly *Sogo* plays '*tegede de dé*' followed by filling beats. The master arranges to play his contribution during the time the *Asiwui* are playing their filling beats. The rhythm of the master pattern is very irregular and he is obviously staggering his accents with the bell all the way through. He seems to be toying with the possible ways of clapping to the *Gankogui*. The last accented note in his phrase in bars 124, 125, 126, and 129 falls where a 4-clap would fall. His first '*to*' in bar 129 and the second note of the first '*gato*' in bar 130 come where a 3-clap would be made—and so on.

There is something to be learnt from comparing *Sogo* and *Kidi* in this pattern. Why are they barred differently? surely we are being perversely complicated? *Sogo* presented no difficulties but this little pattern of *Kidi*'s took half a morning to unravel. Mr. Tay refused *at once* both of these, though the incidence of the beats is equivalent:

(a)

(b) ti gi di ki di gi

that is, he refused to have a main accent on either the third or the sixth syllable of the pattern. Nor would he tolerate an accent on both, thus:

(c) ti gi di ki di gi

Played in these ways, Mr. Tay says that it makes him feel uncomfortable. He wants the rhythm given in the score. The result is that while *Kidi* and *Sogo* are both crossed with *Gankogui*, they are also playing with each other in the relation of 2 to 3.

When the master first enters Pattern B, *Kidi* and *Sogo* must wait till he finishes his second phrase before beginning to reply (bar 125). Though they recognize what he is playing they have to cover the preceding beats of the master with waiting beats of some sort. But having started in this way, they carry on their pattern without any alteration when the master makes his repeats. It will be noticed that right through this dance, though the song's basic time-unit is half as long again as that of *Gankogui*, none of the drums uses this unit, with the exception of the master who lapses into it for a fleeting moment in Pattern A (bars 109 and 110).

Both Master Pattern A and B enter at the same point in the song, that is, half-way through the cantor's first line (bars 109 and 124).

Master Pattern C has a different entry point, namely at the end of the cantor's first line (bar 135). The actual pattern covers fourteen *Gankogui* bars (135–48). It may be repeated at once, or (as we have scored it) after waiting for two *Gankogui* bars. Mr. Tay says that you cannot wait just for one *Gankogui* bar. Its total length

therefore may be fourteen or sixteen but *not* fifteen *Gankogui* bars
It keeps in phase with *Gankogui*, though the insertion of the
crotchet rest near the end of bar 143 throws the pattern temporarily off-beat with the bell. The pattern opens in a rather slow
and stately way, uses quicker rhythms in the middle and steadies
down again towards the end. We notice in bar 139 the reappearance
of the motif '*ga hlebegi*' which seems to be a feature of *Adzida* as
it figures in both the previous patterns as well.

Kidi enters his pattern on the last note of the first phrase of the
master drum (bar 135). *Kidi*'s pattern is perfectly straightforward
and keeps in phase with *Gankogui*. When he first comes in the
master is obviously echoing his pattern. Each of the accented
master syllables '*dey*' fall on *Kidi*'s accented beats, while in the
latter half of bar 136 the parallel between the drums is complete
as to rhythm and nearly so as regards pitch. The same parallelism
occurs in bars 137 and 138: thereafter the master has a fling, but
from bar 145 to the beginning of bar 148 he once again establishes
a clear rhythmic relationship with *Kidi*.

Sogo's pattern is almost identical with *Kidi*'s but includes an
interesting departure from it both in pitch and in rhythm in the
second half (bar 136). The final nonsense word of *Kidi* is '*kide*'
with the accent on the first syllable. *Sogo* at this point reverses
the accents, putting his stress on the second syllable of '*gede*'.
This causes *Sogo*'s pattern to be rhythmically irregular and though
it is rather charming, with its suggestion of tripleness in the
phrase '*te te gede*', it is difficult to bar on the score so as to show
this clearly. By this device *Sogo* creates a temporary cross-rhythm
with the bell, which is an advantage in Pattern C where there is
a good deal of synchrony in the overall barring.

We cannot go on to consider the end pattern for *Adzida* because though Mr. Tay could perfectly easily invent a suitable one
for this dance, he does not know or cannot recall the authentic
one. So we will end this description of *Adzida* by considering the
changing signals. Incidentally, we hope it is realized that though
for convenience we have scored all the three master patterns as
separate units, yet in practice in a dance the drumming goes on
continuously. Each pattern and its variations leads without a
break via one of the changing signals to another pattern, and so
on right to the end of the dance.

Atsimevu has three possible patterns for the changing signal which he may use at choice, and they are all in phase with *Gankogui*. In the first (bar 152), the familiar *Adzida* motif '*hlebe gede*' appears once more, though it can be simplified by deleting the nonsense word '*hlebe*' and playing '*gede gede* . . .' all the time. For this version the master drummer uses both sticks. He may stop and keep silent after covering one *Gankogui* bar, letting the *Asiwui* carry on till the time comes for him to start the next pattern : or he may go on playing '*gede*' till that time arrives, but this is dull and the longest stretch he would play would be three *Gankogui* bars : instead of doing this he could, after playing bar 152, put in some other suitable beats while waiting. *Atsimevu*'s second changing pattern (bar 153) is simpler still. He uses what is about his highest drum-note and merely beats the 6-clap. His third pattern (bar 154) is produced by making a free centre beat with the stick and immediately after muting in zone 2 with the left hand, thus raising the pitch. This makes quite an attractive sound.

For all the changing signals, *Kidi* uses one and the same pattern which is duple and in phase with *Atsimevu* and the *Gankogui*. It is very much of a marking-time and has no intrinsic rhythmic interest. *Kagaŋ* keeps on as usual, and so in the changing signals the whole orchestra is in phase—except for *Sogo*. Playing in triple time he is of course crossing the master drum and *Kidi* and *Kagaŋ*, but he also plays out of phase with *Gankogui*, his bar-line falling one quaver after the low bell-note. He plays the glide-beat '*deŋ*'. In Changing Signal 3, when *Atsimevu* is also playing the glide beat we have a pretty play of rhythm, *Atsimevu* playing it once every four quavers, and *Sogo* once every three. No doubt, owing to his cross-rhythm, *Sogo* cannot enter anywhere : he has to *start* playing on the first quaver beat of the bell-pattern.

So ends our investigation of the club dance music. Reviewing the score as a whole, and comparing it with the Yeve cult music, one's impression is that *Adzida* drumming is simpler and weaker in dynamic force than the cult drumming. Mr. Tay agrees and says that many *Adzida* patterns are taken from cult drumming being altered to fit the words of the Adzida songs. All real *Adzida* songs are specially composed. When a club composer brings a new song to his master drummer, the latter will have to consider the drumming and he may, for example, think of a pattern which fitted another song well and will not quite suit this new one. He therefore modifies the drum-pattern. This may of course be to the good, but by and large the net result seems less rhythmically magnificent than the highly professional cult drumming. At the same time one must remember that club music is not ordinary village music such as one gets in Central Africa and which is performed without rehearsal by a chance collection of musicians. The clubs are organized musical societies which strive competitively for a high standard. Indeed, their popularity depends on this, and the music they make is correspondingly better than that of the purely recreative dancing we are about to consider.

ADDITIONAL NOTES

Two matters of interest which do not fit directly into the subject of any particular chapter are worthy of mention:

A. 'Taking the Arts' of a master drummer

If a lad shows promise of being a good drummer and has already reached a good standard he may be invited to 'take the arts' of a dead master drummer. If his father or his uncle were master drummers it may well be one of these whose art is to be taken over. The occasion suitable for the ceremony is when a master drummer has just died. The officiant must, if possible, be a master drummer and a member of the lad's family: a retired master drummer is preferred. Mr. Tay has not actually witnessed the ceremony but he says it is like this. The dead man is propped up in his hut, a drum-stick is put in his hand and a drum is placed in front of him. The master drummer shakes the dead musician's arm, so as to beat the drum. The son or nephew then takes the drum-stick from the dead man's hand and touches the drum with it at the very spot where it had been beaten, saying certain words. At the libation, which is customary for all funerals, a special petition is added in this case to the dead master drummer to pass on his art to the lad and to bless him. On future occasions when the new master drummer plays unusually well, people will be pleased but not surprised at his prowess: they know from where his art derives.

B. Vuyoyro

In all non-cult dances there is a custom which serves much the same purpose as the cult signal. It is called *vuyoyro*. It is not an organized drumming but nevertheless acts as an announcement or reminder for a dance. For instance, suppose there has been a dance in the morning and people break off for lunch, intending to dance again at 2 p.m. At, say, half past one, the master drummer seeing they are still eating

will say to himself, 'I had better remind them'—and he plays *vuyoyro*.
It consists of a bout of free-rhythm solo drumming on the master
drum. After the drummer has beaten it, a small boy using two sticks
will play *vukɔgo* on the wooden side of the drum. This is a rhythm of
the same length of phrase as the *Gankogui* pattern which will be used
in the dance, though not necessarily the exact pattern. Here is the
vukɔgo for *Adzida*: notes with two tails indicate that both sticks are
used: we include the *Gankogui* pattern to show the relationship but of
course *Gankogui* is not used here:

While the small boy plays *vukɔgo*, the master drummer plays a few of the
standard patterns of the forthcoming dance together with variations
on them, thus indicating to the people what the dance is going to be.
The *vukɔgo* takes the place of *Gankogui* and adds spice to the master's
beating. It is not essential and he could do without it if he wanted to:
but the usual custom is to play it.

Incidentally, *vukɔgo* is used in any dances in which *Atsimevu* is used
and which are not cult dances. For example, *Nyayito* (funeral dance) has
one which goes like this—the phrasing is Mr. Tay's:

7

THE SOCIAL DANCE—*AGBADZA*

AGBADZA is a derivative from the old traditional After-War Dance called *Atrikpui*. Formerly strong restrictions limited both the time and the place for the performance of the *Atrikpui* dance. It could only be danced after a war when the soldiers were reaching home and it had to be danced at the outskirts of the town where the people would go out to meet the returning soldiers. Moreover it was restricted to men. The only circumstances under which a woman could take part were that if the throne happened to be occupied by a woman, or the direct heir to the throne were a woman, these women could join in the dance. *Atrikpui* is still danced and even today the songs are the repositories of military folk-lore—how the Ewe people left Benin on the Niger and reached Ɖotsie, and later the coast—and so on. Nowadays the occasions for *Atrikpui* are still ceremonial but no longer military. It is danced *at the outskirts* of the town at the funeral of a person who has died an unnatural death. It is also now danced *in* the town when a member of the royal family dies, or for certain ceremonies like the Washing of the Chief's Stool, which is done periodically, say, once a year or once in three years, according to custom. It is also danced in the town when a big controversy has been settled by the chief, and his supporters wish to express their joy that he has brought strife to an end. A relic of the military nature of *Atrikpui* is still seen in the male dance regalia: a man has to wear a knife in his belt. But as there is no longer tribal war, *Atrikpui* has also undergone another and separate development and has emerged as *Agbadza* which is today the normal and very popular general dance for social recreation. During the process the *tempo* of the dance has changed: *Agbadza* is slower than *Atrikpui*. Although until recently *Agbadza* clung to the old tradition of being a specifically male dance, during the last few years women have started taking part in it. Anyone can join in *Agbadza* and any members from any dance clubs can combine to play it as it is a tribal drumming and belongs to everybody. Nowadays in towns Agbadza Societies are formed, but none of them has the right to claim *Agbadza* as its own preserve.

In line with its popular character, *Agbadza* demands no special dancing regalia. You can more or less dress as you like, though the men must wear the dancing shorts with 'peaks' on them as already described, with a cloth, or several cloths according to taste, tied round the waist. But you cannot dance in European suits, more especially European trousers and shoes. An exception may be made in the case of the dance patrons who are probably used to wearing European suits and anyway are not much addicted to dancing. If a spectator dressed in European style feels the impulse to join in, he asks of anybody 'can you give me a change?' He will be taken to their house and provided with suitable attire. These small details give an insight into the attitude of the Africans to their art. However much the European customs are adopted, when it comes to dancing a strong conservatism is manifest: and quite rightly so, for the costumes are part of the whole spirit of the dance and it is a tribute to the aesthetic sense of the African that he realizes where to draw the line. No doubt shorts are of European origin but how incongruous it would be to invade the African dance with European suitings!

Agbadza songs still show their ancestry. Sometimes the reference is very remote—for example, a song about a coward who does not stick to his word. The link in thought is, of course, Coward—Cowardice—War. Many of the *Agbadza* songs are real *Atrikpui* songs (Mr. Tay puts the figure as high as 95 per cent.) and some are really old, as, for instance, this song about the Franco-Prussian war which is still being sung:

> Yanu gbɔgbe doku na agbo
> Dzamawo ɖu Frasea wodzi
> Gbɔgbe baɖa doku na agbo
> Dzamawo ɖu Frasea wodzi to hiame.

A weak animal (*sc.* Germany) has secured the death of a ram (*sc.* France)
The Germans have defeated the French

Note. *Yanu gbɔgbe*: an old expression. We do not know its literal meaning but Mr. Tay knows it means Germany.

That bad Gbɔgbe (Germany) has indeed secured the death of the ram
The Germans have defeated the French at this season.

As in the case of the other dances, *Agbadza* songs are in two
classes, the *Hatsyiatsya* songs and the main dance songs. More
than half are in the former group. Their characteristic feature is
that they are free songs, so they cannot be accompanied by clapping. Some of the songs are semi-free: the first half is free and
in the middle it becomes metrical and the people start clapping.
Such songs cannot have repeats and are sung only once. The free
songs could be forced into the *Gankogui* pattern but that would
spoil their musical appeal. For example, the free song in the score,
though it could be forced by slight changes of time to fit the
Gankogui simply will not do for the main dance. Mr. Tay says you
dare not sing it like that. People would laugh at you and say, 'Is
this man trying to create a new thing, or what?' We transcribed
the forced version and found that the forcing consisted of turning
it into a rather jerky triple time. Yet it cannot only be the jerkiness
which spoilt it for Mr. Tay. He sang it to the *Gankogui* another
way: this time it went much more smoothly, but still he felt the
song was ruined by this treatment. It must, he said, be free. This
is very odd when so much African music is patently based on a
rigid metrical concept. Certainly more attention should be paid
to this free music. One great difficulty in analysing and transcribing it is the impossibility of finding a counter-rhythm by which
to determine the exact lengths of the notes.

We have a particular objective in this study of the *Agbadza*
dance. From all that has gone before, it would seem hardly necessary to describe in detail yet another series of drum-patterns. But
there is one very important subject to which we have made passing
references, but which is the very life of all master-drum playing,
and that is the master-drum variations. It is the variations which
will claim our chief attention in this chapter, and for that reason
we shall pass as swiftly as possible over the formal standard
patterns.

The orchestra for *Agbadza* comprises *Gankogui*, *Axatse*, *Kagaŋ*,
Kidi, and *Sogo* which is used as the master drum.

There are three possible ways of starting. The first is this: the
people sing some *Agbadza Hatsyiatsya* songs. After a time the
patrons will say, 'Let us start.' The master drummer will give a
signal to stop the singing and then plays the *Agbadza* signal. He

plays it as a solo: nothing else is happening. As soon as he quits this and has begun to play the introduction pattern, the rest of the orchestra joins in and the cantor starts the first main dance song. The second method of starting is simply to omit the *Hatsyiatsya* songs and in this case the whole performance starts with the master playing the solo *Agbadza* signal. The most popular way, which is recognized as the really proper start is this: the cantor and chorus sing two or three free *Hatsyiatsya* songs. During these, the master drummer playing solo, and in his own time and with no reference to the time of the latter, plays the *Agbadza* signal. He enters on any suitable word in the earlier part of the song. When the signal is finished he waits in silence till the cantor starts the main dance song. Then the *Gankogui* and *Axatse* come in, entering at a suitable point in the song, and the master plays the introduction pattern, being joined by *Kidi* and *Kagaŋ*. This official way of starting is the one adopted in the music-score.

Sometimes, the *Agbadza* dance is preceded, as in the case of *Adzida*, by some *Afãvu* drumming. In *Agbadza* this is called *Avɔlu nyanya* and, as in the former case, is always played three times. It is played in conjunction with the *Agbadza Hatsyiatsya* songs and follows them in this way. There may be a few good dancers singing the *Hatsyiatsya* song, putting in actions as they do so and going round inside the ring of seats surrounding the dance-area. On completing the circle, one of these, the cantor, will line the *Afãvu* song in free style. Then he starts it again in strict time with claps: all join in the chorus and the drums come in. After a couple of minutes or so they all stop and this *Afãvu* is repeated and then repeated again. After that the main dance starts.

THE SONGS

1. *The* Hatsyiatsya *song—free rhythm*

> Esɔdotɔ medo to o
> Be sɔdotɔ medo to o
> Be adzadotɔwo minɔ agboa dzi
> Ee masi hã hã, ee masi hã
> Oo—hee—, be adzadotɔwo minɔ agboa dzi(e)!

The horse-rider could not ride a buffalo—
But certainly the horse-rider could not ride a buffalo
Those of you who ride horses can always be expected to arrive home.
Before I could hear 'What! what!', before I could hear 'What!'

O dear me! surely those of you who ride horses can always be expected home!

> Note: A story lies behind this song. There was a prince fond of horse riding. One day while riding with his father he saw a buffalo and said, 'I want to ride on the buffalo.' His father replied, 'Though you can mount a horse, that does not mean you can ride a buffalo.' Nothing daunted, the prince jumped on the buffalo, but could not control it. It took him here, there, and everywhere, till they came to an *Okro*-tree farm, where the prince, entangled in the trees, was pulled off his mount and the buffalo made off. Presently the farmer came and asked what he was doing on his farm. Then he noticed that the prince had a mark on his belly (a custom of the Mossi tribe) which showed he was a prince. The farmer sent word to his father, but all the king said was, 'What! my prince!', meaning, 'It serves him right.' The moral of the song is, 'No man can say he knows everything.'

The music can be seen in the score from bar 2 to bar 8. The cantor first sings the whole song and then the chorus sing it all several times, not exceeding perhaps three repeats. Now although we have marked it to be sung in free time, yet anyone singing it is bound to feel how strongly rhythmic it is. Like all these African songs it is a serious tune, and we think, a good one.

2. *Main dance song I—strict time*

Avugbe menya be kpɔ̃ le avea me lo ho
Sotua do gbe miwɔ aya ŋudɔ
Avugbe menya be kpɔ̃ le avea me—oo—e
Ahɔ̃tua do gbe miwɔ aya ŋudɔ
Sohɔ̃tua do gbe vɔ
Miwɔ aya ŋudɔ: sotua do gbe: miwɔ aya ŋudɔ
Avugbe menya be kpɔ̃ le avea me
Sotua do gbe: miwɔ aya ŋudɔ.

The red-flanked duiker does not know there's a leopard in the forest
The war gun is sounded, make use of your cutlass:
The red-flanked duiker does not know there's a leopard in the forest
The war gun is sounding, make use of your cutlass.
The war gun is already sounded
Make use of your cutlass: the war gun is sounded: make use of your cutlass
The red-flanked duiker does not know there's a leopard in the forest
The war gun is sounded: make use of your cutlass.

Note the military theme of the words.

Let us look at the score. The song extends between bars 9 and 24 and is then repeated. Its overall length is exactly sixteen *Gan-*

kogui bars and it divides itself into two main sections (*A* and *B*) each of eight *Gankogui* bars. It can be further subdivided, yielding the following analysis:

Main Sections: *A*   :   *B*

Internal structure: $[M+N]+[M+N]+[O+P+N']+[O+P+N']$

Gankogui bars: $\begin{cases} [2+2] + [2+2] + [1+1+2] + [1+1+2] = 16 \\ 4 + 4 + 4 + 4 = 16 \end{cases}$

It is a call-and-response song in still another form not previously met with in this book. Section *A* behaves normally, being a call and response both repeated. Section *B* contains new melodic material at *O* and *P* which are also call and response, but to the latter is added a recapitulation of section *N* in a slightly variant form. This procedure besides being musically interesting, gives a strong sense of stability to the whole song.

In bar 12 and corresponding places, where the melody has alternate forms, while either may be sung, the lower is the better according to Mr. Tay. If desired both may be sung simultaneously, in which case we have not only a fourth but also a third.

Apart from the opening phrase (bar 9) and its reappearances, the whole song is consistently in 3/4 time. But this 3/4 time is staggered with the *Gankogui*: the first beat of the *Gankogui* bar falls on the second beat of the song-bar (see e.g. the beginning of bar 10). When the 6-clap is going, as shown in bars 9–22, the clappers can obviously be considered as in phase either with *Gankogui* or with the song. On the score we have shown them in phase with *Gankogui*. In actual practice the clapping has no accented beats, nor would the performers be aware that the song-rhythm crosses the bell. An accentless regular clap fits both cases equally well. When we deal with the claps, however, we shall see that they ultimately derive from the *Gankogui*.

3. *Main dance song II—strict time*

           Ahɔme sukawo ta avi ɖe dzogbe dzie
           Kagãwo yi vo ɖu ge
           Amegã megãwo ta avi ɖe dzogbe vɔ
           Kagãwo yi vo ɖu ge tagba.

The great war-leaders are crying on the battlefield
The vultures have gone to their scavenging

The great and the mightiest are now weeping on the battlefield
The vultures have gone to their scavenging on the battlefield.

Note: The meaning behind this song is that the warriors who boast of their prowess will be killed and eaten by vultures: in other words, 'Pride comes before a fall'.

Here is another song with the military content of the *Atrikpui* tradition. We have included it for the following reason. We want to demonstrate the exploitable possibilities of the *Sogo* master drum Pattern B. This pattern *could* be played to the first main dance song, but it does not suit very well. The cantor would not normally change the song to suit the drum: the contrary is what happens. Therefore in the score we imagine that during the dance, as is customary, the cantor changes the song. The master drummer, noting that Pattern B would suit the song very well, plays the changing signal and leads into it.

This song is very short indeed taking only four *Gankogui* bars (49–53) and is in the simple form $A+B+C+D$, each section being one *Gankogui* bar in length.

Theoretically, the song will be repeated without any waiting, as we have it on the score at bars 53 and 57. In actual practice, the cantor will wait one *Gankogui* bar and then repeat as in bars 61 and 66. Now, to anticipate the drum analysis, *Sogo*'s Pattern B covers, like the song, four *Gankogui* bars and therefore if the cantor inserts one bar's rest between repeats, *Sogo* will be thrown off his relation with the song. Realizing this, the master drummer will play, as an interlude, a *piece* of Pattern B: he would play *gitegi gaga gi* (see bar 51) at the end of Pattern B: as this phrase is one *Gankogui* bar in length, it will ensure his keeping in phase with the song. Though normally one expects a break between the song repeats, Mr. Tay remarked that 'the continuous singing of this particular song goes very well': and that is our justification for scoring it in this way.[1]

Suppose the cantor is repeating the song without waiting, and the master drummer is playing variations, and wants to bring in the standard pattern again, which would necessitate his entering it at the right point in the song. Suppose he says to himself, 'I will do it on the next song-repeat'. What happens, we asked Mr. Tay, if the cantor suddenly decides to insert the extra waiting bar, or conversely, if he has been using this waiting bar, what happens

[1] See also p. 177.

if, at this juncture, he comes in before the *Sogo* player expected? He said, 'A master drummer does not think in that way'. He is *not* calculating in advance that he will re-enter his standard pattern at such and such a point. He just goes on playing and adjusts his playing to the circumstances. Moreover, a good cantor will mutually assist the master drummer: he knows how things are going, and they both work together in that instinctive collaboration which is the authentic badge of true musicianship. Thus, for example, there are some master-drum patterns which go very well with certain songs. If the master changes to one of these patterns, the cantor may change the song and bring in one which specially suits it. This is not often done, but it is an example of the mutual co-operation between the two leaders.

This is a suitable place to make a digression. We have just considered the question of repeats to a song: we now ask what happens in the course of a dance when the cantor wants to change the song and sing another. Let us imagine they are singing the second song (bars 49 ff.) and the cantor wants to change to the first one (bars 25 ff.): he may do so in two ways. When the chorus gets to '*tagba-e*' (bar 53) and while they are actually singing this word, the cantor singing *rubato* in free time, and rapidly, lines the next song '*Avugbe menyabe*'—singing it right through. Meanwhile the whole orchestra continues as usual. The cantor then comes in with the new song in strict time and everyone takes it up. Mr. Tay says it would be very poor for the cantor merely to leave a gap of silence between one song and another.

Mr. Tay says there is another beautiful way of making the change. At the end of the first song, the cantor holds up both hands and sings 'Ooooh' for about one *Gankogui* bar and then starts the next song. If it is a popular one he can start it in strict time and the people at once join in: if not, he will first line it in free time as already described.

Hand-clapping in Agbadza

In *Agbadza*, hand-clapping occupies a more prominent place than in any other dance except those dances which are accompanied by hand-claps alone. There are no obligatory clap-patterns. The claps are performed spontaneously, as the spirit moves: for instance, Mr. Tay says if he and I are seated side by side in the dance and he starts clapping, I shall think to myself that I must put in a different clap *'which crosses his'* (*ipsissima verba*). We have included quite a number of these claps on the score but, in order to appreciate them better and to facilitate comment, the ten clap-patterns which are used are set out below.

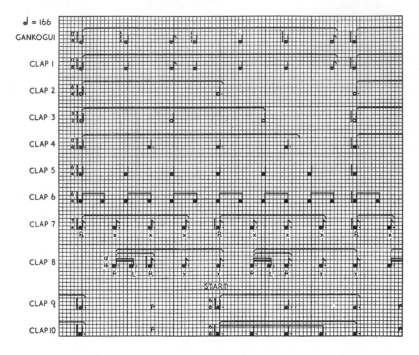

Note first the metronome mark: *Agbadza* is a hot dance with a brisk *tempo*. Claps 1 to 6 need no comment as they are by now familiar, except to point out that sometimes (clap 1) the clapping actually duplicates the *Gankogui* pattern, and that clap 6, going at 232 claps per minute is very rapid. Claps 9 and 10 are an interesting variant of the 4-clap (clap 4). The introduction of a rest in place of the fourth clap in each bar makes a very effective pattern, to which added piquance is given by placing the pattern athwart that of *Gankogui* so that it always starts exactly in the middle of the latter. Clap 10 is a very pretty one: its first half is, of course, going 2 against 3 with relation to *Gankogui*.

Claps 7 and 8 are in a class by themselves: to make the patterns you have not only to clap your hands but also to hit the left breast with the appropriate hand held flat. This makes a dull thud, and the striking contrast in sound is not only fascinating to hear but also produces a powerful rhythmic urge. The signs on the paradigm mean this:

R = hit right hand flat just above left breast
L = ,, left ,, ,, ,, left ,,
X = clap both hands together

Clap 7 is a straightforward clapping at a rate of 2 against 3 to *Gankogui*. Clap 8, however, is astonishing. Without the *Gankogui* and bereft of its dotted notes, it appears perfectly simple. Its essential time is more easily grasped if written thus:

But its time-units are the same as those of clap 7 and it goes 2 against 3 to *Gankogui*. Yet whereas clap 7 is in phase with the *Gankogui* bars, in clap 8 the bars are staggered in such a way that every alternate clap-bar lies exactly athwart the junction between one *Gankogui* bar and the next. The key to this disposition of the pattern is to be seen in clap 4, which consists of four dotted crotchets to the bar. As clap 8 is built on dotted quavers, it is obviously related to the former. Clap 8 *vis-à-vis* clap 4 has shifted its bar-line one dotted crotchet to the right, so that its main beat of the bar falls on the second dotted crotchet instead of on the first, and consequently on repeat, clap 8's main beat falls on the fourth dotted crotchet of clap 4 instead of on the third: with the further complication that the clap-phrase in clap 8 starts one beat before the bar-line. In short, this is playing 2 against 3, staggered by one beat, with a weak-beat start. Surely here is a remarkable piece of staggered rhythm and yet when the *Gankogui* is playing, Mr. Tay claps it with perfect ease and smoothness. Incidentally, clap 8 suits the first main song and also Master Pattern A.

THE DRUMMING

The Agbadza *signal (bars 1–8)*

The *Agbadza* signal is a solo performance by the master drummer on the *Sogo* drum, using his two bare hands. It is in the nature of a declamation and is in absolutely free time, the note-values depending on the aesthetic impulse of the player. The note-values on the score represent Mr. Tay's own performance and were arrived at in a manner similar to that used for the Yeve cult signal. It is therefore approximate and can only be so, for the time-values, while preserving their outline, are likely to vary from one performance to another.

There are two possible entries for *Sogo*: he may come in as on the score. The interesting feature of this entry is that the drum starts just *before* the word *Be* which starts the second phrase of the song. Mr. Tay shook his head at the very idea of starting exactly on *Be*. Why is this? Is it because at all costs the rhythms must cross? Alternately the master could enter in bar 5 approximately where the second group of *gadagada* starts. His third possible entry is towards the end of bar 7, about a quaver before the printed figure 8. The signal is calculated to arouse excitement: it is rapid, and half-way through it accelerates, then dies off with a very rapid roll which keeps at a constant speed.

The introduction signal

When the cantor, having lined the main dance song, starts again *a tempo* (bar 9) the orchestra enters when he sings the word *lo*. The master drummer could also start here but he will not do this as he wants the *Gankogui* and rattle to be heard a little by themselves before he enters. He therefore comes in on the cantor's last word *yudo* (bar 11). The master is now of course playing on time and indeed sets the pace, for if he does not approve of the speed of the *Gankogui*, he will pull everyone up to his own pace. The signal is all in 2/4 time and, except in the middle, is in phase with the *Gankogui*. *Sogo* does, however, cross over for just two *Gankogui* bars (14 and 15): he does it by slipping his main beat one quaver late. We have placed the slipping quaver in a bar by itself (bar 14). He resumes his original relation with the bell by playing his last bar in bar 15 a quaver short. There is one other point to note, and that is his last syllable *ge* (first note of bar 18). Mr. Tay says you *cannot* stop on the final syllable of the word *gede* at the end of bar 17. You either omit the latter syllable, or, as on the score, add one more *ge*. This is analogous to ending the *Gankogui* pattern on its beginning note.

Kidi duplicates the opening of the master signal, adding interest to the pattern by playing alternately fairly loud, and soft (bar 11), and continuing it until the master reaches *hlebe gede* (bar 16). He accompanies the latter either by playing the 4-clap rhythm as on the score or the 6-clap rhythm thus:

maintaining the rhythm till the master enters on his first standard pattern. All this time *Kidi* is in phase with *Gankogui*. The permanent cross-rhythm is provided by *Kagaŋ* who plays his standard pattern right through the dance and who, as usual, shifts his main beats one quaver early so that his bar is always straddling the low bell-note. The place indicated on the score where *Kagaŋ* starts is not arbitrary. He starts on the first quaver in the bell-pattern. This is because it helps him to get his time as, by starting here, his first three beats double those of the bell, a fact which Mr. Tay confirms.

Returning to the master drummer (beginning of bar 18), when he reaches the end of the introduction signal he waits, if necessary or if he feels like it, before entering his first standard pattern. It is best not to wait very long as this is bad musicianship and is likely to provoke a taunt from the women such as—'he is waiting for his mother to put a rhythm in his head'.

Master Pattern A

The entry for this pattern is after the song syllable *ɲudɔ* at the end of the first line of the song (i.e. in bar 27) or, as on the score, at the end of the first line of section B of the song (bar 18). Though its predominant time is 3/4, it contains irregular bars, and it is thoroughly crossed with *Gankogui*. Not a single one of the first beats of the 3/4 bars falls on a main beat of the *Gankogui* bar. In spite of this there is a unifying factor. This is the nonsense word *kiŋ-kiŋ*, which occurs at the end of master-drum phrases no less than nine times, plus the variant *gakiŋ* at the end of bar 21. In each case it falls so that the final syllable comes on a low bell-note. The only exception is bar 18. Nor is this all. If the student will compare the master's bars with clap 4 he will see that there is a relationship between them. The master's accents are either a quaver late on the 4-clap (e.g. bars 18–20 and 22), or actually on it (bars 21, 23, 26). Mr. Tay agrees that it is based on the 4-clap, which situation may be compared with Pattern B which is based on the 6-clap: but he added that there would be nothing wrong if the dancer danced to the 3-clap during this pattern. Moreover, there is added interest in the frequent admixture of playing 2 against 3. Wherever there are dotted notes on the score, 2 against 3 is being drummed. Without exception, each time there is a lapse into 2 against 3, the master drum is exactly in phase with the 4-clap. Finally, at the start of the pattern, the triple repetition of the phrase *Aze degí tegí* seems to help *Kidi* or to reflect his rhythm, as the accented beats in both cases are simultaneous.

Kidi's response to this pattern has three forms, any of which may be used, and all of them emphasizing the *kiŋ-kiŋ* theme of the master pattern. In fact *Kidi*'s pattern is merely playing two firm beats per bar, with filling quavers in between, and these firm beats always occur together with the master's *kiŋ-kiŋ*. The semiquavers on *Kidi*'s stave are really reinforcements of the preceding crotchet, played with the other stick. They are like grace-notes except that they follow instead of precede the note they are attached to, and are a frequent feature of *Asivui* playing. For example, *Kagaŋ* may strengthen his main beat of the bar in a similar way if he wants to, by playing:

One might call them 'after-grace-notes'. *Kidi* plays in phase with *Gankogui*.

The overall rhythmic situation in Pattern A is that *Kagaŋ* is in cross-rhythm with the bell, *Kidi* agrees with it, and the master freely crosses everyone, except that on each low bell-note he pulls himself temporarily into line with *Kidi*.

The master-drum variations

We now come to the question of the master-drummer's variations. We must therefore leave the analysis of the score for a while, in order to consider in a general way the whole matter of variations not only in *Agbadza* but in all dances.

Playing variations is the main occupation of the master drummer when there is dancing. While he has to play his dance signals, introduction signals, and so on, yet for the major part of the time he is playing variations. In one sense therefore, all the scores we have given so far are to some extent misleading. Except for some elementary examples of variations in *Nyayito* we have restricted ourselves to the standard patterns of the master drum. It must be clearly understood that no dance would be played in this way. To play a string of master drum standard patterns even if each is repeated several times is simply not African music. The full flower of the music is in the variations of which the standard pattern is the nucleus. The musical technique is this: the master announces a standard pattern and repeats it several times to establish it. Now each standard pattern consists of several phrases or sentences. Any one of these can serve as a nucleus for variations. But the first phrase is all-important. It is the SEED of the pattern. The whole standard pattern grows out of this seed. So also do the variations on that pattern. Thus, after establishing a standard pattern, the master drummer, by extension, simile, or any other artifice at his command, using the first phrase as the germinal idea, builds up spontaneously a series of variations which continue as long as the inspiration of that particular phrase lasts. Having started with this 'seed', as Tay puts it, the master drummer can go anywhere he likes, for everyone will know that your plant has grown from this seed. Normally you cannot start variations by improvising on, say, section B or section C of a standard pattern. Some drummers might do this, but sooner or later they *must* introduce the 'seed' which is section A. The worst course is to start your variations on some part of the standard pattern other than section A and then go on without bringing in the seed at all. Mr. Tay says this will be 'just playing in the air without any background. People would hardly know on what pattern you were playing variations.'

After starting the variations in this way, having exploited section A you return to the full standard pattern and play it once or twice. Then you may take, say, section B, and play variations on it for quite a time: then return to the standard pattern. You keep on like this till you have exhausted the possibilities of the whole pattern. To put things in proportion and as an indication of the astonishing fecundity of a good master drummer's musical imagination we may mention that the second variations to Pattern B given on the score filled one side of a 12-inch gramophone disk (78 r.p.m.) and were wholly devoted to section A of that pattern. Mr. Tay explained that he could have gone on to variations of other sections of the pattern but it would have taken a very long time, though he also said that these sections 'would not have gone so far' as section A.

While he is playing variations, the master drummer will not trouble much about his relation with the song: the only thing to avoid is to play any beats which clash unsuitably with the singing. Near the end of the dance, however, he will deliberately draw attention to the song by his beating. As we explained before, he will want to arrange that the drumming shall end before the song does.

The standard patterns which best lend themselves to variations are the very short ones. Thus, in *Agbadza*, Pattern A is not very good for the purpose, but Pattern B is.

Obviously if one is to give an account of African music, such a vital matter as the master-drum variations must be tackled. We want to know just what the African does when he is playing them, and for that purpose we need a musical score. But this is no easy matter. The drumming is going at nearly five quavers a second. Neither the transcriber nor the drummer knows what the latter is going to play. It comes into his head at the moment of playing and he cannot afterwards remember what he played. To make a gramophone record will not, by itself, help us because no European, unaided, could analyse it. Moreover, we want to put down not only the correct time-values of the beats but their pitch. The only way to do this is to discover exactly what hands made each beat and in what position on the drum-skin: what notes were muted or secondary-muted, and so on.

We made two separate attacks on this problem, involving different techniques, the results of which are seen in the *Agbadza* score, in the variations to Pattern A and the first variations to Pattern B on the one hand, and in the second variations to Pattern B on the other.

Our first method was this. With the standard pattern in mind, Mr. Tay considered some suitable variations and wrote out their nonsense syllables. He always writes them without our prompting in separate lines, like a poem, thus showing how keenly he feels the phrasing and incidentally indicating where the phrasing is. He then played the first phrase, from his paper, on the drum against the *Gankogui* and we transcribed its rhythm. He then repeated it a few beats at a time and we noted the hands and positions used for each beat. In this way we patiently went through all the syllables he had written. Of course there is an objection to this method of which we were keenly conscious. It is artificial: these are not exactly spontaneous variations, though they occurred to him spontaneously while he composed them. Nevertheless they are genuine variations.

Our second method was an attempt to avoid these drawbacks. While the *Gankogui* was being played, Mr. Tay played Standard Pattern B and then launched out into spontaneous variations, with no anterior written preparation. All this was recorded on a disk. This was stage 1. Stage 2 rested entirely with Mr. Tay. He worked at the record and wrote down the entire set of variations as nonsense syllables. This did not give him any difficulty. The next stage needed the drum recorder. Taking a few lines at a time he tapped out the rhythm while the *Gankogui* rhythm was also played. This enabled us to transcribe the whole variations in terms of note-values only. The fourth stage was to play all this a few beats at a time on the drum while the transcriber noted down the hand positions for each beat, thus determining its musical pitch. We were at last by this means able to present, for the first time as far as we know, the musical score of a set of spontaneous master-drum variations.

We made one mistake. In recording the variations we should have recorded the song as well. As the song was not being sung, Mr. Tay based his variations solely on *Gankogui*. The result was that, on writing the full score, the question of the gap between the song repeats came up. Would the variations clash with the song? Mr. Tay went through them and found that if the cantor left a gap of one *Gankogui* pattern, there would be clashes and it would entail altering the variations in numerous places. But if there is no gap, it falls all right. Theoretically, he says, it is correct to repeat the song with no gaps between repeats, but in actual practice a wait of one or two *Gankogui* patterns is inserted. As our object is to study the variations and as the song in any case during variations is not of much moment, we have scored it with no gaps between repeats. The variations as written fulfil the necessary conditions of arising out of the 'seed', of not clashing with the song and of being spontaneous.

The Sogo *variations on Pattern A*

We now consider in detail the variations on Master Pattern A.

Running from bar 31 to bar 46, they cover sixteen *Gankogui* bars. It is certain that Mr. Tay made no mathematical reckoning when composing them, yet his sense of aesthetic fitness produces once again the sort of number familiar to us in African music.

To understand their structure we must return for a moment to Standard Pattern A. In Mr. Tay's mind this pattern can be subdivided into five sections as indicated on the score. The variations are based on these sections, starting of course with the seed. In order to show the relationship, the sections of the standard pattern on which *Sogo* is improvising are marked on the score in the variations. To appreciate this relationship more directly, we give below the standard pattern together with the derivative sections of the variations.

Pattern A	Bars	Variations
§ A. Aze degi tegi, aze degi tegi, aze degi tegi, gaga kiŋ-kiŋ ga kiŋ-kiŋ gaga kiŋ-kiŋ	31 to mid. 33	Aze degi tegi, aze degi tegi, gada, gada gada gada kiŋ-kiŋ ga kiŋ-kiŋ
§ B. gazegle gazegle gazegle gakiŋ ga kiŋ-kiŋ gagaga kiŋ-kiŋ		Nil
§ C. gatsya gatsya ga kiŋ-kiŋ gatsya gatsya gaga kiŋ-kiŋ	mid. 39 to mid. 40	gaze ga tsya tsya gatsya gatsya ga kiŋ-kiŋ
§ D. ga kiŋ-kiŋ gaga kiŋ-kiŋ, gaze tegi tegi tegi tegi te kiŋ-kiŋ	33 to 39	gazete kiŋ-kiŋ, gazete ga hlebegi kide gaga, gazete ga hlebegi gada kiŋ-kiŋ gaze gaze gaze tsya tsyatsya gaze tete
	40 and 41 43 and 44	gaze tegi ga gadagla kiŋ-kiŋ gaze tegi gaze tegi gazete gi gaga kiŋ-kiŋ
§ E. gatsya gatsya gaga kiŋ-kiŋ ga kiŋ-kiŋ gaga kiŋ-kiŋ	42 46	ga kiŋ-kiŋ gaga kiŋ-kiŋ ga kiŋ-kiŋ gadagla kiŋ-(kiŋ) The final syllable is suppressed on the score by the changing signal.

There is a point of technical interest in the way the master plays *kiŋ-kiŋ*. These syllables coincide with *Kidi*'s *kiŋ-kiŋ* and are an imitation of it. In order to imitate on *Sogo* the tone of *Kidi*, instead of muting as usual with four fingers of the left hand, the master uses the last three only. This shows how susceptible African ears are not only to pitch but to timbre and it also shows the limitation of the European staff notation when used for African drumming. The timbre is all-important: it makes the pattern what it is. This is one reason for writing the nonsense syllables on the score. In order to make a given pattern recognizable as such, every single note in any and all instruments must be produced with the appropriate timbre.

Judging from the nonsense syllables alone, as given above, there is nothing very remarkable in the variations. But the score shows them to be a good deal cleverer and more subtle than the syllables appear to indicate. There is great playing with the time-values: compare for instance the dotted semiquavers in bar 26 which become dotted quavers in bar 43: or note how in section D the duple words *gaze tegi* whose accents are on the first syllables, combine and change to give the triple form *gazete* (*gi*) in bars 33 to 35 and 44, and appear in yet another rhythmic triple form in bar 41. Similarly the actual positions *vis-à-vis* the *Gankogui* which are occupied by the standard pattern phrases are freely altered and bandied about in the variations. Reading them through on the score, one can see clearly that though firmly rooted in the standard pattern they are a free and, one might say, whimsical comment and play upon it.

The dependence of the variations on their standard pattern is emphasized by the other drums who always go on playing the response to that pattern during the whole time the master is improvising on it.

Is there any definite point in the song (e.g. the end) where the master should terminate his variations? There is no rule about this. He may, if he wishes, make them end at the conclusion of a song-repeat, but he will not trouble about the song so far as the variations are concerned. Thus, in our score, he stops them at a suitable drum-phrase which happens to occur soon after the beginning of the song-verse.

The changing signal

We have this time incorporated the changing signal with the preceding variations to show how the transition is made (bars 45 and 46). The master drummer's last phrase should be *gadagla kiŋ-kiŋ*. The final syllable disappears because the changing signal opens on the low bell-note, thus occupying its place. There is an alternative place in the *Gankogui* pattern for *Sogo* to enter his changing signal and that is exactly half-way through it. He is guided in his choice partly by the amount of time he will have to wait before entering on his next pattern.

Kidi, when he hears the syllables *hlebe gede*, changes as soon as possible to the correct response. In this case it is easy as all he has to do is to move from 3/4 to 3/8 time in the same phase. *Kagaŋ* goes on as usual. We have met this signal before: it is exactly the same as the latter half of the *Agbadza* introduction signal. The vertical relationships on the score are these: both *Sogo* and *Kidi* are in phase with the *Gankogui* but are playing 3 against 4 to each other (3 bars of *Sogo* = 4 bars of *Kidi*): *Kagaŋ* is crossed with *Gankogui* as usual and is also crossed with *Kidi* even though both are playing in triple time and at the same speed.

Incidentally there is a choreographic detail in connexion with changing signals. In any dance of any kind, cult or otherwise, while the master plays the changing signal, custom decrees that people cannot dance. They just stand and wait till a new pattern comes. If anyone is actually dancing at the time, he does not suddenly stop: he comes gracefully to a pause in his dancing.

Master Pattern B

Pattern B does not suit the first main song: accordingly on the score we have imagined that the cantor has just changed the song, and the master drummer enters with a pattern which suits it. This short pattern of only four *Gankogui* bars (50–53) is based, says Mr. Tay, on the 6-clap, which fact can be verified by comparing the two staves on the score. As usual it avoids entering on the beginning of the *Gankogui* phrase, but otherwise is in phase with it. Consisting of only four short phrases separated by minim rests, to a European it looks indivisible, each phrase ending in exactly the same way. But Mr. Tay says it falls into two equal sections, and we shall find that he observes this division in the variations. During the minim rests the master will probably make two crotchet beats to fill up but they are not counted as part of the pattern.

Kidi's response to the master-drum phrases comes after the minim rests which follow them. It looks in section (*b*) as if *Kidi* is merely doubling the *Sogo* pattern. This is not so: he is echoing it one bar later. During the rest which follows the opening *Sogo* phrase, *Kidi* plays the single beat *kiŋ* (bar 51) followed by some filling beats. He *must* play this note here, though he does not play it again once he has started. Both *Kidi* and *Sogo* are in phase with *Gankogui* and with each other: the only cross-rhythm is produced by *Kagaŋ* who goes on as usual. The reader has probably realized by now that this popular general recreative dancing is much simpler than the others we have studied. There is much more synchrony between *Gankogui* and the drums. The principle of cross-rhythms is indeed maintained throughout by *Kagaŋ*'s elementary beating: apart from that, the rhythmic interest lies mainly in the hands of the master drummer with his free variations. This is what we should expect in an amateur and 'scratch' performance. There is no trained orchestra. All you need are a number of instrumental players who can play sufficiently well to keep the dance going, together with a master drummer. He is the only professional man required, and he can provide all the subtlety of rhythm-patterns which will put life into the dance. If the *Asivui* players happen to be competent musicians so much the better.

The first variations on Pattern B

These, like the Pattern A variations, were pre-arranged: that is to say, Mr. Tay came with a paper containing the nonsense syllables he intended to play. His drumming of these patterns provided an illuminating comment both on the value and also on the limitations of this African syllabic notation. He had great difficulty in recapturing just what he had meant to play and watching him actually playing the drum from his written sheet, it was clear that it was the recapturing of the rhythm (not the note pitches) and its relation with *Gankogui* which was the difficulty. He said that the difficulty about variations is that they come into your head at the moment of playing and then are forgotten. Here then is the limitation of the syllabic notation. Though it can indicate qualitatively much more than staff notation and is in this respect much superior to it, yet it is imperfect in its quantitative aspect. It is not an absolute system of rhythm indication and therefore it needs to be coupled with another factor which is memory. As an indication of standard patterns whose rhythmic shape is, of course, remembered, the system works perfectly. Otherwise, though it says far more than the old European neumatic notation did, it resembles the early form of the neums in being no more than an *aide-mémoire*.

The short set of variations we give on the score are only a mere sample of what the master drummer would do in the actual dance. They cover fourteen *Gankogui* bars and once more we point out that this figure was arrived at quite unconsciously by the drummer (bars 54–67). They start, as they should, with a statement of the 'seed' which is section A of the standard pattern, and then go on to develop it. Nearly the whole of the variations are an exploitation of section A, only the last two and a half *Gankogui* bars being based on section B.

A careful study of the score reveals what the master drummer is doing. Section A of the standard pattern contains two little motifs—*gitegi* and *gaga gi*, the latter occurring in two separate contexts. In the variations the master drummer plays with these two motifs. Only twice (bars 59 and 62) does he state them in their original form. In bar 61 he preserves the time and accentuation of *gitegi* but expands it so that it becomes *gitegiga*. In every other case while still keeping to the original stress and relative note-values, he reduces the speed of the motifs by $33\frac{1}{3}$ per cent. so that the crotchets and quavers become dotted notes and the little patterns instead of being synchronous with the *Gankogui* time-units are now played 2 against 3 to them. This happens twice in bar 58: also in bars 60 and 64. In bars 59 and 60, *gaga gi* is expanded to *nyaga nyagara gi*. At the end of bar 63 and over into bar 64, there is a pretty play on *gitegi*. The first syllable is detached and appears as the end-syllable of the phrase *gahlebe gi*: the two remaining syllables now stand on their own, and form the nucleus of the phrase *tegi tegide*. The last two and a half bars so clearly arise from section B of the standard pattern that little comment is needed. In the first phrase the melodic interval is widened, the low beat *ga* replacing the mid-tone beat *ki-*; and the single phrase *kitsya gaga gi* is expanded into two phrases, the unity of thought being preserved by the time of the two first syllables *gatsya*, the identity of the end-syllable *gi* and the pitch of the intervening material, thus:

> *Standard*:   kitsya   gaga,   gi
> *Variation*:   gatsya   gadagla, gagla gi

The last phrase in bar 67 is rhythmically the same as its prototype but varies the pitch of its notes.

The technique of variations seems so simple when broken down by analysis in this way, but going at speed and continuously, and with no time to think, and all linked with *Gankogui* and the song, it is an exhibition of true and subtle musicianship.

The second variations on Pattern B

We now examine the more extended and completely spontaneous second variations (bars 69–144). Mr. Tay went to the recording room, and to the *Gankogui* accompaniment he just let fly on the drum for four and a half minutes: we then set to work to find out what he had played. He covered seventy six *Gankogui* bars: bearing in mind that with a flourish he finished by using both hands on a strongly accented beat obviously meant for the very end, this number, a multiple of 4, is another unsought testimony to the thesis we have advanced on this matter.

While Mr. Tay was actually drumming his variations they appeared to the European listener to be a fascinating and effortless flow of kaleidoscopic patterns in very free rhythm which crossed that of *Gankogui* with complete abandon and yet which were obviously harnessed to it as the periodic reappearance of the little phrase *gaga gi* ending on the low bell-note bore witness. When he had translated what he had played into nonsense syllables and written them down, he divided them into lines and then into eleven sections, and when we proceeded to analyse the drumming he treated each section as a unit separate in itself though still part of the larger whole. We give below, first the Standard Pattern B and then the variations.

Standard Pattern B

§ A. Aze geglegi tete gaga gi
       gitegi gaga gi

§ B. kitsya gaga gi
      kitsya gaga gi.

Variations

§ 1. Gitegi gaga gi
    gitegi gaga gi
    azeglede gitegi gaga gi gi gigi,
    tetete tete tete
       gitegi gaga gi:

azegi tegi tegi gaga
azegi tegi tegi
gazegle gi-gi-gi gaga gi
    gi-gi-gi-gi gaga gi,

§ 2. azegi gazegleegi
azeglezegi, gitegi tegite
tegi, tegi, tegi, tegi
tegi tegí tegí
gaga te te te te te te
gaga te te, gitegi gaga gi,

§ 3. gi gi gi gi, gaga gi
azegi gada gada gada gadra
azegi gada gada gada gadra
azegi gaga, azegi ga
azegi gaga, azegi gazegle
to to to gaga gi-to
gaga gi-to, gaga gi-to te
    gitegi gaga gi,

§ 4. azeglege gitegi gaga gi, to toto
gitegi kito to toto
kito to kito, to toto
    gitegi gaga gi,

§ 5. kito gakito, kito gakito
kito gakito, kito gakito
to to to, to to toto, toto
    azegegleegi
to to toto
    azegegleegi
to to toto
gitegi gagagi, to to to to gaga gi
azegle gitegi, gaga gi
    gitegi gaga gi,

§ 6. azege gi-te-gi, ga-ga gi
ga-ga-gi ga-gi
ga-ga-gi ga-gi ga-ga gi
gitegi gaga gi to to
azegi tere zegi, tere tere tere tere
zegi tere azegi, tere tere tere tere
zegi tere azegi, tere tere tere tere
    gitegi gaga gi to toto,

§ 7. azegle gi, to toto
gadaga, gaze te-te
gadaga, gaze gaze gaze gaze gaze gaze
      gitegi gaga gi
      zegegle gitegi gaga gi,

§ 8. azegaze, azegegle gitegi, to to to
gada glaga gi, gi gi gi gi gi
gazé gigí gazé gi gada gada
ze gi-gi-gi-gi-gi gi
gazé gi gigi
      gitegi gaga gi
      azegle gitegi gaga gi te tete,

§ 9. azegegle, azegegle, azegegle, azegegle
gaga gi gi-gigi
azegegle, gaga gi-gi-gi-gi-gi-gi
gate gi-gi-gi-gi,

§ 10. azegegle gi-gi-gi-gi
gagagi gagagi ga gaga
gagagi gagagi te tete
azegi tegi tegi
azegeglee gi, tegi tegi
      gitegi gaga gi to
      tɔte gaga gi to
      tɔte gaga gi to,

§ 11. gitegi gaga gi to toto
gitegi gaga gi, zegeglc, gitegi gaga gi, to-to
gitegi gaga gi, teŋ
to to to to to, teŋ
to to to to to, teŋ
      gitegi gaga GI!

What have we here? it is none other than a spontaneous yet closely organized poem in pure sound. This is no random collection of rhythmic patterns loosely based on the standard original. Let us examine it in more detail.

Though he actually said so, we have no need merely to take Mr. Tay's word for it that the whole variations are based on section A of the standard pattern: we can see it for ourselves. We notice particularly the conjuring with every single syllable of section A, played in a great variety of groupings and contexts and extensions. We also notice the complete absence of any reference to the rhythm-form *kitsya gaga gi* which belongs to section B. Mr. Tay said he could have gone on to play variations on this latter section too, though he adds that 'they would not have gone so far'. It is fairly obvious even to a European that the rhythm of section B is much simpler and less suggestive of development.

There are two apparent reasons why Mr. Tay appointed the sections of the variations as he did. The first is the opening of each section. Nearly all the sections start by stating the first notes of the 'seed' in one form or another. The original *Aze geglegi* becomes *Azegi* in section 2, *Azeglege* in section 4, *Azege* in section 6, *Azegle* in section 7, *Azegaze* in section 8, and *Azegegle* in sections 9 and 10. In the remaining sections, the master drummer does what we have already given as an alternative treatment. He starts the section with some rhythm-pattern other than that of the seed or some later part of it, but introduces the initial germinal element later in the section. Thus section 1 starts with the latter half of the germinal pattern, but states the beginning of the seed-pattern in its third line; section 3 is similar, using the form *Azegi* as the variant of the original; section 5 opens with new material but introduces the seed in its fourth line; finally, in section 11 the treatment is similar to that of section 1, the second half of the seed appearing first, and the opening syllables of the germ coming in the middle of the second line in the form *zegegle*.

The second reason for the section divisions is seen in their closing line. For the most part they use the second half of section A of the standard pattern as a refrain, either in its original form or in a variant. In its unaltered state we see this pattern as the refrain to sections 2, 3, 4, 5, 7, and with great emphasis on the final note in section 11. In section 1 it occurs in a truncated form, and in the remaining sections it has some form of *Coda*-like extension. This may be merely a phrase as in section 6, or an extended sentence added as a sort of modified reiteration seen in section 10. The only section which does not contain this refrain in an obvious form is section 9. Even here we can see what has happened: the phrase *gate gi-gi-gi-gi* is in six dotted quavers (i.e. nine quavers' value) which is virtually the space occupied by *gitegi gaga gi* (eight quavers) and is obviously a reflection of it (see bars 129 and 130 on the score, and compare bars 51 and 52).

So much for the start and close of the sections: they are like

the beginning and end of the verses of a poem each cast in the
form 'X+variable material+Y'.

We next look at the content of the verses and find that this also
is in poetic form, consisting mostly of couplets or triplets. Thus
section 1 has the construction:

> couplet
> couplet
> > refrain
> couplet
> couplet

Again, section 5 consists of five couplets, but there is no need to
labour the point as it is self-evident. There is not a single verse
which is not carefully balanced, one line drawing its inspiration
from some syllable or feature in the line preceding.

After reading through the whole poem one might be willing
to award it a high mark had it been a consciously premeditated
composition. When we realize that it is a spontaneous creation
born of the passing moment, we have surely to admit that this
is great musicianship. Yet Mr. Tay regards these particular variations as less than his best. They are all right, he says, but adds
that a few days previously he had been playing some very beautiful
ones. Not a few European musicians might envy this great gift
of cogent improvisation on a given theme.

We are now ready to look at the musical score (bars 168 ff.).
First a word about the phrasing. All the phrase-marks were put
in under Mr. Tay's direction. Even when his phrasing seemed to
go against what appeared to us to be the natural dictates of the
rhythm we bowed to his judgement. For example in section 6,
bars 109–12, the natural phrasing seemed to be that given in the
upper line of phrase-marks. He said this was possible but preferred
his own which is the lower line. The reason we include the upper
line is just because in this particular case he said it was possible
from the African point of view. Within many of the phrases there
are sub-phrase marks. These also are Mr. Tay's. He would say of
any such phrase, when asked if it could be split up, 'Yes, it can
divide here and here . . . but still it must all be counted as one piece'.
Occasionally one encounters that curious overlapping in which
the African treats the end as the beginning: in bars 83–85 we
have one long phrase-mark which overlaps the beginning of a

new section, so that bar 84 and the next note are not only the end of section 2 but the beginning of section 3. For the most part, he places his main phrase-marks in just the same way as we should ourselves. It is in the sub-phrases where his African idiom differs more from ours. Many times we could not guess where he would make his division. Sometimes (e.g. the repeated syllables *gi* in bar 121) he would say 'that note is by itself'. Compare the same repeated syllable in bar 129 where the syllables are now grouped with a phrase-mark. Then there is the sort of case not infrequent in drumming, illustrated in bar 81. Within one phrase the word *tegi* comes three times. When spoken, its accent is on the first syllable. Yet he insists on the sub-phrase-mark as given on the score binding the last three syllables for musical purposes, while not recognizing this grouping in speech.

As one's eye travels along the stave, one can see how the master drummer takes a germinal motif and exploits it for a while, surrounding it all the time with reminiscences of Pattern B to keep it in context. Then he takes another little motif and does likewise—and so on all through the variations. In section 1 (bars 69–77) he is playing with the motif *gitegi*. In section 2 (bars 78–84) he harps on *tegi* and *tete*. In section 3 (bars 84–92) he exploits the various ways of building a phrase starting with *Azegi*, which itself comes from the seed, following on to expand the second part of the seed. Section 4 (bars 92–96) introduces a new motif *kito*, which is expanded to *kito gakito* in section 5 (bars 96–105), all the time playing upon the seed-pattern in one way or another. In section 6 (bars 105–13) he plays with two motifs: the first is *gaga gi* which forms the end of the first part of Pattern B and there occurs as two quavers and a crotchet; the second is the clever triple motif '*tere*' built into a most attractive pattern with a descending sequence. At this point his unit of time is a semi-quaver: taking them three at a time, and playing *tere* four times, he covers twelve semiquavers which of course means that at the end he is still in phase with his original quaver time-unit. In section 7 (bars 113–19) he is exploiting the jump from low G to the F above in the syllable *gaze*. Section 9 (bars 126–30) is based directly on the seed-pattern. Section 10 (bars 130–8) starts in a similar way but then proceeds to harp on *tegi*, and later, the very distinctive phrase *tote gagagi*, where the interest lies in the wide melodic sweep which is very noticeable on a drum. The final section 11 (bars 138–45) opens with the unadorned statement of the second half of section A of the seed-pattern and then revolves round the two separate motifs *toto* and *teŋ*, the latter being that rising glide which is very attractive to hear. The variations end with the restatement of the end of the germ-pattern whence they arose, reinforced on the final syllable by playing it strongly with both hands.

There is no need to emphasize how free is the time of these master-drum variations. But, true to African tradition, we find that this freedom is by no means licence. In spite of the varying length of the phrases, there is an integrating factor which keeps them harnessed to the general swing of the dance, and this factor is the low *Gankogui* note. Looking at the score we can see how the master uses this note to keep himself within bounds. Usually after several *Gankogui* bars during which he lets himself cross his rhythm freely, he comes into line with *Gankogui* by ending a phrase on this low bell-note, in most cases with the phrase *gaga gi*. At other times he uses it as a jumping-off beat for a new phrase (e.g. bars 79, 82, 100, 101, &c.). Except for these obvious points of contact with *Gankogui*'s divisive rhythm, the master drummer seems deliberately to arrange that when those low bell-notes occur, with which he is not at pains to establish his contact, he staggers both his phrases and his accented beats. He rides roughshod past them. It would be intolerable to an African listener if the master drummer *kept on* making his phrases fit the incidence of the low *Gankogui* note.

Comparing the master drum with the song, we see how independent the drummer is. Yet inasmuch as the song is related to the claps, and the claps to the *Gankogui* pattern, the master drummer by establishing a periodic contact with the latter will *ipso facto* preserve some relationship, however loose, with the song.

As to *Kidi*, he goes on playing his standard response right through the variations: and if any proof were needed to show how cunningly integrated are these free outpourings of drum-rhythms with the whole dance, one has only to look at the staves of the master drum and *Kidi*, and note the relationship of their playing. Sometimes the master's playing shows no consciousness of relationship: but over and over again one finds that the two patterns fit admirably. This is so whether it is a case of exactly doubling the rhythm of *Kidi* as in bar 90, or of doubling the note-values but altering the accents as in bars 84 or 89, or of staggering the rhythm in a more complicated way as in bars 93 and 94 or 96–98.

We have been laying emphasis on the rhythm of the drums. The melody of the drums is equally important. It remains for the reader therefore to look once more at the full score and try to conjure up the total effect of the ensemble, taking especial note this time of the actual tune which the drums are playing. Surely this is interesting music. What with the measured tread of the bell and claps, crossed by the thin alto beats of *Kagaŋ*, the free-rhythm song, and the musical poetry of the master drummer, with *Kidi*'s steady tenor reply, we are conscious of a fine yet, to us, strange musical idiom, free yet organized, conservative yet spontaneous. And that sums up the whole attitude of the African to his music.

The ending pattern (bars 148 and 149)

We first notice that the *Gankogui* ends in a way we have not met before. It ends not on the low bell-note but on the high quaver which is the last note of its phrase. This unusual behaviour is explained by the fact that this quaver coincides with the final note of the drums whose pattern, whose inherent rhythm dictates that it should end just at this point.

Axatse does the same as *Gankogui*: it ends in a way which in isolation from the drums would sound most incomplete.

The custom for the hand-clapping is also unusual. In *Agbadza* they normally end on the nearest clap before the last beat of the drums. There is, however, no rule laid down and if the song is particularly enhanced by clapping, this may continue with the song till it ends. In all our other dances this is the normal procedure. The master drummer usually waits till near the end of the song-verse before starting the ending pattern. This means that the song will only have a few notes left to be sung after everything else has finished. The ending as it falls out on the score hides this fact, for it happens that this particular song actually ends on the final drum note: this is just accidental.

The ending pattern played by *Sogo*, the master drum, divides into two sections, the first being played by *Sogo* alone and the second by all the drums. On the score we imagine that *Sogo* in bars 146 and 147 is playing Pattern A or variations on it: we can tell this by *Kidi*'s beating which is one of his variants for this pattern. The song is our first main song, which suits Pattern A. The master waits till a suitable place occurs near the end of the song, which is the syllable *yudɔ* in the last chorus line. Here he enters on the first section of the ending, while the other two drums continue what they were playing. When he has finished it, he and the other drums, which break off whatever they were doing, play the final section in synchrony, and play it *forte*, *Kagaŋ* producing high notes for the purpose. The final crotchet rest on the master-drum stave is there on purpose. Keeping time with the two previous crotchets, on this rest he presses the butt of his left hand on the centre of the drum without striking. Mr. Tay says this signifies the very end of the drumming.

NOTE ON SUITABILITY IN PATTERN A

The only way to probe the question of suitability seems to be to make a critical investigation of any likely point that occurs during research. The cumulative evidence afforded by a number of such analyses may eventually lead to a consistent theory. This note is concerned with the suitability of multiple clapping in Pattern A: reference should be made to the music-score at bars 18–28.

Mr. Tay says that if you clap the 6-clap and the 4-clap simultaneously, this makes a very congenial accompaniment to master-drum pattern A because the claps hit the key beats of the pattern—the particular clap coming now from one clap-rhythm and now from the other. But the real cause of the suitability appears if one considers the resultant pattern produced by the claps, in relation both to the master drum and to the song.

The 6-clap and the 4-clap are of course playing 3 against 2 to each other, the resultant pattern of which is:

Take first the motif marked 'A': this coincides in the drum-pattern with the two-quaver nonsense word *degi* in bars 18 and 19 and with *gatsya* in bar 24 and twice in bar 26. The motif 'B' falls on the two-crotchet nonsense word *kiŋ-kiŋ* at the end of bar 19 and again at the end of 20, 22, and 25. While the two motifs taken together as one unit coincide with the master pattern at the words *gaga kiŋ-kiŋ* in bars 24 and 27, and, in a modified form of these word-rhythms in bars 19, 20, 21, 22, 23, 25, and 28. Thus there is a very close relationship between the resultant of the claps and the drumming.

The same phenomenon is observable in the relation of the clap-resultant and the song, though here it is motif 'C' which is the co-ordinating factor. This motif emphasizes the rhythm of the song at the words '*miwɔ aya ŋudɔ*' in bars 18, 20, 21, 22, 24, 26, and 28: it emphasizes, the words '*sotua do gbe*' or '*sohɔtua do gbe vɔ*' in bars 18, 20, 21, 22, 24, 26, and 28 (modified words): and similarly it underlines the words '*kpɔ le avea me*' in bars 19, 23, 25, and 26.

Contrast with this what happens if instead of using the 6 and 4 claps you beat the 4-clap and 3-clap together and sing the song. Mr. Tay said at once, 'It will *never* go' and added graphically that if someone added the 3-clap to the 4-clap in these circumstances, folk would exclaim, 'Take that man away'. Probing further, we tried the 4-clap alone with the song and likewise the 3-clap alone with it. In both cases Mr. Tay said the result was not bad, though the 3-clap produced a more graceful effect with the song than the 4-clap. But as soon as we put both claps together with the song he said it was hopeless: 'you have to force yourself' he said, because the two claps together say something quite different from what they say if taken separately. We suggested that the clue might be the resultant rhythm of the claps and he at once agreed, saying spontaneously that the 4 against 3 resultant pattern

just will not agree with the song, while the 3 against 2 resultant does do so.

The same applies, says Mr. Tay, to the master-drum pattern. He tried the 4-clap alone with this and found it went well: the 3-clap went 'very gracefully': but immediately the combined claps were used for the drumming he said 'It will baffle you', and that the combined claps seem to be wandering, with no relation to the drum-beats. So once again it is the resultant of the clap-patterns which is the determining factor.

What are we to conclude from all this? One example obviously will not justify a theory, but nevertheless there may be a pointer here. On the one hand nothing would be more foreign to the general practice of Africans than to make a song-melody in a divisive rhythm exactly emphasized by the clap-pattern. On the other hand we have just seen that they do recognize the suitability when certain motifs arising from *combined* clapping actually, in time and rhythm, coincide with either the song-melody or the drum-pattern. Our tentative suggestion is that the African will allow a synchrony of this sort if it arises incidentally as a resultant of the combination of more than one contrasting rhythm. If this is right it is most illuminating. In the welter of conflicting rhythms in an African ensemble, though as we have seen, there are co-ordinating factors present, one may well wonder what *aesthetic* cohesion there is. What is there which makes Mr. Tay shudder at the thought of certain 'unsuitable' combinations? Perhaps it is that the principle of incidental synchrony is part of their musical system. With Western music, deliberate synchrony is the norm from which our music develops: that is why it is possible for one man with a baton to conduct a whole orchestra. If our suggestion has any truth, then the African also uses synchrony of pattern but in a much more subtle way. His norm is the cross-rhythm and the synchrony is derivative. The synchrony arises from the exploitation of its very opposite principle.

8

A COMPARISON OF DRUMMING

EWE TRIBE, WEST AFRICA: LALA TRIBE, CENTRAL AFRICA

SEVERAL years before making contact with West African music, we investigated in detail a dance in Central Africa. This is the *Icila* dance of the Lala tribe who live to the east of Broken Hill in Northern Rhodesia.[1] The Ewe in Ghana and the Lala in Northern Rhodesia live some 2,000 miles apart as the crow flies. The territory of the former tribe lies near and on the coast, while that of the latter is right in the heart of the continent. Linguistically the Lala are a Bantu-speaking people and the Ewe are non-Bantu. The object of this chapter is to compare the dance-music of the two tribes. It is a test case: on the above grounds there is no reason to expect a similarity of musical culture: but if there is, then obviously this is a fact which will need to be taken into consideration not only by musicians but by all who study African culture.

In order to make a proper comparison it has been necessary to rewrite the *Icila* dance music-score. The original attempt to reproduce in print by means of diacritical signs and a modified stave the *quality* as well as the pitch and rhythm of the drum-beats, gave a score which is not as clear as one could have wished. It is too radical a departure from convention. In the present work we have translated this score in terms of conventional music-writing, and have also written out the complete orchestral performance in full. This has of course involved assigning exact pitches to all the drum-notes. When the *Icila* dance was originally transcribed we avoided giving exact pitch values to the drum-beats because we had not become expert enough to find what they were. So far as pitch is concerned, therefore, the present score is an approximation and is not as accurate as are the other dance-

---

[1] A. M. Jones and L. Kombe, *The Icila Dance, Old Style*, African Music Society, P.O. Box 138, Roodepoort, Johannesburg, S. Africa, 1952.

scores in this book. But as to the rhythm, not one single beat has been altered in any way.

We do not propose to describe the *Icila* dance in detail for that has already been done. We shall concentrate attention on certain features of the music-score. The general orchestral ensemble with singing and hand-clapping is typical of musical practice over a very large area of Bantu Africa. The occasion for the dance itself is also typical: it is a normal recreative village dance.

Let us look first at the song-melody. It is in the familiar call-and-response form and it is in free rhythm. In both these respects and also in its tonality it is indistinguishable from the sort of music sung by the Ewe people. Even the *organum* in parallel fourths is typical of Ewe polyphony, though perhaps it is used more continuously by the Lala. The song is accompanied by hand-clapping. The normal clap (clap 1) occurs on every alternate dotted-quaver unit of the song. Thus there are two time-units of the song to each clap, in other words the song is in essentially duple time *vis-à-vis* the claps. The complete song uses sixteen claps which are equally distributed between the call (eight claps) and the response (eight claps). In order to equate the song time correctly with the drum-beats it has been necessary to use a dotted quaver as the underlying time-unit of the song. This means that the song is going at a relationship of 2 against 3 of the drumming and it also gives a total of forty-eight quavers for the duration of the whole song. So the song agrees with the rule of multiples of 2 and 3 which we derived from Ewe music. This feature is further exemplified by clap 2 which may be added at will, and which is going 3 against 2 of the first clap (bars 6–8: 22–24).

We turn to the drums, of which there are three. There are two minor drums, *Akache* and *Icibitiku*, and the master drum—*Ikulu*, which incidentally means 'big', as contrasted with *Akache* which means 'the little one'. *Icibitiku* starts playing first: it sets up the foundation rhythm and is the easiest to play. It has two possible patterns (bars 1–29, cf. 29 ff.) but these are played without reference to what the master is doing. The least experienced player will probably be playing this drum. In pitch, the drum sounds midway between the full deep sound of the master drum and the high crisp beating of *Akache*. Obviously *Icibitiku* among the Lala is the counterpart of *Kagaŋ* among the Ewe. It fulfills the same functions, providing a steady divisive beating which serves as a background to the rhythmic colours of the other drums. Only in pitch does it differ from *Kagay*, though it does occupy a more important place in the orchestra than the latter. This is because among the Lala and as far as we know in Central Africa as a whole, south of about lat. 7 deg. S., the iron bell is not used as a foundation rhythm in dances. Consequently *Icibitiku* usurps this function and that is why it starts playing first. We do not imply that this drum leads or controls the orchestra. Just as with the Ewe, it is the master drummer who is in command of the whole orchestra: having once started, *Icibitiku* accommodates itself to the whole ensemble, but nevertheless it continues to preserve the basic unit of time on which the other drums build their patterns.

The middle drum *Akache* plays a more extended pattern than *Icibitiku*. For the *Icila* dance it has a shorter and longer form which can be used at choice and without reference to what the master is beating (bars 1–10: cf. 11 ff.). Its patterns are additive in structure, though their frequent repetition is a divisive factor. Owing to its high pitch the *Akache* drumming is always clearly discernible. It does not 'reply to the master' in the way that the middle drum of the Ewe orchestra does: nevertheless if we examine the score, it is obvious that *Akache* occupies a position in the orchestra precisely similar to, if less highly organized than, that of *Kidi* or *Sogo* among the Ewe. This is further confirmed by the limited tonal range of the drum—and this applies to *Icibitiku* also: in tonal range the minor drums of both orchestras are similar. In short, a non-Bantu Ewe drummer would find himself perfectly at home in the heart of Bantu Africa.

When we look at the master-drum score, we find again that he is beating in exactly the same manner as his West African counterpart. He has a standard pattern to work from (bar 3): he employs waiting beats or links of various sorts (bars 10–11: 11–12: 16–17, &c.): he plays variations on his standard pattern: he uses an additive approach to pattern building: and the passages in our book on the *Icila* dance which describe how he suits his patterns to the dancers and works up the whole enthusiasm of the dance might just as well have been written in reference to the Ewe master drummer (e.g. op. cit., p. 24, first para.).

If we compare the master-drum scores of the *Icila* dance and any of the Ewe dances two differences are observable. On the *Icila* score, the master drummer's performance looks rather a bewildering jumble: he keeps jumping from one little piece of pattern to another, which is in strong contrast with the organized and ordered progression of pattern-making exemplified in Ewe technique. This must not be taken as typical of Lala drumming: it is accidental to the conditions of recording. A big Lala dance may go on all night from sunset to sunrise: for the recording, the master drummer had only two minutes in which to show his paces. He told us that he had deliberately packed into this short time as many changes of pattern as he could and that he would not normally do this. From the point of view of comparative research, therefore, this feature carries no weight and may be dismissed. The other difference is of importance. It concerns the length of the patterns. In the *Icila* dance, all the master-drum pattern-making is on a small scale: the standard pattern is very short and the variations are not an extended development of it but a number of short variants. Yet the difference is quantitative rather than qualitative. The essential nature of the drummings of the two master drummers is identical. One special feature common to both drummings sets the seal on this identity, and that is the use of the 'seed' in the variations. The Lala drummer creates his variations by building up on the 'seed'. They start from the nonsense word *Tumbulumbu*. There is only one exception (bar 41) where the variation includes the last motif of the standard pattern, the word *ntuwa*, and this again is in line with Ewe practice.

Reviewing the drumming in *Icila* as a whole, we cannot but conclude that while simpler, this is essentially the same music as that of the Ewe people.

It occurred to us to wonder if the identity went deeper than appears merely from the music-score. The Ewe use of the *Gankogui* usually means that there is an underlying division of the music in groups of twelve-quaver phrases. The Lala have no such background instrument. In spite of this, is their music organized intuitively on a similar basis? To put this to the test, we attempted to superimpose on the *Icila* score the West African *Gankogui* pattern. The prime question to determine is, of course, at what point shall we place the low bell-note. We already know from Ewe master-drum technique that there is likely to be a certain point in the song where the low bell-note falls, which is felt to be a key position so far as the master drummer is concerned, and at which he enters his standard patterns. On page 10 of *The Icila Dance* we have a clue. The passage runs, 'There is, however, one vital link between the song and the drums. In the words "*Yalila ẁa-Sota*" the syllable -*la* is crucial: for that syllable, which you note coincides with a clap, *must* also coincide with one of *Icibitiku*'s main beats. The cantor ... starts singing "*Yalila*" in such a way that the syllable -*la* lands on *Icibitiku*'s main beat.' On the presumption that this might be the Lala equivalent of Ewe practice we placed the low bell-note on this syllable -*la*, and proceeded to write in the *Gankogui* pattern over the whole length of the *Icila* score. The result is revealing.

Look first at the song-line *vis-à-vis* the *Gankogui* stave. The first sentence, 'It has sounded, Mr. Sota, the drum has sounded' ends with the word *ŋgoma* whose final syllable falls on a low bell-note. This is what we should expect, given the tendency we have observed to end on the low first beat of the *Gankogui* phrase (bars 3–6). The same happens at the end of the next line (bar 8): the feminine ending carries one single stress on the syllable -*mpe* which again coincides with the low bell. In bar 8 there starts the chorus vocalization about which we wrote (op. cit., p. 14) 'An observer would say the music absolutely clamours for the chorus to enter on the clap coinciding with *Icibitiku*'s main beat' (sc. the first beat of bar 9). 'But no: the singers anticipate this and sing "*OOH*" on the clap before.' In other words one instinctively felt the underlying swing which is plainly revealed here by the *Gankogui* bars. Moving on to the end of the song, we find that the final syllable coincides with a low bell-note (bar 12). The whole song fits the *Gankogui* in the typical West African manner like a glove. Is this mere coincidence? For answer let us look at the master drum.

The standard pattern of the master drum (bar 3) enters, just as in Ewe practice, not on, but after the low bell-note and the phrase finishes on the following low bell. This is repeated till we come to bars 10–12, where we have a link pattern and some waiting beats. In bar 13 the master drum enters at precisely the same point in the bell-pattern as he did in bar 3, this time playing a variant. In bar 16 he shifts on to waiting beats which finish in time for him to enter in bar 18 with the standard pattern once more exactly in the right relation with *Gankogui*. In bars 22–25 the variants all start correctly *vis-à-vis* the bell. As Variant 5 is longer than the others, the drummer plays a few waiting beats (bar 25) and once more comes in at the same entry point in the bell with his standard pattern. There is no need to labour the point. He consistently marches with *Gankogui*. At bar 51, with Variant 7, he introduces still another feature we have noted in Ewe music. This time the drum-pattern's first main stress actually coincides with the low bell. We found an example of this rather unusual technique in *Nyayito*. After this the drummer goes on in step with the super-imposed *Gankogui* phrases right to the end of the score.

This cannot be fortuitous coincidence. If the Lala drummer had actually been accompanied by the *Gankogui* he could hardly have drummed in a manner more thoroughly consistent with West African Ewe musical practice.

The behaviour of the minor drums still further confirms the identity of the two musics. We remarked before that in the absence of the bell, the small drum *Icibitiku* takes over its functions. Recalling that we wrote in the *Gankogui* stave with reference primarily to the song and not the drums, we look at the *Icibitiku* bars *vis-à-vis Gankogui*. For his normal standard pattern (e.g. bars 1–28) is it not remarkable to find that they are coincident? When he introduces his variant in bar 29 he slips one quaver, thereby making a permanent cross-rhythm with *Gankogui*. Not only is this typical of Ewe practice but the cross-rhythm he sets up is the exact counterpart of that made by the Ewe small drum *Kagaŋ*. There are two ways of crossing two similar triple times: you can slip one quaver or you can slip two, thus:

Foundation Rhythm, *Cross 1*, *Cross 2* (musical notation in $\frac{3}{8}$ time)

Both the *Kagaŋ* of the Ewe and the *Icibitiku* of the Lala use Cross 1:

Gankogui ($\frac{12}{8}$), *Kagaŋ* ($\frac{3}{8}$), *Icibitiku* ($\frac{6}{8}$) (musical notation)

To the evidence of this chapter there can be only one conclusion. The music of the Western Sudanic-speaking Ewe people is one and the same music as that of the Bantu-speaking Lala tribe.

This conclusion does not rest merely on the evidence of this one isolated example nor does it seem necessary to provide further analyses in its support. Rather it is a conclusion which was already evident but which has received powerful confirmation by our experiment. Anyone with even a moderate ear could tell without analysis that the musics are similar. Anyone familiar with the tribal music of Africa knows that the music of any one tribe is extraordinarily homogeneous in its principles. The *Icila* dance is absolutely typical of the dancing one may hear on any moonlit night in hundreds upon hundreds of villages in Bantu Africa. That the two musics are one, anybody could have guessed by listening. That they can be held musically and scientifically to be identical in principle needed the evidence which analysis alone can provide.

The effect of the present discussion is to shake some accepted barriers. In whatever categories or families we divide the Africans, whether from the point of view of material culture, racial history, or linguistic affinity, the position must be faced that certainly as between the Western Sudanic Ewe and the Bantu as represented by the Lala, in the world of music there exists no barrier at all. The Ewe belong linguistically to the Kwa family which includes the Yoruba, Twi, and Akan peoples to mention only some. It can easily be ascertained even from gramophone records that, provided we delete any musical traits deriving from Arab influence, the real African music of all these peoples is essentially one and the same.

This means that musically, a large part of West Africa forms an indivisible whole with Bantu Africa. What is the inference to be drawn? Is it possible for a very characteristic folk-music to spread and to be assimilated by peoples of divers origins? Or is this music part and parcel of the heritage of Africa? In the first case we have a merely superficial unity: the second hypothesis goes much deeper.

One has only to think of the Western musical system to realize that it is possible for a musical style to spread over a large part of the world. But this is sophisticated music which has been reduced to writing and can be studied from textbooks. Could the same thing happen in the realm of folk-music? Is there evidence in any part of the world that this sort of assimilation has taken place? As far as Africa is concerned, its very characteristic treatment of polyrhythms demands a specially acute rhythmic sensitiveness for its execution. Only those peoples possessed of this faculty could possibly perform it. For this reason we do not think the African musical system could ever take root, for instance, among the peasant peoples of Western Europe. We find it hard to believe that its prevalence in Africa could have been due merely to cultural assimilation. To accept the theory of assimilation is indeed only to force the argument one stage further back, for then one would have to admit that the African peoples who assimilated the system all shared a common attitude to, and facility in, polyrhythmic cross-accentual combinations: would this not also indicate a common heritage? The only alternatives to this unity-of-Africa theory seem to be these. To maintain that the peoples of the world fall into two classes—those who think in terms of staggered polyrhythms and those who do not: and that all the African peoples whose music exhibits this trait happened in the past to belong to the former group. Or, to hold that those peoples whose music does not exploit this rhythmic dexterity have lost to a greater or lesser extent a faculty which was once the heritage of mankind as a whole.

But we have, in the case of Africans, actual contemporary evidence as to the relative permanence of music and language. What has happened to the American Negroes? Knowing only their own language and music they were transported thousands of miles to a land where both music and language were foreign to them. They have been there some hundreds of years. In recent times American scholarship has given much attention to the Africanisms in jazz. The result may be summarized in the words of Richard A. Waterman,[1]

The demonstration that the tradition of 'hot' rhythms born in Africa has survived the tremendous social, economic, and religious changes that have fallen to the lot of the carriers of that tradition, is no less important in indicating the almost incredible toughness of basic musical culture-patterns than it is in attesting the genuine musical value of the concept. For the 'hot' rhythm of Negro music, now so influential in the music of the New World, has proved its strength by the sheer fact of its survival.

On the other hand, the American Negroes have lost their old languages.

[1] Richard A. Waterman, *Hot Rhythm in Negro Music*, Journal of the American Musicological Society, vol. i, No. 1.

Both language and music are expressions made in the same medium—sound. Yet in this case folk-music has proved to be far more permanent than language. Is there any reason to suppose that on the African continent, the African reaction to outside influences would have been different? *Prima facie* the influence of Moslem music on Africans seems to weight the scales the other way. It is obvious that tribes which have adopted Islam imitate its characteristic music. Yet this Moslem influence is highest in the more important cultural centres such as towns and chiefs' courts, while in the countryside, the repository of traditional elements, the old music of Africa still persists. There is need for research to find out how completely Moslemized are the apparently Moslem musics performed by Africans. It may well be found that they have treated this music in the same way as the younger generation has treated European choral singing or as the American Negro has adopted the divisive rhythms of our music while at the same time infusing them with his own polyrhythmic attitudes. The case is non-proven for lack of evidence and therefore cannot at present be used for or against our hypothesis. Meanwhile, as to the relationship between the linguistic cleavage and yet the musical unity of the various language families of Africa south of the Sahara, one fact is clear: the fundamental identity of the musical system is as certain and as striking as the disparity in languages. In our opinion, with Africans, music is more permanent than language. The unity of musical practice therefore suggests a common past and not the assimilation of a dominant culture.

The argument for this musical homogeneity arose, in this chapter, from the consideration of the internal structure of one special musical form—the dance. This is by no means the only evidence we have. In the next chapter we shall extend the evidence by reviewing a number of other characteristic musical features.

'. . . Dancing and beating time are engrained in their (the Africans') nature. They say: were the African to fall from heaven to earth he would beat time in falling.'

A statement made by Ibn Butlañ, an Arabic-writing Christian physician who was active in Bagdad during the thirteenth century. Quoted by G. E. von Grunebaum, *Medieval Islam*, from A. Mez, *Die Renaissance des Islams*, and printed at the head of an essay by H. E. Hause in the Supplement to the *Journal of the American Oriental Society*, No. 7, Jan.–March 1948.

9

THE HOMOGENEITY OF AFRICAN MUSIC

I N the last chapter we studied the similarity in general rhythmic
structure of the music of two widely separated tribes. This,
in Africa, is of course a matter of basic principles. The characteristic staggered beats of polyrhythmic music are an acid test—
you either use them or you do not: the Europeans in Africa do
not use them, the Africans do: and therein lies the essential
cleavage in their musical traditions. But in the world of those who
do use these polyrhythms, the music may express itself in many
different ways. For instance, one could beat polyrhythms on
instruments of widely differing forms: one could build additive
repeating patterns of almost infinite variety: and there could arise
all sorts of local and discrete mannerisms in vocal music deriving
from the *tempo*, the harmony, the form-structure of songs—in fact
from a specific exploitation of any of the elements of which music
is composed. Such features are not essential principles of the
music: they are various forms of its concrete expression in sounds.
If one or more of these features occur in more than one tribe they
assume the character of typological features and provide us with
a very interesting series of criteria for the study of musical practice. It is this musical typology with which we now concern ourselves. Much of our evidence depends on hearing the music: for
this reason we have appended at the end of the chapter a numbered list of gramophone records which illustrate the points dealt
with. The bracketed numbers in the text refer to this list.[1] So vast
is the area of African music and so lamentably uncharted are its
musical manifestations that what we have to say is bound to be
but a mere fraction of what ought to be and could be said. Nevertheless even so imperfect a review may gather a cumulative force
whose weight cannot be ignored.

[1] Much, but not all, of the material in this chapter appeared as an isolated essay:
see A. M. Jones, 'East and West, North and South' in *African Music*, Journal of
the African Music Society, vol. 1, No. 1, 1954.

To appreciate the significance of the evidence, it has to be pictured against the linguistic background. The radical diversity of tongues in Africa is very great, even when we confine ourselves, as we do here, to Africa south of the Sahara. The Bantu area to which we have referred accounts for not more than a third of the area. The omnibus term 'Bantu languages' is deceptive. While contiguous tribes might understand each other fairly well in spite of their linguistic differences, the coefficient of comprehension decreases, as a general rule, inversely as the distance. A Zulu from South Africa and a mu-Bemba from Northern Rhodesia would not be able to understand each other's mother tongue. When we find Professor Guthrie[1] listing some 700 separate tribes each with its own form of speech we begin to realize how great is the diversity of the linguistic background to our musical study.

Then there is the huge area of the West African languages[2]— Westerman gives some 900 of them—where it is not merely a case of tribal differences within a general family language-kinship, but where there are a number of distinct language families each containing a large number of local variants. The third large area comprises the Eastern Sudanic languages[3] where Professor Tucker lists about another 800 speeches. It is against this multi-lingual patchwork of many hundreds of languages that we set the musical evidence.

We must at the outset draw a distinction between musical typology and the more general subject of the distribution of musical instruments. There are only a limited number of ways of producing music by mechanical means within the framework of a scientifically undeveloped social culture. The ordinary classification of instruments adopted by ethno-musicologists presupposes this. Thus in any community we are likely to find wind or string instruments, idiophones, aerophones, linguaphones, and membranophones, and the fact that widely separated peoples use instruments of these categories in itself indicates no direct kinship. If, however, we find a characteristic method of making these instruments, or a characteristic shape or any special decorative motif applied to them which occur in more than one place, or a

---

[1] M. Guthrie, *The Classification of the Bantu Languages*, International African Institute, 1948; *The Bantu Languages of Western Equatorial Africa*, ibid. 1953.

[2] D. Westerman and M. A. Bryan, *Languages of West Africa*, ibid. 1952.

[3] A. N. Tucker, *Non-Bantu Langua es of Eastern Africa*, ibid. 1956.

common type of music played on them, these constitute true typological data and provide strong grounds to suspect a mutual relationship.[1] There is a fair amount of published literature on African instruments[2] which might serve as a basis for the preparation of distribution maps based on typological data though, as far as we know, only one attempt has been made to extend the research, as indeed it must be, to cover at least the whole of Africa south of the Sahara. This is a map of the distribution of the African xylophone [18] made by Dr. Olga Boone. If the xylophone occurred generally throughout Africa, it would at least support the somewhat negative argument that the linguistic differences do not indicate an antagonism in musical culture such as we find, for example, between African music and Arab music. But in fact the xylophone does not occur everywhere: there are large areas where it is not used at all. Presumably, therefore, its distribution has a story to tell, but what that story is we do not know. Is it connected with tribal kinship, and does it therefore bear witness to ancient migration? Or is it a stream of culture which for some reason has been assimilated by some tribes and not by others? We cannot say, but the accumulation of data such as this may result in evidence which will be of service to studies other than that of music.

Wherever it occurs, the African xylophone in its developed form (i.e. with fixed and not free keys) appears to be constructed in the same sort of way, and in all the examples we have heard from widely different parts of Africa it plays the same sort of music. It thus qualifies to be considered as a typological feature. Dr. Boone shows the use of the xylophone in a broad belt between lat. 5–10 deg. N. right across Africa from the west coast almost to the Nile, right outside the Bantu area. It is used by the Duala and the Fang on the west coast at the eastern end of the Gulf of Guinea, thus bringing the stream within the Bantu line. The whole

---

[1] For a notable example, though not connected with Africa, see Jaap Kunst, *Cultural Relations between the Balkans and Indonesia*, Royal Tropical Institute, Amsterdam, 1954.

[2] To mention only some: P. R. Kirby, *The Musical Instruments of the Native Races of S. Africa*, Witwatersrand University Press, Johannesburg, 1953; Trowell and Wachsman, *Tribal Crafts of Uganda* (Part II), Oxford University Press, 1953; Olga Boone, *Les Xylophones du Congo Belge*, Tervueren, Belgium, 1936; Hugh Tracey, *Chopi Musicians*, International African Institute, 1948; J.-N. Maquet, 'Note sur les instruments de musique congolais', *Mémoires de l'Académie Royale des Sciences Coloniales*, n.s., tome vi, fasc. 4, Brussels, 1956.

of the South Congo area uses it and it occurs among the coastal tribes on the east coast between lat. 5 deg. N. and 5 deg. S. It thus spreads itself through and right beyond Bantu Africa both to the north and to the west. It is another testimony to the proposition that African musical practice is not circumscribed by linguistic boundaries. We would draw particular attention to Dr. Boone's map. In a general way it bears a resemblance to our own map based on the entirely different data of African harmony, and which we shall consider later. The resemblance is close enough to raise the question as to whether there is not some connexion between the two.

Take again that other favourite African instrument the Sansa or Kaffir piano. It is widely distributed and not only in the Bantu areas, yet as in the case of the xylophone, it is not used by some tribes at all. Common as it is over much of Central Africa from the Sotho in the south, the Manyika in Southern Rhodesia, over the whole of Northern Rhodesia and into the Congo, it is yet found in West Africa—to mention only two cases—among the Ga and the Ibo, which are outside the Bantu line [19]. Wherever it occurs it has the same general shape and construction, whether it has a wooden sound-board and metal prongs or a reed raft with split reed keys. The wide distribution is itself significant but added to this is the fact that the music played on it, whether inside or outside the Bantu line, is in one and the same tradition. It would be impossible from gramophone records to distinguish between what comes from one language family and what from another.

In Northern Rhodesia the Bemba make a special use of axe-blades in music. Three men, each holding a pair of axe-blades chink them together, forming three interwoven rhythm patterns as a charming rhythmic background to a song and chorus. In Ghana, the very foundation of the drum–dance orchestra is the iron gong [8]. Sometimes, among the Ewe, several gongs are used without drums, to form a sort of rhythmic orchestra. Ghana is outside the Bantu area, but the Bemba axe-blades and the Ewe gongs are unmistakably manifestations of the same musical technique. Go right across Africa once again, to the Luo tribe near Lake Victoria and we find them making an iron chinking sound as a background to their singing [9]. It is just the same sort of rhythmic bell-like background. In this example the sound is produced by different means: but the sound in all three cases is similar and each time it is used for a precisely similar purpose. Though we have given instances from only three tribes, the use of the gong is very widespread in West Africa. How general it is elsewhere we do not know. Yet to find the custom in West, East, and Central Africa is added testimony to the overall unity of the musical system.

In gauging the extent and depth of this musical unity in Africa we are fortunate in being able to compare the African tradition with the strongly contrasted musical system which is more or less predominant wherever Islam has penetrated. Islamic music in Africa is based on principles manifestly far removed in several respects from the music we have been studying. It has its roots in the East and its kinship lies more with Persia and India. The four characteristics which most clearly differentiate it from African music are first, that it rests on a formalized rhythmic framework which is much simpler than the complexity of rhythms we have been analysing. In any typical recording of Islamized African music we hear a *single* rhythm as a background to a song, and this rhythm will usually sound fairly comprehensible to a European ear. Second, the typical accompaniment to singing: instead of the hand-claps and the multiple and full-voiced drum-patterns we have the thin wavering sound of a solo stringed instrument attended by a drum—often of the hour-glass variety. Thirdly, and most marked of all, is the characteristic voice production and the embellishment of the melody-line. Africans, like Europeans and the West generally, sing all their own songs with open tone and a perfectly natural way of singing. The Islamic tradition can at once be recognized by the very nasal and stringy quality of voice that is invariably used. But added to the nasal vocalization there is the very frequent use of mordents to embellish the melody notes. Never, in the whole of our experience, have we come across a single example of a shake of this sort in the Africans' own music. It is not part of their system, just as it is not a normal part of our Western conception of melody. Fourthly, in the Islamic tradition there is no harmony.

Africans are as prone to imitate Islamic musical practice as they have proved themselves adept at absorbing modern American dance music and Western four-part choral singing. We should expect the position *vis-à-vis* Islam to be similar to that of the African and Western music—namely that he has taken its more obviously characteristic features and infused them with his own attitude to music. Whatever be the truth of the matter, the fact still remains that wherever Islam has penetrated in Africa, it has made a powerful musical impression. So totally different is the sound made by the two several traditions that it needs but a modicum of musical skill to be able to separate a pile of gramophone records into the two sets.

The strength of this Islamic influence is a curious phenomenon. One would be inclined to attribute it to the Mohammedan religion. But this cannot be so because music plays no vital part in that religion at all: indeed the only music to be heard in a mosque is the chanting of the Koran. In the Islamic world music is altogether secular. If the affected tribes had been converted directly by Arabs living amongst them, they might well have copied to a certain extent the music of their co-religionists. Yet even this cannot have happened, because the spread of Islam though emerging from the Arabs was apparently propagated from people to people: from the Berbers to the Tuaregs: from them to the Fulani, and from the Fulani to the Hausa and so on. The driving force of the phenomenon remains an enigma.

A large part of West Africa has been musically influenced by the incursion of Islam from the north. Much of the Hausa music is uncompromisingly Islam in style (e.g.[3]). The Mossi, the Mandinka, the Kissi, Dyula, and Mano people have been similarly affected. This forms a broad belt of Islamic influence running inland from the west coast of Africa roughly from lat. 15 deg. N. to 10 deg. N. In between this belt and the northern extremities of the Bantu line there is a belt of country 5 degrees in width from north to south where the situation is mixed. At first blush many tribes would be classed as in the Islamic tradition: but if we look closely at, say, the Yoruba we find that while there is plenty of Islamic style, with its unisonal singing and the use of mordents [4], yet side by side with this there is the typical music of the Bantu style [5]. We believe the same to be true of the Hausa and indeed of all the Islamized African tribes whose music we have been able to hear. On the other hand the enormous area covered (from west to east) by the Mende, the Kru peoples, the Akan group, the Ewe, the Urhobo, the Igbo, and the Duala is all in the pure African style and untouched by Islamic features. Here we find vocal harmony everywhere and the typical centrality of the drum ensemble. The broad conclusion seems inescapable that the original style of the whole area was the sort of music we have been dealing with in this book and that any deviation from this traditional norm has resulted from the impact of Islam.

Exactly the same happens on the east coast of Africa. The Swahili-speaking peoples have to a greater or lesser extent absorbed the Islamic musical idiom where Arab influence has been strong, particularly in the coastal belt lying between 5 degrees north and 5 degrees south of the latitude of Zanzibar, yet at the same time one can play numerous records of their music which are pure Bantu in principle and in execution [7]. Whereas on the west coast we were confronted with non-Bantu people who had been influenced by the Islamic musical system, here in the east we find tribes which are right in the Bantu area responding in exactly the same way.

This discussion on the presence of the Islamic musical tradition among Africans brings into focus several important points about African music itself. The particular manifestations of Islamic music we chose in order to trace its influence are of course typological features. The great contrast between these features and the typical features exhibited by African music generally throughout the continent south of the Sahara, itself brings into greater prominence the essential homogeneity of the Africans' own music. The Islamic style is patently an influence imposed from outside on a musical system which is by and large a homogeneous entity. Again, the fact that Africans belonging to different language families, when under Islamic influence all behave in varying degrees in the same way lends support to our thesis. Lastly, all who know Africans are aware of their propensity for imitation and the adoption of the latest fashion. Such an obviously powerful force as Islamic music would surely be expected to have spread far and wide: but it has not. The map of its distribution emphasizes the extraordinary tenacity of the African musical tradition: even in areas where Islam is the predominant religion we have shown that usually the African system still persists alongside its rival.

We have so far considered the musical typology of African music mainly in the realm of musical instruments. Musical instruments belong to material culture, and therefore their appearance in different tribes might be due to cultural forces other than that of musical aesthetics. So we will now turn to other typological features which are more deep-seated, features which are inherent in the very music itself.

Our first example is a short rhythm-pattern. This pattern is sometimes made by hand-clapping, sometimes it occurs as a bell-rhythm, and it is even played on the drums. It occurs in various forms but always it is basically one and the same pattern. It is found widely in West Africa, in Central Africa, and in East Africa. In fact both its ubiquity and its typically African form qualifies it to be called the African 'Signature-tune'. It consists of a twelve-quaver phrase subdivided either as $[2+2+3]+[2+3]$ or, conversely, as $[2+3]+[2+2+3]$. Its simplest expression is in these forms:

One of the Ewe dances which we have not dealt with is called *Abuteni*. It is in the same class as the *Adzida* dance, being one of the club dances, though compared with the latter it is a very stylish one. The dancers move slowly and, still dancing, gradually assume a squatting position, with one foot farther forward than the other, then gradually rise again. It uses three drums, *Sogo*, *Kidi*, and *Kagay*, one or two *Gankoguiwo*, and the rattle. If two bells are used this is what they play:

The first *Gankogui* plays the pattern we are considering.

The Ewe have another dance, which they took over from the Akan people, and which is called *Asafo*. It is a royal drumming, and is danced by men only. There are two parts to it, first the processional which is always very slow, and then the main dance *in situ*, which is fast. Both parts use the same *Gankogui* pattern played at suitable speeds. Here is an extract from the ensemble-playing during the processional:

The small drum is playing a standard and invariable pattern which is none other than the pattern we are dealing with. The *Gankogui* rhythm is essentially the same pattern though treated in a different way as is indicated by the accent marks. The fact that it starts with a crotchet and not two quavers does not alter the fact that it is *au fond* the same pattern.

This pattern, doubled in time, occurs also as a clap pattern in the same *Asafo* dance: here it is with, for comparison, the 'Signature Tune':

One might be tempted to transcribe it more simply as:

but this is a travesty of what the African actually claps. He treats his clap-pattern as existing in its own right and not as an off-beat derivative.

There is hardly need to point out that the standard *Gankogui* pattern used by the Ewe and which figures so frequently in our musical scores, is also a form of the same pattern:

Recently we met Mr. Omideyi, a Yoruba from Lagos, and said to him, 'In Northern Rhodesia we have this clap

$$\frac{12}{8}$$ ♩ ♩ ♩. ♩ ♩. |

—do you know it?' He replied, 'Yes: but in the Yoruba tribe we do it in this form'—and he tapped:

$$\frac{12}{8}$$ ♩ ♩ ♪♩ ♩ ♩ ♪|

The important point is that he recognized the Rhodesian pattern *as being the same* as his although it was (*a*) inverted and (*b*) without the quavers. It is occurrences such as this which make it clear that this particular pattern is very deep down in the African musical mind and is indeed part and parcel of their music.

In West Africa its use is not confined to the two tribes cited: it is widely known.

Moving over to Central Africa we find it as a very usual hand-clap accompaniment to Ila and Tonga songs in the south of Northern Rhodesia.[1] It is used also in the north of Northern Rhodesia by the Bemba in a compound clapping pattern where it appears in still a new form, both the accentuations and the phrasing being different, though the actual spacing of the claps proclaims its identity. Here is the Bemba clap with the basic form below it: the latter of course is not used in performance:[2]

♩. = 120   *Bemba Tribe*

Clap 2: $$\frac{12}{8}$$ ♩ ♪ ♩ ♩ ♪ ♩ ♩ ♩ ♪ ♩ &c.

Basic Pattern: $$\frac{12}{8}$$ ♩ ♩. ♩ ♩ ♩. |

The Bemba also make a rhythmic background to a song by chinking together three pairs of axe-blades.[3] the third axe-player uses a pattern which is the same as that given above only it is in reverse—that is, the second phrase is played first and is followed by the first phrase.

The unadulterated basic pattern is used by the Lala in the centre

---

[1] A. M. Jones, 'African Rhythm' in *Africa* (International African Institute), vol. xxiv, No. 1, Jan. 1954, p. 34.
[2] For the compound pattern see op. cit., p. 38.　　　　[3] Op. cit., p. 37.

of Northern Rhodesia. They also do something rather remarkable. In a compound clap-pattern they clap the basic form together with a variant whose phrasing and accentuation are different from any we have mentioned and produce a pattern whose feel is so unlike the basic one that we should, without close inspection, judge it to have no kinship with it. Here is the clap with the basic form printed below:

When, however, the two claps are combined in actual performance, the basic pattern does not occur in the position printed here: it is reversed, the second phrase in the above example being played first, thus producing a clash of rhythm with the other clap.[1]

It might be objected that if you take the basic pattern and re-arrange it, phrasing it in different ways and placing the stresses in different places you are in fact producing a number of different patterns. From the standpoint of the sound actually heard this is so, but what is important is that in all the cases quoted, in spite of the variety of forms, there is no rearrangement of the actual sequence of time-values represented by the formula [2+2+3]+[2+3]. At whatever point in this formula you choose to start, if you repeat your pattern, this sequence will appear. Were the Africans to *change the order* of the long and short notes, then the basic pattern would be upset. For example, the sequence 2+3+3+2+2 makes an entirely different basic rhythm and at whatever point you start in it, you will never, by repetition, produce the familiar [2+2+3]+[2+3] form. It is this particular sequence of short and long basic units which is so clearly a typological feature of African music generally.

We have met the same basic pattern in East Africa. But there is no need to labour the point. Is it not powerful evidence of the homogeneity of the musical system?

The remaining examples of musical typology are all concerned with vocal music. We made passing reference to this when dealing with Islamic influence: we have now to consider the style of rendering vocal music in more detail.

[1] For the whole compound pattern see op. cit., p. 44.

To those accustomed to listening to singing in the Bantu area there is something in the general style of the music which, though hard to analyse or to describe, yet is unmistakable. Listening, for instance, to two records, one can say at once, 'That is typical Bantu music and the other is not'.[1] Particularly useful is this 'style' in discriminating the presence or absence of Arab influence. The Yoruba provide examples sometimes in one and sometimes in the other style, but even though they live far from the Bantu area, when they sing in the style which is not Islamic, one recognizes at once that this is typical Bantu music. The same style is used by the huge Akan group of tribes in West Africa, and going still farther west, by the Mende, the Temne, and the Susu, to mention but a few tribes of which we have had concrete evidence. We have now arrived almost at the most westerly point of the great bulge of Africa, some 1,500 miles away from the Bantu line and we still find the same basic style of singing. We go right over to the east of the continent, still outside the Bantu line and we visit the Teso, a Nilo-Hamitic people living on the east of Lake Victoria, or the huge tribe of the Masai, or the Kipsigis in Kenya, or going farther to the centre and the north, the Azande and Bandiya peoples in the Southern Sudan. They all live outside the Bantu area but their music is indistinguishable in its essential structure from that which we find both in Bantu Africa and in West Africa.

So far, this is typology only of the most vague sort. We now come to three clearly defined features which are to be observed within the general tradition. In Bantu Africa there are at least three characteristic kinds of chorus-singing. First, there is that four-square, virile, rather slow but very forceful type of chorus sung by the Zulus in South Africa [12]. A different type of chorus is exemplified by the Bemba in Northern Rhodesia [13] whose choruses, in parallel thirds, have an even, *legato*, wave-like flow which is intensely musical. Yet again, a third type of chorus-work is employed by the Nsenga [14] on the eastern border of Northern Rhodesia. This is a rapid style of bright cheery singing which is clearly distinguishable and could be recognized any-

---

[1] To say that certain music of, say, West Africa is 'typical Bantu music' is not in the least intended to suggest that West Africans acquired it from the Bantu. It is merely a case of convenient terminology. One could just as well say that Bantu music is 'West African' in build: but as West Africa has two styles—Arab and non-Arab—both used by Africans, one cannot use this term without ambiguity.

where. Now these styles of chorus-singing are not restricted to the tribes mentioned, nor to the Bantu area. The Bemba style is used by the Ciokwe on the western side of Northern Rhodesia, the Cuabo about 1,000 miles away to the east on the far side of the Zambesi delta, and yet again by the Ibo near the mouth of the Niger, and again by the Yoruba to the west and north-west of them, both of the latter being right out of Bantu country [15]—to mention but one or two examples. The forthright heavy pounding Zulu style (South Africa), occurs among the Nandi [16] and the Kikuyu far away in Kenya, also among the Gisu in eastern Uganda and among the Caga on the slopes of Mt. Kilimanjaro in Tanganyika Territory. We do not omit to notice that the Nandi are outside the Bantu area, and the others widely scattered within it. This same Zulu style is found among the Ibo of West Africa, who are non-Bantu. In the same way the Nsenga style of rapid cheerful chorus-work occurs also among the Ganda on the eastern side of the continent in Uganda, and right away over in West Africa, once more among the Ibo.

An interesting consideration arises out of the widely scattered distribution of these very distinct types of chorus. The examples quoted can by no means be taken as exclusive. There are hundreds and hundreds of tribes whose music we have not heard. If we had samples from every tribe, we are certain that there would be plenty of other examples and that we should be able to make distribution maps for each type. But the lack of information does not imply that if we had it, we should find that all tribes use all three types of chorus. The evidence does not point that way at all. In Northern Rhodesia where we had opportunity to observe tribal singing at close quarters over nearly a quarter of a century, we never heard the Zulu style at all. We never heard the Nsenga rapid choruses sung by any tribe except the Ansenga. At St. Mark's College, Mapanza, we had members of at least six tribes living together: these included the Bemba proper and the Usi and Cisinga who are culturally so close to them that they call themselves Bemba, and musically are in one group with them. None of the other tribes either sang in the typical Bemba chorus style or attempted to imitate it. We thought for a long time that these chorus styles were single and individual tribal characteristics. It was with a real sense of discovery that we later found the same styles used in various tribes all over Africa.

This differentiation in chorus style might seem to indicate that the music itself differs in principle. But it does not: in each case, the rhythmic structure, the musical form of the songs, the whole general ethos of the music is identical. It appears, therefore, that within the general framework of African music there are several streams characterized by the chorus-work. There may be other streams which we have not noticed. How this has come about we cannot say, but the existence of these streams has at least a two-fold significance. In the first place, the fact that this chorus typology applies all over Africa argues very strongly indeed for the homogeneity of the African musical system. If we think of individual tribal music as such, we must think of it as falling within the general context of the unity of African music as a whole. In the second place, we find it impossible to believe that the emergence of these well-defined chorus styles all over Africa is merely fortuitous. Does it point to some close kinship in the remote past? Or is it a key to the movement of migrations? That is not for a musician to say: but the facts are there and may be of interest to others whose studies lie more in the field of ethnography and history.

We have left to the last a typological feature which in view of its importance might well form a separate chapter. Our thesis is strikingly illustrated by the distribution of African harmony in choral music. This discussion is based solely on the indigeneous African folk-music. Where the practice of harmony has been influenced by Islam we shall say so, for such cases have nothing to do with the matter in hand. We must also carefully distinguish between the harmony which belongs properly to African folk-music and that which has emerged in the African neo-folk tradition as a result of contact with the Western musical system. The harmony used in this sort of music is totally ignored here. Our question is, what is the traditional harmony of African folk-music, and what is to be learnt from it?

Normally, African chorus-singing is diodic, that is, in addition to the song-melody itself, some people are making harmony by singing at what we in the West recognize as consonant intervals, usually, but not always, below the melody-line. That is the essence of the matter: in practice both the melody and the harmony-line are usually doubled at the octave so as to suit the pitch of both men and women for both parts. Thus the women are singing in harmony and the men are doing the same an octave lower. Dr. André Schaeffner prefers the term 'polyphony' for this African chorus-work, reserving the term 'harmony' for choral combinations which include triads. As polyphony suggests a distinct discipline belonging to Western music this seems confusing: we would suggest the term 'diody', though 'harmony' seems the easiest word.

Though there are one or two exceptions which do not concern us here, generally speaking all over the continent south of the Sahara, African harmony is in *organum* and is sung either in parallel fourths, parallel fifths, parallel octaves, or parallel thirds. Leaving aside the question of the exact tonality of African melodies, which anyhow does not affect the present argument, African songs are diatonic: there are no accidentals except the sharpened subdominant which can only be used when preceded and followed by the dominant and which functions not as an accidental but as a leading note transposed down a fourth. In using this Western terminology we are not suggesting that the Africans use a diatonic major scale in the sense that their series of notes rests on the tonic, with the dominant as an important subsidiary point of repose. All we intend to say is that their melody notes are all notes of the diatonic major scale without accidentals. When the Africans sing in parallel fourths the lower voice always sharpens the subdominant, thus avoiding a tritone fourth. This is a complicated way of saying something very simple. When the African makes harmony in fourths all he does is to sing the melody at the right pitch and at the same time to sing the very same melody a fourth lower. He thus has a succession of perfect fourths which inevitably means sharpening the subdominant. If he sings in parallel fifths he proceeds on the same lines. In this case the lower voice would flatten the leading note, making a perfect fifth with the subdominant above. In fact those who sing in either parallel fourths or fifths do exactly the same as those who sing in octaves. The lower voice sings the same tune in a lower pitch. This is a very simple way of harmonization but we stress the essential nature of it because when we consider parallel thirds we find the situation is, musically, totally different. When the African sings in parallel thirds the lower voice introduces no accidentals whatever. This means that, following the diatonic major scale, some of the thirds will be major ones and some minor. Two important considerations arise from this. First, in *organum* in thirds, the lower voice is no longer singing the same tune as the higher. Second, as a major third has four semitones, and a minor third only three, a succession of thirds in a diatonic major scale is a series of two quite different intervals. We in the West recognize both major and minor thirds as partaking of a quality of 'third-ness', and it is interesting that Africans feel the same about it. Only when they sing in parallel thirds do they depart from the custom of singing the main melody at a lower pitch to produce the pleasant sound of harmony. This means that any tribe who sings in thirds is doing something essentially different from those who sing in octaves, fifths, or fourths.

Now let us see what the African tribes actually do in singing harmony. It is very arresting. Some tribes sing in parallel thirds. The tribes who sing thus, do so to the total exclusion of any other interval, with the exception of some border cases we shall deal with later. We have dubbed them 'Thirds tribes'. Usually the thirds-tribes sing *all* their choruses in thoroughgoing *organum* in thirds, including even the submediant for the lower voice at the end of a song where the upper voice comes to repose on the tonic.

Some tribes sing in continuous *organum* in fourths. These tribes never, by any chance, sing even an isolated third. Some of them sing partly in fourths and partly in unison. Sometimes we get a more sophisticated ending in the harmony to a song where the upper voice sings the *cliché* tonic—leading note—tonic. The harmony in this case may occur as:

but it may also be:

i.e. fourth, fifth, and octave. This is particularly noticeable with the Nsenga of Northern Rhodesia. The point to observe is that the fourths tradition, while totally excluding thirds, has definite links with fifths and octaves.

Some tribes sing in parallel fifths. Here again we often find the songs partly in unison and partly in fifths. Sometimes they are isolated fifths at strategic points in an otherwise unison song.

But the fifths-tribes never on any occasion use thirds. There are quite a number of tribes who sing only in unison and use no harmony whatever. They are to be sharply distinguished from tribes whose unisonal practice derives from Islamic influence. The unison songs they sing are in the true idiom of African folk-music.

The above analysis is a summary of the experience gained not only from personal contact with Africans but by listening to a considerable number of records. Experience in listening makes it evident that the octaves-tribes, the fifths-tribes, and the fourths-tribes all belong to the same harmony family, which we dub the '8-5-4' tradition. The typology of harmony thus divides Africa into two distinct streams—the thirds-tribes and the 8-5-4 tribes.

This divergence of harmonic practice does not in the least mean a difference in essential musical principles as a whole. Just as in the case of the three streams of chorus styles, so in harmony, whatever be the form adopted, the whole structure of the music in every other respect is entirely and absolutely one and the same. The only, yet absolute, discriminating factor is the harmony. Here indeed is a paradox. All the tribes are obviously one in the general character of their music both rhythmic and melodic. Yet just as surely they fall into two streams in respect of their harmony. One simply cannot accept this as fortuitous chance. The whole sound of the two musics is so different: and if it were chance, why has not one form of harmony become the fashion and spread over the whole continent? Why is it that even tribes living in the same compound would not and virtually could not alter their harmonic customs so as to be able to sing together? One can hear African music recorded at schools where tribes are mixed, and where children of more than one tribe have learnt the same African song. The probability is that that record will be useless for typological purposes. The two harmony traditions, in some cases, have become confused and we get thirds or fourths occurring (though not simultaneously) in the same song.

The traditions are so conservative that one often gets tribes living side by side where one tribe sings in one tradition and one in the other, with no fusion at all. Moreover, so tenacious is the custom that it is virtually axiomatic that to hear one single record of a tribe is to hear dozens of records so far as harmony is concerned. One needs to hear the singing for but a few seconds to be able accurately to assign the tribe to its harmony family. Additional listening merely confirms that choice.

There exist some tribes—the border cases referred to above—who live between tribes singing severally in the two traditions, and whose harmony has been influenced by both. In these cases one sometimes gets some songs entirely in parallel thirds, and some in the 8-5-4 style, sung by the same tribe. We have not so far tried to find out whether the borrowed harmony is used to accompany words borrowed from and in the language of the other tribe. Alternatively, a given song may contain some thirds and some fourths introduced into what would otherwise be unison singing. Compared with the total evidence we have collected, such occurrences are of minor significance.

We next inquire into the geographical distribution of these two streams of harmony. Does it in any way coincide with the location of language families? There are two answers to this question. In the first place it is quite clear from the map that the thirds tradition is not confined to any one language group. It occurs plentifully among the West African languages, there is indication that it is to be found in the Southern Sudanic group, and it sweeps right across the Bantu area. In its present day distribution it is a phenomenon of Africa as a whole: it overrides the main linguistic divisions. The same obviously applies to the 8-5-4 tradition. Yet at the same time—and this is the second point—closer inspection suggests that the harmony practices occur often in large patches including more than one tribe and that therefore there may be some link between language and harmony. Let us look at the distribution of the thirds tradition, starting from West Africa, and moving eastwards. In the area classified by Dr. Westermann, the Kru people sing in thirds, so does the whole of the large Kwa language family west of the Volta River. East of the Volta the Kwa people use the 8-5-4 style except at the extreme eastern end of their area, where the Ibo sing in thirds. Thus the Kru and the western Kwa language families form one big area which sings in thirds.

Coming to the Bantu area as classified by Professor Guthrie, the whole of his area C sings in thirds (with some cases of admixture with 8-5-4). In his area D, there are parallel thirds in the north-east, north-west, and south-west: we have no evidence on the remainder of the west and central part of area D. It is significant, however, that in the east of area D immediately we cross the Rift Valley (approx. longitude 30 deg. E) there is a dramatic change: the parallel thirds abruptly cease and the whole area is 8-5-4. This fact is bound to prompt the question, 'Was the thirds-tradition a spreading movement which was halted by the geography of the Rift?' Dr. Guthrie's areas L and K and M show large patches of parallel thirds. To area K we may link the thirds tribes marked in area R (R 21 and 22): these two tribes are both classified by Dr. Guthrie under group R 20, showing linguistic kinship and we know that the Ndoŋga (R 22) migrated to their present position from farther east. Apart from these areas of parallel thirds, virtually the whole of the remainder of Central and South Africa of which we have sampled records is in the 8-5-4 tradition.

What are we to make of all this? Our map is too incomplete for clear deductions to be drawn, but what evidence we have accumulated suggests certain considerations.

Dr. Westermann and Dr. Guthrie have both been concerned with the classification of languages into families and linguistically related groups. The study of African harmony is an entirely different approach. Yet the two disciplines do seem to point to some sort of relationship. Where the thirds occur they seem to do so not merely sporadically in isolated tribes, but more in larger areas which on linguistic grounds are also grouped together by the language scholars. More than that the evidence will not allow us to say definitely.

At the same time the evidence leaves some impressions on the mind which are no more than hypotheses at present but which seem to be distinct possibilities.

We have a strong feeling that the 8-5-4 tradition is the main harmony tradition of Africa as a whole and is probably the older. It seems to us that the thirds tradition is something which has impinged on the former. We have already pointed out the general resemblance between the location of thirds-tribes on our harmony map and Dr. Olga Boone's map of xylophone distribution. We are not suggesting that where there are xylophones there are thirds in singing, for this is not always so: for instance, the Tiv in West Africa use xylophones but sing in the 8-5-4 style. Nevertheless the two maps show a general sweep of musical tradition across the continent from west to east. Does it point to a

migration in the distant past? Both maps point to two streams of
tradition issuing from West Africa. Let us trace these by following the thirds on our harmony map—the reference in brackets
are Guthrie's classification.

The west–east stream would run thus: Kru, West Kwa, Ibo,
Cameroons, Nzeli (C 16), Ŋgombe (C 31), Mangbetu and Yogo
(3 deg. N.: 27½ deg. E.), to the Bira (D 30).

The west–south-east stream runs: Kru, West Kwa, Ibo,
Cameroons, Nzeli (C 16), Moŋgo (C 61a), Nkundu (C 61b),
Manyema group (C 70, D 20, D 50), Luba (Katanga) (L 33),
Hemba (L 34), Bemba group (M 42), Biisa (M 51), Nyanja (N 31a),
Teŋgo (N 13) to the Cuabo (P 34). It has a south-westerly diver-
sion from the Luba (L 33) which goes via the Ciokwe (K 11), the
Luena (K 14), and the Lucazi (K 13) to the Kuanyama and
Ndoŋga (R 21 and 22).

As we are concerned with African music, the problems of
language and history are not our immediate business. But it may
be that the musical evidence has some contribution to make to
these studies. The sharp cleavage in harmony tradition may be
additional evidence in support of language classification: it can
hardly be neglected. The evidence would be greatly strengthened
if our map were to be completed. To acquire the information is
no mean task. Recordings exist in such widely scattered collec-
tions. But the task should be done and the author will welcome
any additional information which will help to this end.

Summing up the whole of this chapter we draw from musical
typology two main conclusions: first, the music of Africa south
of the Sahara is one single main system. Second, within that
system there exist streams of typical expressions of it, the most
notable and discrete being the two mutually exclusive streams of
harmony.

APPENDIX I

THE African clap-pattern which we represent thus:

is often scored in West Africa as:

We have to ask three questions: first, are these two transcripts identical in time-values? second, if not, which if either, can be proved to be correct? third, which of the transcripts would be better able to help a reader to capture the time and the lilt of the real clap-pattern?

We may set them out graphically in this way:

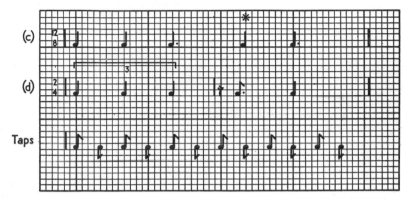

Only the two top lines of this diagram concern us at the moment. The scale used is eight squares per crotchet of example (c): therefore, in (d) as the first three notes are *ipso facto* equal in time to those of (c), the bar will contain twenty-four squares: so, in the second bar of (d) the semiquaver rest will equal three squares and the dotted quaver nine. To our surprise we see how very nearly equivalent the two versions are: but they are not exactly equal, (d)'s fourth clap entering sooner than (c)'s. African percussive rhythm is very exact in performance and so we can say at once that if one of them is correct, the other is wrong. Let us test the matter in a thoroughly African way by asking someone to tap six equally spaced taps to this pattern with one hand, and to intersect these with six taps played with the other hand. The result expressed graphically will be seen in the lowest line of the above diagram. The crucial test is at the point marked with an asterisk. Does the clap coincide exactly with the intermediate hand tap or not? Any competent African will have no hesitation at all in agreeing that it does indeed coincide. This admission automatically proclaims version (d) as inaccurate while the whole tapping is found to confirm version (c).

The third criterion by which to judge the versions is that of reading the score: does the score give us the lilt of the original and is it reasonably easy to read? No one who has heard a party of villagers clap this pattern could possibly think that there was the slightest suggestion of syncopation in it, that is, the suggestion that it is 'out of step' with some primary background existing in the performer's mind. It simply sounds like a smooth irregular pattern existing as a complete conception in its own right. The scoring in version (*d*) does not in the least convey this impression, in fact it looks like a travesty of the real thing. Moreover, besides being wrong in time-values it is extraordinarily difficult to read.

APPENDIX II

KEY

B = Bantu style	5 = Use of fifths in harmony
A = Arab style	4 = „ fourths „
8 = Unison singing	3 = „ thirds „

WESTERMANN'S AREA

Tribe	Language Group	Harmony	
Mandinka	Mande	8	A and B
Susu	„	8	B
Mende	„	4, 5, and some 3	B
Mano	„	8, some 3 by overlap	A and B
Dyula	„	8	A
Mwa	„	3	B
Temne	West Atlantic	8	B
Kissi	„ „	8	A
Gola	„ „	8, 4	B
Mossi	Gur	8	A
Kru	Kru	3	B
Akan	Kwa	3	B
Baule	„	3	B
Anyi	„	3	B
Guang	„	3	B
Asanti ⎫	„	3	B
Twi ⎭	„	3	B
Ga	„	3	B
Ewe	„	8, 4	B
Yoruba	„	8	Partly A, partly B
Gu	„	8	B
Fɔ	„	8	B
Urhobo	„	8, 4	B
Igbo (Ibo)	„	3	B

Tribe	Language Group	Harmony	
Adaŋme	Kwa	3	B
Hausa	Chado-Hamitic	8	A, and some B
Tiv	Isolated	8	B
Tuareg	Berber	8	A
? ?	Fr. Cameroons	3	B

GUTHRIE'S AREA

These are of course all BANTU style, but note that the list includes Pygmies.

Tribe	Language Group	Harmony
Duala	A 24	3
Faŋ	A 66	4
? Mbede	B 21	3
Yanzi	B 40	8 (mostly) and 4
Nzeli	C 16	8, 5, and a few 3
Ngombe	C 31	5 (and one 3)
Moŋgo	C 61a	8, 3 (plenty)
Ŋkundu	C 61b	8, 4, and mostly 3
Manyema area {	C 70	3
	D 20	3
	D 50	3
Genya	D 15	3
Bira	D 30	3
Amba	D 22	8
Tutsi	D 61 and 66	8, 5, 4 (mixed Arab and Bantu)
Nyoro	E 11	8, 4
Toro	E 12	8
Nyaŋkole (Hima)	E 13	8
Ganda	E 15	8
Haya	E 22	8, 4
Luo	E 25 and 43	8
Gisu	E 31a	8
Wanga	E 32a	8
Gusii	E 42	8
Kikuyu	E 50	8
Meru	E 61	8
Caga	E 62	8, 5, 4
Nika	E 72	
Giriama	E 72a	8

Tribe	Language Group	Harmony
Conya	E 72c	8
Sukuma	F 21	4
Nyamwesi	F 22	8, 5, 4
Gogo	G 11	8, 5, 4
Zaramo	G 33	8, 5
Swahili	G 42	8
Hehe	G 62	8
Bena	G 63	8 and some 3
? Kisi[1]	G 67	3
Kongo (N.E.)	H 16e	8, 5
Ciokwe	K 11	3
Lucazi	K 13	3
Luena	K 14	3
Mbunda	K 15	4
Lozi	K 21	4
Luba—Kasai	L 31a	8, 5, 4
Lulua	L 31b	8, 5, and 3
Luba—Katanga	L 33	3
Hemba	L 34	3
Kaonde	L 41	5, 4
Ŋkoya	L 60	4
Fipa	M 13	8, 4
Mambwe	M 15	4 and 3
Nyika	M 23	8, 5, 4, and 3
Nyikyusa	M 30	5, 4, and 3
Bemba	M 42	3
Cisiŋga	,,	3
Usi	,,	3
Biisa	M 51	3
Lala	M 52	5, 4
Lenje	M 61	4
Soli	M 62	5, 4
Ila	M 63	4
Toŋga	M 64	4
Manda	N 11	4
Ŋgoni	N 12	4
Teŋgo	N 13	3
Toŋga (Nyasaland)	N 15	3
Tumbuka	N 21a	8, 5, 4
Kamaŋga (Heŋga)	N 21c	8, 5, 4
Lambia	N 21h	4

[1] Marius Schneider spells the tribe 'Kesi'.

Tribe	Language Group	Harmony
Nyanja	N 31a	3
Cewa	N 31b	8, 5, 4
Mananja	N 31c	3
Nsenga	N 41	4
Kunda	N 42	4
Sena	N 44	8, 5, 4
Cuabo	P 34	3
Kuanyama	R 21	3
Ndonga	R 22	3
Venda	S 10	8, 4
Tswana	S 20	4
Pidi (Pedi)	S 22	8
Suthu	S 23	4 (and one 3)
Xosa } Mpondo }	S 31	8, 4
Zulu	S 32	8, 4
Nguni	S 32b	8, 5, 4
Zezuru	T 12	5
Manyika	T 13a	8, 5
Karanga	T 15	8 (also 5 and 4 by overlap)
Shangaan	T 23a	8, 5, 4
Copi	T 31	8, 5, 4
PYGMIES		
Batwa } Mambuti }	Belgian Congo and Ruanda	8, 5, 4
Bahutu	,,	8, 5, 4, and some 3

NON-BANTU EAST—CENTRAL AREA

Tribe	Language Group	Harmony	
Yogo	N. Congo	3	
Mangabetu	,,	3	
Bandiya	,,	8, 5	B
Azande	,,	8, 5	B
Nandi	Kenya	8, 4	B
Masai	Kenya, Tanganyika	8	B
Arusha	,, ,,	8	B
Kipsigis	,, ,,	8, 5	B
Itesio	,, ,,	8, 5, 4	B
Ateso	,, ,,	8, 5, 4	B
Sebei	Uganda	8, 4	

NOTE: *A few entries contain a remark like 'and one 3' (e.g. for Suthu). This means that among the records listened to, we did actually hear one third. In these cases the probability is that the third does not really belong to the tribe and is borrowed perhaps from European music or a neighbour, and should be discounted. But it is printed for the sake of honest accuracy.*

APPENDIX III

LIST OF GRAMOPHONE RECORDS

1.	Hausa (Nigeria)	Decca WA 180, *compare*
	Bantu (Sukuma tribe—Tanganyika)	Gallotone GB 1327 T
2.	Arab	Gallotone GB 1547 T
3.	Hausa	Decca WA 182
	Shirazi (Zanzibar) (Bantu style)	Gallotone GB 1255 T
4.	Yoruba (Arab style)	Decca WA 1506 or WA 1632
5.	Yoruba Bantu style	Decca WA 212
6.	Twi	Decca WA 528
	Ewe	Decca WA 140
	Ibo	Decca WA 196
7.	Nguja (Dar-es-Salaam) (Arab style)	Gallotone GB 1242 T
8.	Ewe	Decca WA 139
9.	Luo	Trek DC 218 H
10.	Ibo	Decca WA 1700
	Ewe	Decca WA 547
11.	Temne (Sierra Leone)	Decca WA 2521
	Nyamwesi (Tanganyika)	Gallotone GB 1312 T
12.	Zulu (South Africa)	Gallotone GB 1037 T
	Twi (West Africa)	Decca WA 645
	Mende (West Africa)	Decca WA 2514
	Susu (West Africa)	Decca WA 2634
13.	Bemba (Northern Rhodesia)	Gallotone GB 1086
14.	Nsenga (Northern Rhodesia)	Trek DC 168 H
15.	Ciokwe (N. Rhodesia)	Gallotone GB 1068 T
	Cuabo (Portuguese E. Africa)	Gallotone GB 1138 T
	Ibo (West Africa)	Decca WA 1559
	Yoruba (West Africa)	Decca WA 200
16.	Zulu (South Africa)	Gallotone GB 1037 T
	Nandi (Kenya)	Gallotone GB 1465 T
	Gisu (Kenya)	Gallotone GB 1502 T

17. Teso (Kenya)   Gallotone GB 1454 T
    Kipsigis (Kenya)   Gallotone GB 1470 T
18. Nguja (Zanzibar)   Gallotone GB 1254 T
    Chopi (Portuguese E. Africa)   Gallotone GB 1046 T
    Luba (South Congo)   Gallotone GB 1112
    Twi (West Africa)   Decca WA 617
19. Zezuru (Southern Rhodesia)   Gallotone GB 971 T
    Nyamwesi (Tanganyika)   Gallotone GB 1315 T
    Biisa (Northern Rhodesia)   Gallotone GB 1055
    Ga (Ghana, West Africa)   Decca WA 626
    Ibo (Igbo) (South Nigeria,   Decca WA 1673
        W. Africa)

NOTE:

(a) The Decca records are listed in their West African catalogue:
    they can be obtained, however, in England.

(b) All the other records are in the African Music Society's Library,
    which contains notes on each record. A set of the Library is
    housed with the English Folk Dance and Song Society at Cecil
    Sharp House, 2, Regent's Park Road, London, N.W. 1. Those
    wishing to play the records should make an appointment with
    the Librarian of Cecil Sharp House, from whom they may order
    copies.

10

TONE AND TUNE

'IL est seulement regrettable,' says M. Tegethoff, commenting justifiably on an earlier book of ours,[1] 'que les courtes remarques au sujet des rapports entre les langues tonétiques et la formation absolue de la mélodie ne depassent pas la constatation du fait déjà universellement connu de leur influence réciproque.' He adds, 'Les résultats de recherches plus poussées ont déjà été publiés par M. Schneider: *Phonetische und metrische Korrelationen bei gesprochenen und gesungenen Ewe-Texten*, dans: *Archiv für Vergleichende Phonetik, Bd. 7, Heft 1/2, 1–6 (1943–1944).*'[2]

Dr. Marius Schneider had the assistance of three Africans and used, as a basis for his study, a number of gramophone records of songs, some of which were made in Berlin by one of the Africans. The investigation dealt with the Ewe dialects in Togoland and Dahomey. The texts and speech-tones were established for him by Dr. Westermann who used a three-tone system (high, middle, low) for the latter. He transcribed the song-melodies, applied the text to them, and from the twenty-two songs treated in this way he made his observations and conclusions which are of considerable interest. There were two phenomena to deal with. First, in the bulk of the music, the melody followed the speech-tones. He points out that the musical intervals agree with the tonal distinctions of speech only as regards their direction and that if this were not so, it would be impossible for a true melody to develop at all. This freedom of the melody takes two forms. On the one hand the melody may make jumps larger or smaller than those used in speech, thus giving musical scope to create a good tune. On the other hand the melody frequently employs a device which he calls a shift of centre. A section of melody will have a mean centre around which it moves in accordance with the tonal

[1] A. M. Jones, *African Music*, Rhodes-Livingstone Museum, N. Rhodesia, 1949.
[2] W. Tegethoff, 'Tendances nouvelles dans la musicologie comparative', in *Aequatoria*, xviii. 1, 1955 (Congo Belge).

features of speech. This may be followed by a section whose mean
centre is higher or lower but in which the tune is still faithful to
speech-tone. The repeated shifts of centre greatly increase the
possible range of the melody. Second, and in contrast with this
general tune-tone agreement, Dr. Schneider observed that: 'In
many instances the succession of high, middle and low notes in
sung Ewe texts fails to correspond at all points with that of high,
medium and low tones in speech—without, however, causing an
impression of irregularity in the hearer.'

Most of his conclusions deal with these 'exceptions' and in
order to rationalize them he states that the whole question of
tone *vis-à-vis* tune is not merely a simple correspondence in pitch-
direction, but is much more complex. There are, he says, four
determining factors any one of which may cause a note to rise or
fall: (1) the linear movement of melody in the direction of speech-
tone, which he does not regard as primary; (2) the really primary
'motor basis', i.e. 'the intensity of utterance of the syllable, which
according as it is strong or weak is realised metrically as stressed
or unstressed, in pitch—and this is secondary—as high or low';
(3) metrical rhythm of the music: 'the possibility of loosening the
purely tonal bonds between music and speech or of replacing them
by metrical factors at last opens the way to the specifically musical
development of melody'; (4) concept and emotion: 'the language
provides the concepts, the music develops the emotional values
of the given context. The result of this is that while the tune starts
in agreement with the speech-tones, as it proceeds, the text is
progressively subordinated to the dictates, sequential or otherwise, of the music.'

All this is highly interesting—and yet? One cannot help feeling
uncomfortable about both the bases of this work, and also many
of the conclusions reached.

To rely on gramophone records for intensive analysis is to
court disaster. They are too impersonal: no questions can be put
to them: all results obtained from them are largely subjective,
depending ultimately on the listener, and in scientific work the
subjective element must, as far as possible, be eliminated. The
only satisfactory way to study these problems is by working
directly with an informant and with the help of apparatus giving
objective readings. This, however, is not our main criticism.

Dr. Schneider has built his theories on two unwarrantable

assumptions as regards speech, which are : (1) that Ewe speech has three fixed tones; (2) that the median pitch of whole sentences in Ewe is, as it were, a horizontal line. To treat the Ewe language as a three-tonal one may be a convenient simplified abstraction for the grammarian but it is certainly not true of Ewe as it is actually spoken. With suitable apparatus it can be demonstrated that one ought to think of Ewe speech not as consisting of three fixed tonal pitches but as three bands of tone—high band, mid-band, and low band. Within these bands there are several degrees of pitch available to, and indeed used by, the speaker. To ignore this is to confuse the musical issue : for a word consisting of two mid-tone syllables, the first lower than the second, would be taken as having merely two middle and therefore level tones. If the melody to these syllables rises, it would be taken as violating the tone-melody relationship, whereas in actual fact it would be faithfully observing it.

We go on to the second point: although he nowhere states it, Dr. Schneider proceeds on the assumption that we can represent a sentence in Ewe as a straight horizontal line, where the mid-tones fall, with the high and low tones occurring above and below it. This again may be a convenience as a linguistic conception but no sentence in spoken Ewe or in any other language known to us behaves in this way. In actual speech there is, of course, always a median or centre above and below or on which we move our voice. But it is never a line of fixed pitch. It is continually moving according to the context or the tribal manner of speaking. For instance, the Tonga in Northern Rhodesia, when reading, start most sentences high and gradually work down the scale till at their end they are speaking very low. This downdrift is a common feature in African languages. In other words the median line is not horizontal but sloping downwards, with the high and low tones still correctly placed above or below it wherever the median happens to be at any moment. The same principle is at work in Ewe. The median line is not a straight horizontal: it is not even a straight downward slope : it is in the form of waves whose peaks are determined by the subject matter. While this fact may have no linguistic significance, its importance when we are relating speech to song-melody is obvious, and of prime importance. It is not sufficient to know the tonal features of a number of words in order to solve the tone-tune problem. We must know the exact musical outline of the spoken words of the whole song. Not until we know this can we test the behaviour of the actual tune to which those words are sung. On these grounds it appears that Dr. Schneider is arguing from false premises. He is arguing from what a linguist thinks the speech-tones ought to be and not from what they actually are. This lands him in serious difficulties where the melody does not behave as it should. But he has an answer in all cases even though he has to go outside music and fall back on 'motor impulse' and 'concept and emotion'. To accommodate cases where the melody goes up when it ought to go down, he has to provide a theory which holds good whether the melody behaves in one way or in exactly the opposite way. The cadences do not follow the speech-tones: they are so intractable that he makes them *ultra vires* and suggests they are a foreign importation. The melodic sequences give difficulty and therefore they are places where musical considerations override tonal ones. All this is highly suspicious. Can it be that the real answer is simpler? We suggest there is a case here for a re-examination of the evidence.

It is obvious that we cannot start to evaluate the problem unless we can be absolutely sure of the reliability of the data we use. In the case of the song-melody this is fairly straightforward as the relatively large size of the musical intervals makes them easy to recognize: even here caution is needed because two adjacent notes which to our ears appear to be the same, may actually and purposely differ slightly in pitch. In the realm of speech we are presented with a very much more difficult problem involving considerable finesse. As contrasted with the relatively sustained and stable sounds produced in singing, speech does not to our ears present a series of defined musical notes. Though we are aware of the major movements of the voice so that we can say one syllable is high and the other low, we cannot assign an absolute value to the pitches used, while the finer degrees of tonal varia- tion will escape all but the acutest European ears. Even if we can hear these relative pitch-variations fairly well, we could not, over a long distance like a complete sentence, determine by listening whether all the high tones used were of the same musical pitch, or whether the pitch of the mid-tones is a constant right through the sentence. Clearly the subjective method of listening is totally inadequate. What we need is an apparatus which will give an ob- jective and mensurable reading of the tones used in speaking.

The tonometer we invented for the purpose has been described in the *Zeitschrift für Phonetik* :[1] its chief features are these. It consists of three units—a microphone, an amplifier, and the tonometer itself. The latter indicates the speech-tones by means of a row of 66 metal reeds tuned between the limits of 70 and 287 vibrations per second, which is what is needed when dealing with adult male voices. The pitch of adjacent reeds is so close that the apparatus will show very fine differences of speech-tone. In the lower notes the reeds are only 2 v.p.s. apart: in the middle they are 3 or 4 v.p.s. distant, while in the top the gap is 5 v.p.s. This has proved to be amply discriminatory for ordinary research purposes. Close to the reeds there is a numbered scale and there are movable pointers which can be slid into position while a word is spoken, thus facilitating the reading of the result. Whatever pitch is spoken into the microphone, only that reed will vibrate whose vibration number is the same as that spoken or is very near it. Suppose a high-middle word is tested: it is repeated several times and two pointers are slid opposite the reeds which are vibrating. The numbers on the scale are read off, and we thus have an indisputable and objective value given to these particular speech-tones.

It has been necessary to give this brief description of the tonometer because upon its objective readings rests the validity of the research we shall now set out. One of the songs in this book was selected at random and the choice fell on the *Nyayito* dance song *'Beble'*, which had been transcribed from Mr. Tay's singing. There lives in Ghana a skilled woman singer, Madame Kpevie. Very fortunately we had a recording of Mme Kpevie singing the same song. We thus had two transcriptions of the same tune.

The words of the song were spoken by Mr. Tay and the pitch of each syllable recorded. If this had been done a word at a time the record would have been useless for our purpose as it would have given the speech-tones of the words spoken in isolation, and there would have been missing that other prime necessity—the relative wave-movement of the median speech-line in continuous speech. To ensure that the list of speech-tones should represent the pitches produced when the song is spoken as a whole, Mr. Tay first recorded the spoken words on a gramophone disk. This was played into the tonometer bit by bit, and the speech-tones

---

[1] Heft 5/6, Berlin, 1955: article 'A Simple Tonometer'. Also under the same title in *Nature*, No. 605, London, 1956.

duly noted. Where any ambiguity occurred Mr. Tay listened to his voice on the record and then repeated the word into the microphone. The result is set out below. The tonometer figures represent semitones or fractions thereof. The lowest reed on the instrument has the figure '1': the reed a semitone above that is called '2': the next semitone is '3'—and so on. The intermediate reeds give the fractional values.

1. *The tonometer scale*

Note	DD	DD♯	EE	FF	FF♯	GG	GG♯	AA	AA♯	BB	C	C♯
Vib. per sec.	72	76	81	85	91	96	102	108	114	121	128	136
Tonometer number	1	2	3	4	5	6	7	8	9	10	11	12

Note	D	D♯	E	F	F♯	G	G♯	A	A♯	B	c	c♯	d
Vib. per sec.	144	152	161	171	181	192	203	215	228	242	256	271	287
Tonometer number	13	14	15	16	17	18	19	20	21	22	23	24	25

2. *Tonometer readings for the spoken words of the* Nyayito *song*

(These are the tonometer pitches plotted on the graph.)
Sliding tones are shown thus: ╲ — slide down: ╱ — slide up.

13 14⅓ 18½ 15 13 10⅔ 13
Be — ble tsi — tsi — e me — nye

12⅓ 14 10½ 10½ 14 11 11 10⅓ 12½ 12½
Nye — la ge — dea — wo ɖo — mee ma — ku do

12 15 13½ (9╲7½)
Ha — le — ya hee

14½ 17½ 15 12½ 15 14 11⅔ 11⅔ 11⅔ 11⅔ 11⅔
Mi — a — wo tɔ — ba — ha zu ma — ke ma — ke

11 15 15 12⅓ 13½ 12 12 10½ 10½
Ʋe — dzia ɖe dza ɖe nyi me ʋe — nu

13½ 14½ 14½ 14½ (13╲10) 12 (12╲10) 11⅓ 13⅓ 12⅓ 14 13 13 (12╲11)
A — nya-koa-wo yi a — dza wu ge na a — kpa — lu ee

11 12½ 11½ 15 12 (10½╲7) 10½ (10½╱15) 10½
Ma — do a — loe — wo gbe na mi — dzro

$$\begin{cases} 14\frac{1}{4} & (14\frac{1}{4}\backslash11\frac{1}{2}) & 17 & 11\frac{1}{8} & 13\frac{1}{8} & 12\frac{1}{4} & 12\frac{1}{2} & 13\frac{1}{8} & 12\frac{1}{8} & (11\frac{1}{8}/8\frac{1}{2}) \\ \text{Me — gbloe} & & \text{na} & \text{mi} & \text{be} & \text{me — dzi} & & \text{ge} & \text{na} & \text{mi} \end{cases}$$

$$\begin{cases} 12 & 14\frac{1}{8} & 16\frac{2}{3} & (15\frac{1}{8}\backslash12\frac{1}{2}) & 11\frac{2}{3} & 11\frac{2}{3} & 12\frac{1}{8} & 11\frac{2}{3} & 10\frac{1}{4} \\ \text{Uu} & \text{ya — wo} & \text{ha} & & \text{me — dzi} & & \text{ge} & \text{na} & \text{mi} \end{cases}$$

$$\begin{cases} 15\frac{1}{8} & 9 & 12 & 13\frac{1}{2} & 13\frac{1}{4} & (10\backslash6\frac{2}{3}) & (9\backslash6\frac{2}{3}) & 11\frac{2}{3} & 14 & 14 & 9 & 13\frac{2}{3} & 7 \\ \text{Tɔ — nye} & & \text{ga} & \text{ku — a} & & \text{me — dze} & & \text{a — xɔ} & & \text{ɖo} & \text{gbe} & \text{lo — ho} \end{cases}$$

$$\begin{cases} 9 & 9 & 12 & 12 & 12 & 12 & (9\backslash5\frac{1}{2}) & (6\backslash4\frac{2}{3}) & 8\frac{1}{2} & 12 & 13\frac{1}{4} & 12 \\ \text{A — dee} & \text{— vu} & \text{na — va} & \text{le,} & \text{me — dze} & & & \text{a — xo} & & \text{ɖo} & \text{gbe} \end{cases}$$

$$\begin{cases} 12\frac{1}{4} & 8\frac{2}{3} & 9\frac{2}{3} & 9\frac{2}{3} & 9\frac{2}{3} \\ \text{Sa — ti} & & \text{na — va} & \text{tsɔ} \end{cases}$$

We now have the information necessary for our investigation. We know the tune and we know the speech-tones. The most convincing way to illustrate their correlation is to do so in a composite graph, which we now examine. To the left of the vertical axis are the tonometer numbers, to the right of it are the musical notes. These two are not correlated musically, because we want the speech graph to lie as near as possible to the melody graph for ease of comparison: but the same vertical distance on the graph is accorded a semitone in both cases, thus making the graphs strictly comparable. The thick-lined graph is the melody as sung by Mme Kpevie: the dotted lines show where Mr. Tay differed from her. The thin-lined graph represents the speech-tones. For ease of reference the syllables are numbered.

There is an obvious trend of agreement in the direction of the two graphs. This agreement is far closer than appears from a cursory glance. For example, the sliding tones make the speech graph appear to diverge sharply, whereas in fact the next syllable as spoken may start in relation to the start of the previous one in the same direction as the melody. One special feature of agreement which stands out is the correlation of amplitude in speech and voice. To a surprising extent, in spite of the musical dictates inherent in creating a good tune, the range of semitones covered by the song and by the speaking voice is by and large remarkably similar. But a superficial glance at the graph reveals only a small part of what it has to show. We must now examine it in considerable detail.

In a sentence we have a number of words whose boundaries are indicated on a printed page by gaps. Does the melody behave in one way in respect of the internal tonal relationship of words and in another way in respect of the gaps? This raises the prior question as to what constitutes a word in Ewe. As a basis to work on we have adopted the word division officially sponsored at present in Ghana. We give two lists: one for the internal and one for the external correlations: single-syllabled words are counted together with the previous gap as one gap.

Table of Tone and Tune correlations

NOTE: 1. M╱ = melody rises: M╲ = melody falls: M— = melody stays on same note. And so for T = tone: also ╲ = sliding tone.
 2. The figures in brackets refer to syllable numbers on the graph.

WORDS (2 syllables or more)			GAPS (and words of one syllable)		
		%			%
Total words counted .	35	100	Total counted . .	70	100
a. Complete agreements of tone and tune	27	77·15	. . . .	44	63
b. M — T╱ (42–45 : 56–57 : 58–60) . .	3	8·6	(37: 42: 52: 69: 76: 84: 95: 106: 108) .	9	12·8
c. M — T╲ (84–85 : 104–5)	2	5·7	(33: 40: 47: 51: 58: 73: 74: 82: 83: 91) .	10	14·3
d. M╲ T — (13–14 : 70–71)	2	5·7	(63)	1	1·4
e. M╱ T — (47–48) . .	1	2·85	(62)	1	1·4
f. M╱ T╲ nil . .	...	...	(20: 64: 78) . .	3	5·7
g. M╲ T╱ nil . .	...	...	(97)	1	1·4

We are at once struck by the fact that by far the largest number of exceptions to complete agreement occur in sections (b) and (c) where the melody stays on the same note while the speech-tone moves either up or down. Evidently there is some special factor present here for apart from these cases there are very few exceptions indeed to the primary rule that the melody follows the speech-tones. We shall consider all the exceptions presently, but if, for the time being, we include sections (b) and (c) in the count of agreements we get:

Words and tune agree . . 32 out of 35   91·45 per cent.
Gaps and tune agree . . 63 „ 70   90 per cent.

Considering that a tune is a musical concept with its own necessary organization of rhythm, phrases, sequences, and cadences if
it is to be a proper tune at all, is not this high percentage remarkable?

Our next step is the laborious one of examining closely all the
exceptions listed above. It is by studying these that the subsidiary
rules governing the tone-tune relationship may be elucidated.
The figures refer to the syllable numbers on the graph: the letter
G stands for 'Gap' between words.

13–14 *domee* $\left\{ \begin{matrix} M \searrow \\ T \underline{} \end{matrix} \right\}$ Melody descends 1 tone: speech is level.

The context is (a)-*wo domee ma-(ku)*: excluding the syllables in
brackets, we have in speech a descending sequence, the tonometer readings being 14, 11, 11, 10⅓. The melody faithfully follows this descent except that it keeps on descending instead of
pausing level on the final syllable of *domee*. The melody is wending
its way from the high note on syllable 12 to the low note on
syllable 15. When it gets to syllable 13, instead of keeping level
it looks forward to its falling relationship between 14 and 15: it
anticipates this fall by dropping down a tone on the level word
domee. This is a feature which we shall meet with repeatedly and
we shall call it the principle of 'melodic anticipation'.

17–18 G $\left\{ \begin{matrix} M \diagup \\ T \diagdown \end{matrix} \right\}$ Melody rises 1 tone, speech descends ½ semitone.

This is the junction between the end of one line of the song
and the beginning of the next. One would expect a melodic
liberty here. However, the melody does work to rule. It is in process of moving up from G to C. As in the case above, it begins
to rise towards C on the previous syllable '*ha*' (18). It is another
example of melodic anticipation.

19–20 G+*ya* $\left\{ \begin{matrix} M \diagup \\ T \diagdown \end{matrix} \right\}$ Melody rises 1 tone: speech descends 1½
semitones.

There are two points to note here. On the following word '*hee*'
the melody, if it is to follow the speech, must descend. In order to
do so, it must previously have been higher. Secondly, it may be
regarded as a change of melodic centre as indicated by Dr.
Schneider. Of the whole phrase '*hale ya hee*' the graph shows that

in the second half, while the melody exactly follows the direction of the speech it has moved its centre of pitch higher. We should be inclined ourselves to take this as another example of melodic anticipation.

32–33 G$\left\{\begin{matrix} M\ — \\ T\ \diagdown \end{matrix}\right\}$Melody level: speech descends ½ semitone.

This is a gap between the end of one song-line and the beginning of the next, a point at which one might expect some liberty in the melody. Yet the speech drop is very slight—only a quarter of a tone. There are two further points. The melody has stayed on one note for five syllables, forming the end of the song-line: this is a feature we shall meet again. At the end of lines the melody often stays constant over several syllables which fall in pitch when spoken. The second point is that the melody is about to rise at 33–34 and therefore 32–33 is a melodic anticipation. The tone-tune discrepancy is justified on either of these two grounds.

36–37 G$\left\{\begin{matrix} M\ — \\ T\ \diagup \end{matrix}\right\}$Melody level: speech rises ⅔ semitone.

34–35 and 36–37 are a melodic sequence. This might, as Dr. Schneider observes, in itself account for the tone-tune variation. But the melody is about to descend in 37–38, so once again this is a melodic anticipation. There is no need to fall back on the influence of the sequence.

39–40 G$\left\{\begin{matrix} M\ — \\ T\ \diagdown \end{matrix}\right\}$Melody level: speech falls 1½ semitones.

This is the end of a song-line. The tonic is the normal lower limit of repose in this diatonic tune. The melody stays level on the tonic for five syllables which include a drop in speech-pitch. This is 'end-of-line' technique.

41–42 G$\left\{\begin{matrix} M\ — \\ T\ \diagup \end{matrix}\right\}$Melody level: speech rises 3 semitones.

This is the start of a new song-line. The melody chooses a new centre by keeping low and starting on the same note as that on which the previous line finished, instead of jumping up with the speech-tone.

42–43 *Anya-*$\left\{\begin{matrix} M\ — \\ T\ \diagup \end{matrix}\right\}$Melody level: speech rises 1 semitone.

Anyako is a place name. Is it possible that it has a variant pronunciation which the melody follows? We note that the next syllable 44 is a coalescence, '*Anyako a-wo*'. Perhaps this influences the melody on the previous syllable. If neither of these hypotheses is right then this is the first tone-tune variation for which we cannot provide a simple explanation.

46–47 G $\begin{Bmatrix} M & — \\ T & \diagdown \end{Bmatrix}$ Melody level: speech slides down on 46; speech on 47 is 1 semitone below start of 46.

This is the gap between '*yi*' which has a down-slide in speech, and '*adza*'. In singing, '*yi*' and '*a-*' are coalesced on one note which, in relation to the previous note is pitched about half-way down the slide: the syllable '*a-*' is also half-way down the slide and therefore this note is the natural one to take in the circumstances. On the average the melody follows the speech-tones.

47–48 *adza* $\begin{Bmatrix} M & \diagup \\ T & \diagdown \end{Bmatrix}$ Melody rises 1 tone: speech stays level but has a down-slide on the second syllable.

After the slide, the speech-tones are going to rise twice in succession. The melody begins to rise on the previous syllable. This is melodic anticipation. A further point is that the rise in melody may be a mirror reflection of the fall in the down-slide. This is not as naïve as might be thought. A slide like that on '-*dza*' has an open expanding feeling in the chest: it is possible that the rise in melody is a symbol of this feeling.

50–51 G *na* $\begin{Bmatrix} M & — \\ T & \diagdown \end{Bmatrix}$ Melody level: speech descends 1 semitone.

The syllable '*na*', in singing, is coalesced with the following one (52). So we have one melody note to two different speech-tones and the note chosen is the average of the two, which is the natural course to take. This statement disposes of both the intervals 50–51 and 51–52.

56–57 *Mado* $\begin{Bmatrix} M & — \\ T & \diagup \end{Bmatrix}$ Melody level. There are three alternative pro-

nunciations: to rise $1\frac{1}{2}$ semitones, to fall by the same amount, or, says Mr. Tay, you may say both syllables at the same pitch. The melody takes the average of the first two and adheres to the third, so there is no exception here.

$\begin{cases} \text{57--58} \quad G\left\{\begin{matrix} M & - \\ T & \diagdown \end{matrix}\right\}\text{Melody level: speech falls } \tfrac{2}{3} \text{ semitone.} \\[2ex] \text{58--60 } \textit{al}\text{ɔ}\textit{ewɔ}\left\{\begin{matrix} M & - \\ T & \wedge \end{matrix}\right\}\begin{matrix}\text{Melody level: speech rises } 3\tfrac{1}{2} \text{ semitones and} \\ \text{falls 3 semitones.}\end{matrix} \end{cases}$

The melody takes the average of these tone shifts and remains
level. To do this seems reasonable if we consider that the word
'*alɔewɔ*' is nearly all elided. The word has been absorbed into the
preceding and following words.

$\text{61--62} \quad G + \textit{na}\left\{\begin{matrix} M & \diagup \\ T & - + \text{previous slide} \end{matrix}\right\}. \text{ Melody rises 1 tone.}$

The slide down on the previous syllable '*gbe*' (61) makes '*na*'
follow the rule: from the bottom of the slide to '*na*' there is a rise
in speech-tone and the melody also rises.

$\text{62--63} \quad G + \textit{mi}\left\{\begin{matrix} M & \diagdown \\ T & - \end{matrix}\right\}\text{Melody falls a fourth: speech stays level.}$

The low D of the melody at 63 is a harmony variant of the G
above: the latter is the same note as that sung on 62. The melody
therefore follows the speech-tones. This statement must be expanded for it contains an important principle of African singing.
Many tribes who belong to the 8-5-4 tradition sing as we have
seen either wholly or partly in *organum* in parallel fourths. Sometimes they sing the bulk of a chorus in unison, only breaking into
fourths at certain places. Whether they do so or not, these Africans
carry in their minds the notion that a fourth below any given
melody note is an equivalent of, or at least an alternative to, that
note, and can be used, if desired, at any moment. It may often
be used as an embellishment and by way of a change when repeating a melody. When he drops to this note the singer is *thinking* in
terms of the original melody. Thus the note a fourth below is
really an alternative way of conceiving the note in its true position.
It *indicates* the original note. It is essential to grasp this important
point in dealing with tone-tune relationship: otherwise we may
be led to regard as an exception, a progression which is perfectly
according to rule.

$\text{63--64} \quad G + \textit{dzro}\left\{\begin{matrix} M & \diagup \\ T & \diagdown \end{matrix}\right\}\begin{matrix}\text{Melody rises a minor third: speech drops} \\ 4\tfrac{1}{2} \text{ semitones.}\end{matrix}$

If one accepts the explanation of the previous syllable (62–63) then this present syllable follows the tone-tune rule. From the top of the speech-slide on '*mi*', the voice falls to '*dzro*'. If the melody note for 62–63 is held to be really G, then the melody also falls in agreement.

65–66 *Megblɔe* $\left\{ \begin{matrix} M \searrow \\ T — \end{matrix} \right\}$ Melody falls 1 tone: speech is level.

This is Mme Kpevie's version. In Mr. Tay's singing, melody and speech agree. The second half of the song is just starting. Mme Kpevie makes a typical African *reprise*, which consists of singing the first note higher than it should strictly be. This sort of thing is often done when the melodic context is suitable, when repeats are being initiated.

66–67 G+*na*. Mr Tay's tune follows the speech-tones: Mme Kpevie sings a harmony variant a fourth below. She therefore follows the rule also.

68–69 G+*be* $\left\{ \begin{matrix} M — \\ T \nearrow \end{matrix} \right\}$ Melody level: speech rises 1 tone.

Of the syllables *na mi be* (67–69), *na* is high, *mi* is low, and *be* is middle: the melody takes the average of the drop from *na* to *mi*, i.e. about the pitch of *be*, and therefore remains level.

70–71 *medzi* $\left\{ \begin{matrix} M \searrow \\ T — \end{matrix} \right\}$ Melody falls a major third: speech is level.

The melody has got to be able to rise on the next syllable and must therefore descend below it. This is melodic anticipation.

72–74. This is the end of a song-line. The melody follows the rule. It remains level during the sequence of falling tones.

75–76 G $\left\{ \begin{matrix} M — \\ T \nearrow \end{matrix} \right\}$ Melody is level: speech rises $2\frac{1}{3}$ semitones.

Throughout the song the melody harps on the dominant of the diatonic major scale. It is this note which is used here and repeated on the next syllable. See also 65–66, 68–69, and 81–85 to mention but a few instances. As the speech rises here, so should the melody, but to where? It has been on G and at 76 it is on C. It cannot go in the sequence G, B♭, C because an upward jump to the subdominant followed by a rise to the dominant is a progression which the Africans do not normally make. The subdominant is freely used in descending progressions or as an *appoggiatura* in the sequence dominant, subdominant, dominant. So also the melody could move up to it and then downwards away from it. The only other available note is the mediant A. This could have been used, but there are two possible reasons why the dominant was chosen : we are at the start of a fresh line of the song and we have seen that there is some freedom allowed in this position: also, the melody is about to enter an ascending sequence and this rise from G to C is a preparatory anticipation. Although in this case the melody will stay on C for the next syllable before rising and it is not therefore quite the same as the cases we have classed as melodic anticipation, we regard it as falling in this category.

77–78 G+*ha* $\left\{ \begin{matrix} M \\ T \end{matrix} \right.$ $\diagdown$ Melody rises 1 tone (Tay): speech descends $1\frac{1}{3}$ semitones.

Let us consider Mme Kpevie's version. On 77 she sings contrary to the speech direction, but her note A is a harmony-note of Mr. Tay's D. She is therefore *mentally* singing Mr. Tay's note D: on 78 she drops to C. Thus she is faithfully following the speech-tones. At this point 78, Tay ascends to E, which is a major third above Kpevie. Although the Ewe are in the 8-5-4 tradition, they live close to a very large area of 'Thirds' tribes and do occasionally use a third as harmony. Thus Mr. Tay's E is a harmony-note and he too is obeying the tone-tune alignment.

80–81 G+*ge* $\left\{ \begin{matrix} M \\ T \end{matrix} \right.$ $\diagdown$ Melody falls 1 tone: speech rises $\frac{2}{3}$ tone (Tay only).

With Mme Kpevie, speech and tune agree. At 79 and 80 Mr. Tay is singing a fourth above her. This is a normal case of the 'harmonic alternative'.

81–83. This is the end of a line. It is a parallel case to the situation in 72–74. The words are the same. There is a descending sequence of speech-tones while the melody remains constant, this time on C instead of G as in the previous case. It is the 'end-of-line' technique.

83–84 G $\left\{ \begin{matrix} M \\ T \end{matrix} \right.$ $\diagup$ Melody stays level: speech rises 5 semitones.

If the melody on the previous words had fallen with the speech-tones, then the present note would be following the normal rule. Mentally, therefore, there is no exception here, and anyway it is the beginning of a song-line and uses the customary liberty.

84–85 *Tɔnye* $\left\{ \begin{matrix} M\; — \\ T\; \diagdown \end{matrix} \right\}$ Melody level: speech falls 6⅓ semitones.

This is a very big speech-leap. There seems to be a tendency for the melody to flatten out these wide speech-jumps. We have already seen in 46–49 how the melody smooths over speech down-slides. We shall see in 93–96 a case similar to the present one, where the flattening-out process preserves a smooth melody. But apart from this, the melody is obeying the rule of melodic anticipation. It is going to rise (Tay) on the next note.

From this point right on to the end of the song the two versions of the melody are in *organum* either of fourths or thirds except for one word at 110–11.

90–91 G $\left\{ \begin{matrix} M\; — \\ T\; \diagup \end{matrix} \right\}$ Melody level: speech rises 2⅔ semitones.

In singing the words *medze axɔ*, the first vowel of the second word is coalesced with the previous syllable and therefore loses its separate melodic identity. Nevertheless, the note on which it is sung takes the average position between the bottom of the slide on 90 and the true spoken pitch of the vowel on 91.

94–95 G $\left\{ \begin{matrix} M\; — \\ T\; \diagup \end{matrix} \right\}$ Melody level: speech rises 4⅔ semitones.

This is the second example of the melody flattening out a big speech-leap. Once again it takes an average position between the low tone at 94 and the high one at 95.

96–97 G $\left\{ \begin{matrix} M\; \diagdown \\ T\; \diagup \end{matrix} \right\}$ Melody falls a minor third: speech rises 1 tone.

Except for 63–64 this is the only example of contrary motion between speech and melody (77–78 being a harmonic alternative). In 95–96 the word *loho* has a steep speech-fall which the melody flattens out. In 96–97 the melody proceeds to a note which in relation to the note at 95 would be eminently suitable to represent the change of speech-pitch in the two cases. Besides, this is a gap between the end of one song-line and the beginning of the next.

104–6. There are two down-slides here in juxtaposition. The melody takes the average of the rapid up-and-down speech movements, i.e. it remains constant. Compare 46–48 : 61 : 63 : 89–90. Obviously in these cases the melody has to take some course of simplification. The alternative would be for it to use *glissando*, a device which African music does not normally employ except for special effects.

107–8 G+*ɖo* { M — } Melody stays level: speech rises 1½ semi-
           { T ⁄ } tones.

The melody is going to fall on the next syllable. Instead of rising on 108 it stays constant, that is, it prepares to fall, and incidentally flattens out the more abrupt speech-fall from 108 to 109. This is melodic anticipation.

111–12 G+*na* { M — } Mr. Tay's melody stays level: speech rises
            { T ⁄ } by approximately 1 semitone in either alternative of pronunciation.

Mme Kpevie's melody follows the speech-tones. Mr. Tay uses the 'end-of-line' technique, the melody smoothing out the speech fluctuations and staying here on the tonic of the scale and thus providing the necessary feeling of rest at the conclusion of the whole song.

We have now examined all the cases where the speech and melody do not move in a parallel direction. But this necessarily lengthy discussion must not be allowed by sheer weight of words to distort the real proportions of the matter. The plain fact is that out of a total of 114 melodic steps, the melody and speech move parallel in 74 cases, the remaining 37 being the ones we have just considered. Let us summarize the tone-tune behaviour in the remaining third: there appear to be seven rules:

1. There may be a change of centre in the melody.
2. At the beginning of each song-line there is melodic liberty: the melody may jump to a new position.
3. At the end of a song-line, the melody moves to a note of repose, around which the speech-tones may fluctuate.
4. The melody flattens out big tonal leaps in speech.
5. The melody takes the average course. This occurs especially:

(a) when two syllables are sung to the same note in semi-
    quavers, i.e. when they share a normal unit of time;
(b) where there are slides in speech.
6. Melodic anticipation. The melody tends to look forward to
    its next move in following the speech, and this modifies the
    position of the previous note.
7. The use of harmonic alternatives. The speech-tones are fol-
    lowed mentally by the singer, but he may express his thoughts
    by using a harmony-note derived from the note which
    actually follows the speech.

All these rules seem to be just plain common sense and, what
is more important still, they fit naturally into the general context
of African musical ideas and practice as it was known to us before
we undertook this particular study. Indeed, rules 2, 3, and 7 could
be either observed or deduced by anyone listening to African
singing, even if he were not aware of the tone-tune problem at
all. The cases where these simple rules apply, added to the cases
where tone and tune are more patently in alignment, account for
every move of melody and speech in the whole song with the one
possible exception of the proper name '*Anyako*'.[1] There appears to
be no need whatever to invoke the imaginary dynamic stresses,
the motor force, the idea of concept and emotion, and all the
elaborate structural factors proposed by Dr. Marius Schneider.
We see that it is not a recondite problem at all. The liberties that
the melody takes are few and perfectly understandable in their
contexts. There is no doubt that the African, in melodizing his
speech feels that the tune does all along conform to the speech
outline. That he is able, in approaching vocal music from this
standpoint, to create such strong, well-balanced, and musically
satisfying tunes is surely a remarkable tribute to his musical
aesthetic.

In basing our conclusions on the analysis of one single song

---

[1] Dr. J. Berry supplies this note: 'It is not unusual to find anthroponyms and
toponyms in a language that are "special cases" from the point of view of the phonology of that language: there are many examples, such as perhaps the French patro-
nymics, which are best considered to be outside the overall phonological system
of the language in which they occur.' One cannot argue from this, that because
proper names are special cases, therefore the music is at liberty to move contrary
to their speech-tones: if the pronunciation is invariable, one might expect the music
to conform. On the other hand, to find that both phonology and music have to
regard a proper name as a special case is perhaps significant.

we lay ourselves open to the charge that it may be a freak and that more evidence is required. We accept this criticism: certainly more songs should be analysed in this detailed way, though only those who have tried it will know the amount of labour involved. African music is such an uncharted field that the pioneer cannot cover the whole ground satisfactorily. But he can point the way, and that is what we have tried to do. We have no reason to believe that this song is exceptional: it is a perfectly normal average specimen. Its detailed analysis shows that it contains plenty of recurring instances which help to show what the African is doing. The field is open for others to hunt in. We do not believe that their conclusions will differ materially from ours.

*   *   *   *   *   *

The last word has certainly not been said on this subject. While we have given what we believe to be the main outline of the matter, there remain other facets of the subject which need investigation. For instance, granted that the tune must follow the tone, what is the relationship between the *magnitude* of the tonal steps *vis-à-vis* the size of the musical intervals between one melody-note and another? Does the melody-jump depend wholly on musical considerations providing it moves in the right direction or are there limiting factors? It is worth while recounting a small exploratory attempt at probing this question.

The first words of Play Song No. 6, '*Abayee loo*', have this speech-tone pattern: _ ‾ _ ‾ : we will consider only the first two syllables where there is a rise in the speech-tones. The melody is this:

A - bayee loo

As the Ewe actually sing these syllables, therefore, while there is a rise in speech, the melody stays level on C. The question we pursued with Mr. Tay was what are the possible alternative melody-notes which an African could attach to the first syllable. The result is as follows:

(*a*) You may sing   but if you do,

this will affect other notes later in the song.

(*b*) On NO account can you sing any of the following:

It is quite obvious, therefore, that there is a limiting factor in the extent to which a melody may leap. The example we have chosen is, in a way, a special case, for it is the *beginning* of a song-line. Nevertheless the example does at least show what may or may not be done in such a situation. Standing by itself it is insufficient material on which to theorize: but it is a pointer to future research. The magnitude of the melody-leap is important. The factors which determine it remain to be discovered.

APPENDIX

THE CONCEPTION OF PITCH AND TIMBRE

EUROPEANS think naturally of pitch in terms of vertical direction: if we wish to indicate it by movements of the hand, we shall put our hand high to illustrate a high pitch, and hold it low to show a low one. This applies whether we think of melodic pitch or the relative pitches in speech. But this concept is not the only possible one. In terms of a keyboard instrument we think horizontally: a high note is on the right and a low one on the left. It would be perfectly possible to think of pitch in terms of volume—a large note or a small note: or again in terms of weight—a light note being what we should call high, and a low one heavy: or yet again in terms of male and female. How does the African think of pitch?

In singing, the Ewe describe a high note as '*Egbe yi dzi*' that is, 'Voice gone high'. A low note is '*Egbe bɔbɔ*, that is, 'Voice low'. This word *bɔbɔ* is used only of the singing voice and not of the act of speaking. It is the same word as would be used to say 'Bend down' if you are standing up. Thus in singing, the Ewe think, as we do, in terms of vertical direction for variations in pitch.

In speech there are three relevant terms. A high voice is called '*Egbe kɔkɔ*', where the sense is a voice high in altitude (e.g. like a mountain). We could find no word directly used for a low voice but there are two terms which throw light on the matter. If a person says the word '*bayee*' using two high tones instead of mid and low, one may say to him, '*Egbea ne vanyi*' that is, 'LOWER your voice'. This word 'Lower' is used with the sense of direction downwards. Alternatively one might say, '*Egbea ne bɔbɔ*' that is, 'Bend your voice down'. In the Ewe mind this connotes 'Make the voice SOFT and low, it was too HARD and high'.

Three more expressions may be used in regard either to song or to speech. *Egbe vi* (*lit.* small) refers to a voice of thin and very quiet quality. Mr. Tay calls it a 'small voice'. This obviously is more in the category of timbre than of pitch. Similarly *Egbe gã* uses the common adjective for 'big': while the term *Egbe lolo*, which also may be translated 'a big voice' means a voice of big natural volume: 'big' is here used in the sense of describing say, a fat man, or the rotundity of a football. In demonstrating the concept, both hands are used to describe a large round object in the air. Mr. Tay maintains firmly that the concept of weight (light and heavy) is not used at all either for speech or for song in his tribe.

We have here two different categories for the conception of pitch. When thinking of the actual intervals made in melody or speech, the Ewe think in terms of vertical direction as Europeans do. When, however, they are classifying the natural pitch and the quality of a person's whole voice range they use the category of volume—big or small.

This mental attitude to vocal pitch and quality is paralleled elsewhere in Africa. The Kikuyu (East Africa) and the Suto (South Africa) both regard change of pitch in speech or song, just like the Ewe, as a concept of vertical direction. In thinking of the high or low natural range of different persons' voices, e.g. a treble or a bass voice, the Kikuyu use either of two concepts: a low voice is *thick* and a high voice *thin*, in the sense of thick or thin porridge: this is the concept of mass. Or, like the Ewe, a low voice is big and a high voice small— which is the notion of volume. The Suto use the former but not the latter concept. In Liberia the Grebo people speak of a low-pitched voice as *heavy*, and a high one as *light*. Contrary to the other cases we have cited, they also use this concept in describing the relative pitches both in speech and in song. Thus they use the conception of *weight* to the exclusion of all others.

Three more Ewe terms are of interest. When a cantor starts singing people may exclaim, '*Gbe na dze ga dzi*' which means 'Sing in a *pleasing* way'. 'Pleasing', says Mr. Tay, means to sing on time, at the right speed and with a beautiful voice. People may also say, '*Akowogbe, akowogbe*' to encourage him. This really means 'Sweet as a parrot'[1] (*akowo* = parrot: *gbe* = voice): or they may say, '*Aloewogbe, aloewogbe*' which means 'Sweet as a lark'. This bird-simile seems to have some bearing on the conception not only of timbre but also of pitch. In

---

[1] 'To sing like a parrot' is the common idiom in Islamic poetry to praise a person's voice. The idea is thus not confined to Africa. We cannot understand why the parrot of all birds should be singled out as the epitome of the melodic aesthetic!

Northern Rhodesia, young boys like to feel they are adults by trying to sing at the pitch of a man's voice: it is very hard to persuade them to sing treble. We found that adjurations to 'sing high' were not understood: but immediately we said, 'Sing like a bird', the boys sang in their proper treble register. To take another instance, in the Grebo tribe just referred to, the usual simile for good singing is, 'You sing sweetly like a Bletoo bird'. The use of this bird-simile is interesting for several reasons. As it is used by Western peoples and by the Islamic world and by Africans, it is obviously widespread. In Africa not always the same bird is chosen: does the geographical distribution of birds account entirely for this, or are there tribal preferences? Further, we in the West have an 'octave-mentality'. Within reason, however high or low the notes if they are in unison we find no difficulty in recognizing their kinship. The African thinks much more in terms of the actual pitch of a note. He knows nothing consciously of octaves. It is therefore surprising that he should recognize in the usually high-pitched call of a bird a sound which is suitable to be compared with his own voice.

In the case of the pitch of drums, the Ewe mental pictures are the same as those for speech. In tuning a drum you strike it and say to yourself, 'Is it *gbega* or *gbevi*?', that is, 'Does it give a *big* tone (= low note) or a *small* tone (= high note)?' You will know by custom and the sense of absolute pitch, the 'just' pitch for that drum. You can go on tuning till you can exclaim '*Egbe lenu*' which implies that the drum now has its proper clear tone and pitch with the required responsiveness to the various notes produced by the different kinds of drum-beat. Two other terms may be mentioned, though not directly concerned with pitch. If the drum is hopelessly out of tune, you say it is '*kpo-kpokpo*', indicating that it sounds as if the skin is not properly dried. You may use the term '*kpoto-kpoto*' meaning that the drum is out of tune and more particularly that it needs water (see the Tuning of Drums).

This application of the concept of size to the musical range of instruments is not confined to the Ewe, in fact we believe it will be found to be general in Africa. Hugh Tracey makes too wide a generalization when he says, 'Where Europeans talk of "high" and "low" pitch, in our Bantu languages we say "small" and "great".' When he is referring to musical instruments, his words are true provided they refer to the individual notes sounded by themselves and not to their relative position in the musical scale. But he later uses this concept in speaking of vocal music: we do not think the concept holds good here.[1]

[1] H. T. Tracey, *Ngoma*, Longmans Green, 1948, p. 19, cf. p. 55.

The Lala tribe of Northern Rhodesia (in the Bantu area) in referring to the individual metal prongs of their Kalimba (usually known to Europeans as the Kaffir piano) speak of the high-sounding prongs as giving a *small* sound. Yet in contrasting the sounds of the prongs in the process of tuning the instrument, they use the concept 'higher' instead of 'smaller' for the upper note sounded.[1]

The conclusion of the whole matter is that the Ewe use two concepts. The natural pitch and quality of a voice is defined in terms of *size*: the intervals actually used by the voice in speech or song or by an instrument are defined in terms of *height*. Such evidence as we have, indicates that these concepts are also used fairly widely in Africa.

[1] A. M. Jones, 'The Kalimba of the Lala Tribe, Northern Rhodesia', in *Africa*, Oct. 1950, pp. 329–30. On p. 329 we endorse Tracey's generalization: we wish to retract the statement and to substitute the more limited use of 'big' and 'small' discussed above.

11

THE NEO-FOLK-MUSIC

IT was about the year 1940 that we in Northern Rhodesia became aware that a new sort of music was coming into the country, though it had been generating elsewhere for some decades before that. It quickly captivated the young Africans in schools and the young men and women in mine and town compounds. At first many of the words of the new songs were in Sindebele which proclaimed apparently the South African origin of this music. It was not long, however, before Cibemba, Cinyanja, and other of the Central African languages took its place. What started as an occasional item in a school or compound concert grew with astonishing rapidity and has now become the standard form of recreational music used by the urbanized African of some education and the student class in Central and Southern Africa. Meanwhile, exactly the same sort of music has arisen not only in East Africa and Uganda but right over the other side of the continent in West Africa. Here it is called '*High Life*' : in Uganda they call it '*Cheta*', while in Northern Rhodesia it was first called '*Makwaya*' (= Ma-Choir) but developing from this *Makwaya* there have been a succession of dance forms each with a distinctive name such as '*Saba-saba*'. At one time in the middle forties, so great was the craze in our schools that frequent and lengthy concerts consisting of twenty-four or more of these dance-songs each of which needed quite a lot of practice were a regular feature of school life. By those familiar with the real traditional folk-music of Africa, this new tradition is instantly recognizable. The essential basis of the new tradition is European, but this Western musical framework is clad in African dress. From the point of view of its European basis this music would not merit consideration in a treatise on African music, but such is the way the African handles it, and so completely has he made the new music his own, and so copious and widespread is the creative urge behind it pouring out a flood of new songs almost from month to month right up and down and across Africa, that one is compelled to treat this music seriously. It is nothing less than a neo-folk tradition and at the present bids fair almost if not completely to displace the traditional music of Africa in towns and compounds and schools. It has even begun to penetrate the country villages and one can now attend a village festivity, for instance in the Lala area east of Broken Hill in Northern Rhodesia, only to find that the music is no longer the old drumming and dancing, but this neo-folk-music of *Makwaya*, *Mganda*, and the like.

But there is another reason why necessity compels us to study it if we are to have a clear grasp of what the traditional music of Africa is and what it is not. Nowadays not only commercial recording companies but Colonial broadcasting officers, to say nothing of anthropologists and other field-workers, make a good many disk and tape recordings of African music. It is natural that sound engineers prefer where possible to call in musicians to a studio where the best recording conditions prevail rather than to go round the villages and produce recordings of second-rate technical quality. Thus it is that the majority of records on sale which purport to be African music are records made by urbanized Africans and are not traditional folk-music at all. While such is the vogue among Africans for records of this neo-folk-music that a field-worker right in the heart of the bush must be very careful in recording or else he will find that what he has been given is this new style music. The Broadcasting Officer at Lusaka told us that during a recent up-country recording tour when he made over four hundred recordings, less than a quarter of these were of traditional music and he had to struggle hard even to get these. Such a proportion does not represent the relative distribution of the new and the old, for taking things by and large, the bulk of African music is still in the traditional idiom.[1] So it is essential that anyone taking a serious interest in African music should know how to differentiate the two traditions. The best way to do this is to study some of this neo-folk-music in detail, but as it exists in such a new world of its own, we will first discuss the matter in a general way.

We believe that the new music owes its origin to the conditions of urban life and in particular to the presence in African town compounds of a Recreation Hall built in the European style

[1] From the commercial standpoint, the sales-value of a neo-folk recording is far and away in excess of that of real traditional music.

complete with a theatrical stage with wings and footlights. The African being a born imitator and noting the European custom of going to concerts where practised performers mount a stage while the bulk of the people sit passively watching in rows of seats, has set himself to produce the same sort of thing within the framework of his own culture. Further, in the towns, he has seen Europeans dancing and has caught the lilt of a fox-trot and all the usual and often banal popular American and European dance rhythms: he has learnt in the towns to sing his version of the latest American song-hits.[1] He has assimilated the basic features of our Western popular dance tradition and then created within the framework of African social life and musical thought something which is in essence on the same lines, and which is, therefore, in its roots quite un-African. Where the real genuine village dance is a corporate social occasion in which everyone takes part and there are normally no professional performers, the new form in essence is exhibitionist. It demands that the majority of people should be spectators and listeners rather than participants. The old tradition does of course have a place, and an honoured place for professionalism especially in solo dancing: but the notion that social recreation should take the form of the bulk of the people looking on at a display given by 'concert artists' is something quite new.

What is extraordinary about the growth of this new music is that it does not seem to have originated in any one place and then spread over the continent. While we in Central Africa see clearly that our *Makwaya* has come up from South Africa, we have no direct cultural contact with Uganda: and it seems most unlikely that there could have been a musico-cultural link between South Africa and West Africa. Yet all young Africa has started doing the same sort of thing. It seems as if, for some unknown reason, the impact of American jazz and Western four-part harmony have suddenly produced more or less all over Africa a simultaneous urge to create the same sort of derivative music.

It is rather difficult to pin down and to describe the form of this

---

[1] Hugh Tracey puts it like this. Our teaching of Western music to Africa has gone awry and young Africans turn to the popular American form of it as it contains something they find agreeable. He stresses the influence of American *films*, and instances the comparable case of the sale of gramophone records in the Mombasa area in East Africa. Recently the sale of Indian records to Africans has been greater than that of all other records put together. This is said to be because of the large number of Indian films they see.

music because it is of such rapid growth and the cult is so alive
and creative that one never knows what form it will take a year
hence. This is thoroughly African: the words of a song may be
varied as occasion demands, and every dancer at a village gathering will have, and indeed invent, a special style of his own, while
the music and drumming of any one dance will gradually change
with the years. No African could bind down his artistic soul to
a fixed choreography, and this attitude to singing and dancing is
maintained on the whole in the new style.

Broadly speaking the earlier form of the new style was this: a
man would gather his friends (or a schoolmaster his more musical
pupils) and form a choir. At first, in Rhodesia at least, this was
a male pastime but after a few years the girls took it up also. The
choir sings special songs in four-part harmony as a spectacle at
a concert or gathering. It may be static, and for this purpose the
choir prefers to sing not in the open but indoors and on a proper
concert platform where the choir comes on the stage in column
of fours singing a 'signature tune' of its own choosing, which is
a *Makwaya* song, goes round the stage, and with various movements of the ranks suggested by the artistic whim of the owner
of the choir it draws up in line, about four deep, facing the
audience, and sings *in situ* one or more other *Makwaya* songs.
This done, at a signal from the leader it turns into column of fours
and sings itself off the stage. A typical concert will consist of two
dozen or more similar performances given by five or six different
choirs, each owing allegiance to a different leader and each
known by a usually bombastic and slightly quaint name, for instance, 'The Twelve Champions Choir' or 'The Nsenga Victory
Choir'. Often each choir will have some special insignia such as
a uniform dress (e.g. all in white shorts), or a coloured sash. On
the other hand the choir may not be static but processional, which
is usually the case at an outdoor gathering. At such times the choir
assembles some distance from the gathering and goes on a processional route chosen for its spectacular possibilities, often with
a home-made flag carried on a thin long bush-pole in front. The
leader (and here we suspect the influence of the military) marches
at the side of this column which may be in twos or in fours, keeps
it in step, and acts as a cantor, for during the whole time of the
procession the choir is singing *Makwaya* songs. The leader loves
to show off and there is an indefinable air of 'Here come the

champion singers from So-and-so's village'. All this sounds and seems as if it is striking at the very roots of the indigenous folk-music tradition and yet in a way it is not. It is an expression of elements all found in that tradition coupled with features drawn from the white man's ways.

What we have just described is the earliest form of the *Makwaya*. After a few years—in the middle forties in Northern Rhodesia—the *Makwaya* became more stylized and a new 'professional' element appeared. This was an exceedingly clever imitation of Western tap-dancing. To call it an imitation is really a misnomer, for though the pit-a-pat sounds of the feet and the general body movements are obviously drawn from the music-hall, the means by which they are achieved are totally and triumphantly African. Some of this tap-dancing is incredibly clever and it is all and always built on thoroughly African conceptions of rhythm. But the fact that these 'steps' are entirely unlike anything to be seen in a village dance and that they depend for their effect on considerable precision, shows that the new tradition is basically a concert-hall art form. When the choirs do songs with 'steps' they wear shoes in order to get clear and incisive tapping. They only do this kind of thing indoors and on a stage. They come on as before and range themselves behind the footlights: the leader starts a *Makwaya* song which the choir takes up and sings several times. The leader then blows a whistle and without any singing the whole choir performs the 'step' which sounds to be in a sort of African free-rhythm. Occasionally the leader blows the whistle as a signal for a change of step-pattern, and after a time suddenly up goes every-one's leg, the whole choir stands motionless for a few seconds and the dance is over. What is not apparent during this performance is that this free-sounding tap-dance is in reality rigidly constructed round the rhythm of the preceding song and that this song is running in the heads of the dancers all through the 'step'. It is this hidden cross-rhythm which so captivates both performers and audience: they are all aware of it and we think the audience is thrilled just as much, if not more, by the consciousness of this rhythmic clash as by the virtuosity of the actual tap-dancing itself. Without being informed, an observer would be unlikely to guess that this is what underlies the performance. The leader of a choir occupies his position by virtue of the fact that he is particularly gifted both in the ability to hold the song-rhythm in his head and in the actual tap-dancing itself and so can be relied upon not to make a mistake. A good leader not only remembers and reproduces 'steps' he has seen done by other choirs but can compose 'steps' of his own to suit any song. Thus a *Makwaya* concert which to the European appears to consist of a boring succession of turns all doing more or less the same thing, can give much pleasure to an African audience.

On the scene there now enters the guitar bought from a European music shop. The young African of today has claimed this instrument as his own. He has taught himself to play it in his own way, and he uses it to accompany songs and dances of the neo-folk tradition. It is everywhere—in schools and towns and mines, on railway platforms and in trains. Now this has had a strong influence on the development of *Makwaya* away from corporate music-making by a group to solo work. Generally speaking, the guitar player is a solo singer and is his own accompanist: at other times he is a solo player for a new-style dance danced by a party of enthusiasts. This has made the choirs rather old fashioned: they have been virtually dropped and everyone is now playing and singing guitar songs at concerts. So the move is still further away from village recreational music, from the communal song-dance-drumming, to the solo concert performer. Yet even when this is said, the guitar still occupies in one way a traditional place in African music. In the old days, in Central Africa, personal music-making for one's own enjoyment had a definite place: the instrument was the *Kalimba*, *Ndandi*, or *Kaffir piano*—a metallophone with a calabash resonator whose tuned metal prongs were plucked by the thumbs. The *Kalimba* is now nearly gone, but the guitar has, for this purpose, taken its place. The young man who in the old days could be seen walking dreamily along with a pre-occupied look in his face playing his *Kalimba* and crooning softly to himself is now succeeded by just such a young man filled with the same emotions—they used to say it was love which prompted it—doing the same thing on a guitar but doing it all in the new style music. Anyone buying a record of 'African music' which contains guitar playing will know at once that he has a record not of indigenous African folk-music but of the new tradition.[1]

[1] Some of the tribes in West Africa—the Ewe in Ghana for example—have gone a stage further. They are now 'swinging' in their dance bands some of their *traditional* songs.

The rhythmic basis of the new style is entirely Western. It is usually a four-square common time. The old *Makwaya* songs made no attempt to disguise this common time. With the passing of the years this rhythmically threadbare basis has been clothed by the African in various ways so as to secure the piquance of the irregular rhythm he so loves. In songs of the *Saba-saba* type rhythmic interest is provided by simple syncopation in the manner of jazz. Mr. Leonard Kombe, one of our teaching staff, told us that if a tune like '*Naŋgu mu mpate*' (Fig. 3) is sung without the syncopation it would be very dull to an African. We took the opportunity, while talking about this, of giving him several examples of syncopation of the usual early jazz sort. He was able to sing them straight away with the greatest of ease and at the same time to keep his hand beating to the fundamental four-beats-in-a-bar. It was quite clear that this sort of jazz syncopation is entirely understood by and congenial to the musical mind of Bantu Africans. With the craze for novelty, the simple syncopation is giving way to more recognizably African devices of rhythm but whatever rhythms he employs in this neo-folk-music they must all fit into and be controlled by the underlying four-square European common time. This of course cramps his freedom of rhythmic invention but also calls forth an extraordinary resourcefulness. It is quite remarkable how un-European some of these tunes can sound, yet basically they are European and not African in their rhythmic framework.

From the point of view of its basic rhythm this new music compared with the kaleidoscopic variety of rhythms in the real folk-music is unutterably banal. It is a pathetic degradation and denial of the priceless African heritage. There are indications, however, that the African himself is dissatisfied with the limitations of this European rhythmic ground-bass and the more recent creations in the new style seem to be trying to recapture the genuine African rhythmic freedom. If this is to be so, all will be well and the African will produce a new music based on a fusion of East and West which will be of real merit. Meanwhile we must wait and watch.

The second characteristic of the neo-folk-music is its harmony. Whereas the indigenous African harmony is in *organum*, since the advent of Christian missions and with the spread of Government and Mission schools, young Africans have heard and have been taught to sing songs and hymns in Western harmony. This musical experience has the most profound effect on Africans who are a very musical race. They are not particularly attracted to a normal European four-part song because, we think, the harmony moves too fast from one chord to another. They want above all to savour, relish, and linger upon the gorgeous sound made by a diatonic triad: the simpler the progression, the better they appreciate it. The wonder is that the vast majority of Africans who make this music have had no training in our theory of harmony, yet nevertheless they get the results.

The normal chords used, and their usual sequence, are these: diatonic triads on the tonic, subdominant, dominant, tonic. This sequence will be sung in song after song or played on the guitar for hours on end.[1] The melody varies and so may its rhythm: but the underlying four-square pattern is this steady sequence of triads. There is a frequent use of the 6/4 5/3 on the dominant preceding the tonic triad as an authentic cadence. This, and the first inversion of the triad on the supertonic, are the most common inversions used in singing, all other chords being in root position. The guitar makes use of the familiar dominant pedal in this sort of music:

Appoggiatura and passing notes and occasionally chords other than those we have given occur, but on the whole what one hears in singing or on the guitar is the eternal sequence we have quoted.

The Africans themselves claim this music as their own, though any African musician knows perfectly well that it is European in origin, and they, just like the European student of their music, need only hear a couple of bars or so, to be able to declare whether or no it is the old or the new style.

Let us now consider some examples of the music. Fig. 1 is a typical *Makwaya* song of the early period, say the late nineteen-thirties. We have given the complete song, which is sung over

[1] This same sequence of chords is used by Respighi in his setting of Gianoncelli's 'Bergamasca' (No. 4 of the 2nd Suite of Old Italian Airs by Ottorino Respighi). There are thirty pages of score composed almost entirely of this sequence, and the whole dance is therefore curiously reminiscent of *makwaya* music.

and over again generally dozens of times. The song consists of
two phrases each containing four bars of 2/4 time, the first phrase
being divided into two sub-phrases of two bars each. The harmony

FIG. 1. ♩ = 108   *Bemba. N. Rhodesia*

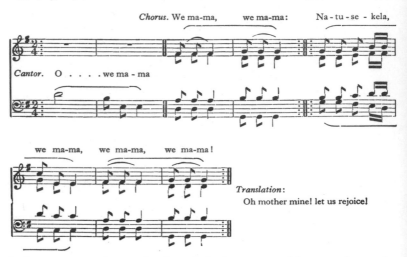

Translation:
Oh mother mine! let us rejoice!

is European, using only the triads in root position on the tonic,
subdominant, and dominant, except for the second half of the
fifth bar where the harmony is dictated by African practice. This
is not the only African feature in the song. The use of a cantor
to sing the first phrase, which is then taken up and completed by
the chorus: then the repetition of this section: then the singing
by the chorus of a second phrase joining straight on to the repetition
of the first: and finally the repetition of the second phrase itself—
all these are genuine African folk-music idiom, and the form

$$(A+B)+(A+B)+C+C$$

is one of the standard ways of singing an ordinary village song
of the old type. The harmony in the second half of bar 5 is really
incidental and arises from two clichés beloved of the African in the
new style, one in the bass and the other in the tenor. The bass progression from tonic to subdominant in a form and time like this:

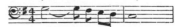

is often used and the Africans seem to love the feel of tripping
down from tonic to subdominant on this running glide. Similarly,

African tenors in the new style have their own pet loves, one of which is a delight in producing the typical high sound of a tenor voice in relation to the other singers. It is this characteristic of European tenor singing which has struck them most. Perhaps arising directly from this, the African tenors have a fondness for dwelling on the dominant: to them it sounds very 'tenor-ish'.

These tenor and bass lines are improvised by the choir leader if he does not know them by heart. He has heard the song some- where and remembers the words and treble. When he wants his choir to sing it he will probably teach the treble line, which is almost always sung an octave lower in Africa if the choir is a male one. While they are singing he will vamp a bass himself and finding a good version, will teach this: and the same with the tenor. Thus the progression in bar 5 emerges fortuitously from setting a bass cliché to the treble and then finding a tenor line which also suits it. The similar motion of tenor and treble is derived from the normal custom of African harmony in parallel intervals. The same remarks apply also to the alto in this bar which is pure village practice—in parallel fourths with the treble. The third chord in this bar, the secondary seventh on the leading note is a chord entirely unrecognized by the African. Even in the new style he would never think deliberately and consciously of such a chord. It simply arises in passing: the two points of interest and relish for the African are the tonic chord at the beginning of bar 5 and the subdominant chord at the beginning of bar 6. In the first chord of bar 6, why does not the tenor sing E? One thing is certain and that is that he is not thinking of making a discord. We think it is just another case of adaptation from European practice. The tenor line, including the dissonant D, does sound quite like the real thing, and if it happens to produce a dissonance at one point, well no one notices it and anyway most of it is all right and it gets there in the end.

A song like this gives enormous satisfaction to the singers, who linger on the luscious diatonic common chord harmonies with undisguised relish. One can see by studying the translation of the words, that they are unimportant and serve only as a vehicle for the part-singing.

For our second example we move from Northern Rhodesia some 500 miles north-east to the Henga tribe at the north-western end of Lake Nyasa (Fig. 2). The song was actually recorded at

Blantyre Secondary School by a mixed 'choir' with the trebles singing in the true treble register and only a bass accompaniment

FIG. 2. ♩= 130   *Henga. Nyasaland*

as far as we could tell from the disk (Gallotone GB 1173 T). But even with the absence of the inside parts the harmonic intention is clear. Once more the time is four-square. The whole song has not been given in this example but sufficient has been transcribed to show the style. Here again we have a cantor and chorus which latter, on repeat, extends its phrases. The whole of the extract consists of three phrases, arranged thus:

$$(A+B)+(A+B)+C: (A+B)+(A+B)+C: D: D$$

Looking at Fig. 2 we observe that in bars 5, 6, and 7 the outline scheme of harmony is:

Here once again is the inevitable tonic, subdominant, dominant, tonic in the bass. The *appoggiatura* bar 6 producing a major seventh on the subdominant and also the 6/4 5/3 on the dominant leading to a final tonic triad are also very typical and frequently used. But there is a further point. There is a subtle flavour about this new-style harmony resulting from the *function* of the subdominant and dominant chords. These often occur as points of rest to which the preceding notes tend: so also does the 6/4 on the dominant before its resolution, and the melody in the treble often emphasizes this by the use of short imitative phrases: bars 5 and 6 are a good example. The number of these *makwaya* songs is just uncountable. Owing to the basically similar harmonic structure, to hear one is to feel that one has heard them all, yet in fact they are different in detail.

Figure 3, a *Saba-saba* song, was in 1950 one of the modern ball-room dances of the younger generation of Africans in Northern Rhodesia. At the time, we did not transcribe the accompaniment.

FIG. 3. ♩ = 78   *Saba Saba. Bemba. N. Rhodesia, 1950*

We have, however, indicated in Fig. 3 the chordal progression of the harmonies as we remember them.

The whole style of the song is on the face of it un-African. It is slow, and is sung with heartfelt and wistful sentimentality: Africans in the villages simply do not sing like this. The words of their songs are often nostalgic, but melody in the old folk-music is markedly impersonal: time is not used to express emotion—a very sad subject may well be sung allegro. The sort of sentimental singing with languorous face and body movements exhibited in *Saba-saba* are features of the new style and have been taken over with warm-hearted enthusiasm from American crooning.

At the beginning of bars 1, 2, 4, 6, and 8 there are runs of three quavers. An African friend, Mr. Kombe says the Africans very much appreciate these little runs and their imitative recurrence during the song. He further said that if the syncopation were flattened out a bit in this way:

the song would be very dull. The syncopation, then, does occupy an important place: in this particular song it not only causes the rhythm of the melody to be well crossed with the underlying common time of the accompaniment, but it also provides the words with a melody which follows the relative time-lengths of the syllables in ordinary speech very closely.

Still another point of interest lies in the four repetitions of the word *mama*: all four have a slightly different rhythmic treatment. This gives piquance to the melody but it also reflects the African's traditional love of slight and subtle variation in his old music.

We now go back to *Makwaya* songs which have a 'step', of which two examples are given (Figs. 4 and 5). The particular interest attaching to these is that in both cases the step was actually composed by a creatively musical African boy who was then in our college and we had an opportunity of discovering at first hand the various factors involved. We take Fig. 4 first. The whole song with the words, which are in Cinsenga, together with the step were composed by Mako Mataliyana, himself a Munsenga, aged about 20, who had spent some time on the Copperbelt in Northern Rhodesia and so had come in close contact with the new style. He says he first made the song and then the steps. He chose as

Fig. 4. ♩ = 150

Introduction

Zani muwone   *Mako Mataliyana. Nsenga Tribe. Dec. 1947*

Za - ni mu-wo-ne a-nya - ma - ta mchi-fi-la, Za - ni

Za - ni

STEP I

Leg up

his dancing party two boys about 16 years old, who were specially good at it, one a Mulala and the other a Mubemba. The singing was done by these three augmented by a choir of students of similar age or rather older. The translation of the song is, 'Come and see the boys at the meeting (sc. concert)'. Mako says that the tune may be harmonized in any way that strikes the singers at the time of performance. Here we see that freedom of improvisation so characteristic of village music. He says it might, for instance, be sung in parallel thirds. Having heard so much *makwaya* we are quite certain that it would generally be sung in the sort of way set out below: the harmonies are ours:

However, the real interest lies in the step. The song is sung three times and then the step starts immediately. During the step there is no singing at all. The leader has to keep the song running in his head all the time he is dancing because he uses the song as an inaudible time-line. To show the relationship between the step and the song, the latter is transcribed in full in Fig. 4, but it must be understood that this is only for analytical purposes and there is never any singing or music of any kind while the tap-dancing is performed. Mako says that while the leader concentrates his mind on the song, the other dancers are thinking only of the step. This no doubt accounts for the regularity and extreme precision of the syncopation. They are thinking of the step rhythm as the main rhythm: hence its notable vitality.

The dancers are lined up on the stage facing the audience with the leader, holding a whistle, at the dancers' left end. They wear shoes with leather soles and heels so as to make clear taps: and they are usually dressed alike, with white or coloured shirts, and shorts or trousers, preferably the latter. They use the typical arm and body movements of the European or American tap dancer, the arms held well clear of the sides and the body bent slightly forward, with the eyes usually fixed on their feet. The dancers are utterly concentrated on producing a synchronous and very strongly emphasized rhythm-pattern with their feet, for which purpose they use both toe and heel, but mainly the whole sole of the foot. They occasionally turn through an angle of 90 degrees, clockwise, and arrange that they will turn to the front in the last section of the dance. At some of the longer pauses, they cock one leg up forward, holding the stance till they are about to carry on dancing. The beginning of a change of step is sometimes anticipated by a jump with both feet coming down on the stage together exactly on time, a few beats before the new pattern starts. All the steps are fairly fast, and right at the end of the dance on the final tap, they alight on one foot, shoot the free leg forward, and at this precise moment shout a triumphant 'Wo' in a descending voice exactly as in Morris dancing, from which our own boys may have copied the custom, and remain balanced in this position for some seconds while the applause starts.

With Fig. 4 at hand for reference, we now consider the analysis of the step. The song having been sung three times by the dancers and chorus, the leader blows the whistle and the dancers dance the introduction pattern. This is repeated three times. It is mostly triple, but its first main beat does not coincide with the first main beat of the song: it is purposely staggered in typical African fashion. This strong beat does in fact occur on one of the song's *weak* beats. This introduction occupies three verses of the song. The whistle blows again and the first step is begun and is danced four times, the last time with a *Coda* attached (bar 13), on the final beat of which all cock the free leg up and stay motionless awhile. The first step occupies four verses of the song. Like the introduction, this first step is composed of step-phrases which extend over twelve quavers. The exceptions to this are the two extra taps when it starts, and the *coda* which is of six quavers time-length. This first step is a mixture of 3/8 and 3/4 time as contrasted with the common time of the song, and is again arranged so that the first strong accent of its pattern does not coincide with the first strong beat of the song. As the first step's pattern is a phrase of twelve quavers (i.e. six crotchets), and as it is staggered against a song with four crotchets to a bar, its repeats lie athwart the song in different positions, but this does not present any difficulty at all to the African dancers. A curious feature of the starting-point of the steps is that the introduction as well as Steps 1, 2, and 4 (neglecting the preliminary semiquaver hop to get them going) all actually start their pattern on the initial note of the song, which is an accented one, though their first two taps are unaccented.

The whistle blows just as the song is about to repeat again (bar 17), and everyone jumps in the air, bringing both feet down and holding the stance 'at the alert' for the interlude. This interlude is a piece of pure Africanism, for it is in common time which however does not coincide with the common time of the song but lies exactly half-way athwart it, and the leader makes sure that this shall be so by calling out, 'One... Two... Three... Four...' at the beginning of each of the tap-dancers' quadruple bars. The interlude is done four times, the last beat of the last repetition (bar 21) being interrupted to start the second step whose pattern-phrase covers a length of fourteen quavers and is danced three times. Its first accented beat coincides with the third beat of the song's bar, so for once there is a coalescence of accent. It is a cleverly arranged step, for though its phrase-length is not the same as that of the song, yet it does secure that a good number of its accents fall on accented beats of the song, though on each repetition, owing to the difference in phrase-length of song and step, these beats are not the same ones. The second step leads straight into the third step (bar 27) which is different from the others in that it is not repeated and consists of a longer phrase. It is really a repeat of Step 2 with the addition of a triple motif at the end. After this there is a break lasting for one complete verse of the song (bars 31 and 32), and then the last step, Step 4, starts. This is rather unlike the others because it has a special beginning (bar 33) and a special end (bars 43–46).

Another remarkable point in the score is where the third repetition ends and the fourth starts, that is, near the point marked 'P' on the score (bar 40). The semiquaver under P and the three notes following it are clearly the end of one of the repetitions as may be verified by comparing it with the two preceding ones. But if you start reading at P itself, and not at the end of the repetition, you will observe that from this point to the end of the next repetition, you have a duplicate of the first version of Step 4, that is, the one danced when this step entered. There is here, therefore, a telescoping—an overlapping of the end of one repetition with the beginning of another. This overlapping technique is once more thoroughly African.

The last place of interest is the last four bars of the tap dance (bars 45 and 46). They consist of two triple bars followed by a duple one and secure that the close of the dance actually coincides with a main beat of the song. Now the actual rhythm of this concluding tap-phrase is an African cliché of doubtless ancient vintage. We ourselves knew of it in the early nineteen-thirties and it existed in West Africa before that date—in fact it was in Africa long before the new style was thought of, at least in Northern Rhodesia. For instance, in a traditional dance called 'Imbeni' the first drum beats a mainly triple rhythm against the quadruple time of the second drum. In order to bring the triple phrase into line with the second drummer, the first man uses the same pattern as the step we are considering, thus:

Imbeni dance   *Bemba tribe: N. Rhodesia, 1933*

Again in a Pangwe xylophone and chorus music from West Africa[1] which was certainly being played before 1929 when it was transcribed, we get:

Here is the same cliché used to bring the two xylophones and the voice, whose rhythms are staggered, into line at the end of the phrase.

Reviewing the 'steps' of Fig. 4 as a whole they do look like a piece of rhythmic virtuosity: and yet they are not, for any party of school lads, in the late nineteen-forties could do this sort of thing. The remarkable point about the whole score is the fusion of completely African dance technique with the strait jacket imposed by the underlying four-square European-type song: four-square not only in bar-time but also in its phrase-length of two bars. Here we see one feature of the new style which has a deep attraction for the African. In spite of the banal European sound of the *makwaya* songs themselves, the step attached to the song does give the performers a chance to exploit the very same techniques they use in their traditional music. The wonder is that a step built on so entirely African and un-European lines, can look and sound so very much like the ordinary tap dance with which we in the West are familiar. But if one were to ask which is better—the European or the African 'step'—it must surely be conceded that the African has evolved a method of tap-dancing whose rhythmic construction is far more interesting than is ours and far more subtle.

Our final example, Fig. 5, is frankly a hybrid, but just because it is, it provided an instructive opportunity to see just what the African creative instinct was capable of in artificial circumstances. In writing our annual College play, it was decided in 1948 to include a burlesque of an African village school. To be up to date

[1] Quoted by E. von Hornbostel in *Africa*, vol. i, No. 1, 1928: and see also A. M. Jones, *African Music*, Appendix 3.

FIG. 5.   *Burlesque 'Makwaya' Song from 'The Charlatan', 1948.*

♩ = 160. *Accents* = ´

Step

(Feet) { R
       { L   R L R L R L R &c.   L

Song

There's no - thing we love more than frac - tions,   Un -

- less   it's a de - ci - mal dot, Per - cent - a - ges have their at -

- trac - tions And graphs are a plea - sure to plot: But the

si - ni - ster de - tails we'll spare yer Of cir - cum - ference, vol - ume and

a - rea.   Yes the si - ni - ster de - tails we'll spare yer   Of cir-

CHORUS

this entailed, of course, a burlesque *makwaya* song. The tune was ours: banal it had to be because these tunes always are: and we were careful to preserve the usual four-square rhythm, and in the main, the inevitable chordal sequence. Having taught it to the cast, we wondered if any one could produce a 'step' to complete the verisimilitude. We called for Mako Mataliyana who said he thought he could do something if given time. Only a few days had passed when he came to say he had made a 'step', which he then taught to four other boys. The 'step' he produced and taught with complete success is set out in Fig. 5. Here we have a song entirely composed by Europeans with a step added by an African. The four verses of the song, interspersed with a chorus in four-part harmony were sung by the dancers in turn, the chorus being a separate body of non-dancing singers in the background. There was a piano accompaniment played by the author. After the second and last verses, in accordance with *makwaya* custom the singing stopped, the leader blew the whistle and the step started. A novel departure from precedent was that we continued to play the song on the piano during the step. The only person who really needed practice in accomplishing this was the pianist. We found it so difficult that the only way we could manage it was to be most un-African. We virtually ignored the dancers and concentrated on trying to play our notes in metronomically exact time. We confess to this inadequacy: what we ought to have been able to do was to hear with ease and mastery both their rhythms and ours so that there should be a real co-operation between piano and dancers.

The score of the tap-dancing shows that while it gives the effect of the fast foot-work and syncopated accented taps of the conventional white man's practice yet at the same time the rhythms are truly crossed with that of the song in the real African way. A careful scrutiny of the tap-dance score will reveal the five main means employed. We start by looking at the first three bars of sections B and B', and the first two bars of C (bars 5, 9, and 13): from these we find that Mako takes the first three notes only of the 4/4 bar of the song and sets against them two bars of 3/8 time: in other words what we have here is simply dancing 2 against 3. To keep this triple time in line with the song, the dancers insert a short bar of two quavers to cover the fourth beat of the quadruple song-bar. That this is what is happening may be seen by looking at the whole of sections B and B', where this process is repeated three times in each section. The C sections show the same thing happening at first, but a different method is used to complete the phrase. While we are looking at sections B and B', it is worth while noting that each of the tap-phrases covers two lines of the song, giving a length of thirty-two quavers, which is just the right length for a bout of tap-dancing, and each starts with a crotchet step on the initial note of the relevant line in the song.

We next look at the second half of section C (bar 14). The first half of section C starts exactly like section B. Then it differs: in the second half, the accented beats of section C coincide with those of the song but the whole 3/4 bar is staggered with the song-bar, starting one beat before the latter. This is typical traditional practice in drumming. If we now look at the second half of section A (bar 3) and the second half of C we again find this motif, though in section A it is now in duple time. But we are indeed surprised to find that this time it is moved just one quaver forward in relation to the song, so that its accents instead of falling on the song-beats, fall right between them.

The particular interest attaching to Fig. 5 is that in it we see the African working within limits deliberately prescribed by a European. It is in itself a justification of our thesis that *makwaya* consists of the application of African musical techniques to a framework essentially European in character: for the 'step' in this hybrid piece is exactly the same sort of thing as the step in Fig. 4.

There is an astonishing precision in these *makwaya* performances. Though we have occasionally seen junior or less musical members of a choir lose the step for a bit, we have never known the step to break down in performance. Taking each tap-phrase of Fig. 5 separately, it would present no difficulty to a European tap dancer; yet one wonders how many of us could dance the complete score to a piano accompaniment of the song: it is just this point which shows the cleavage between African and European music. Taken individually, the rhythms used by Africans usually sound reasonable enough to us: but in their combination the African displays a subtlety in which we cannot begin to claim to be his equal.

Reviewing the *makwaya* step as a whole, we see that the 'step' enables the African to treat a four-square quadruple song in a way typical of his traditional music, using a mixture of duple and triple times and staggering the main beats of song and dance. What is indeed remarkable is that this combination of old African and modern American stage-dance technique should produce a show which, both to look at and to hear, is exactly like the article it imitates. It is a piece of genius on the part of the African to be able to get this result from the ingredients he uses.

This chapter has been concerned merely with the bases of the neo-folk-music: it is not intended to be a complete survey. The study of the new music is really a subject on its own. What we have tried to show is first, the chief ways in which it differs from the traditional music, and second, that in spite of its basic difference, it is in some ways truly African. Banal though it is at present, and degrading an art form as it undoubtedly must appear to anyone knowing what Africans can really do in the villages, this neo-folk tradition is a vital one. It is a true fusion of Africa and the West.

APPENDIX
PERFORMANCE SCORES

Nota bene:

These performance scores give detailed information to *each separate player* in the drum ensemble, to show him what to do and how to do it.

They do not show exactly how these separate strands are combined in a full drumming.

They are therefore useless without a study of the full score in volume II. But once they have been mastered, and the way they make their entry has been observed from the full score, there is no reason—given the necessary skills—why a recognizable performance should not be attained.

NOTES ON THE TABLATURE

1. For the three zones of the drum skin see Chapter 2.

2. L = Left hand or stick: R = Right hand or stick.

3. ALL Stick-beats are Centre beats for all drums.

4. ATSIMEⱴU: all *Right* hand beats are Centre beats.
   Left hand: a Centre beat is always a Palm Beat.

5. Unless otherwise indicated, make all *hand* beats in Zone 3.

6. C   = Free Centre beat.

    CM   = Muted Centre beat.

    RD   = Play a Free beat with the stick on the wooden body of the drum.

    RMD = Play a Muted beat with the stick on the wooden body of the drum.

    SM   = Secondary Muted beat.

$\begin{cases} \text{R} \\ \text{SM2} \end{cases}$ = Play a Free Centre stick beat while muting with the left hand on the skin in Zone 2.

$\begin{cases} \text{R} \\ \text{F—S} \end{cases}$ = Play a Free beat with Right hand and immediately *after,*
      M   mute the drum with the Left hand: i.e. it is a delayed secondary muting.

    SMC = Secondary Muted Centre beat, i.e. play a Free beat and at the same time mute the skin in the centre with the other hand.

7. In playing, try to recapture the *pitch* of the beats as written on the music stave, and the lilt of the pattern.

8. In these performance scores, each drum pattern is integrated with the *Gankogui* to show their inter-relationship. This is all that *Kagaŋ* and the master drum need to worry about as beginners. But *Sogo* and *Kidi*, though preserving this relationship ought to think *primarily* of *answering the Master* at the right times. This correct attitude of mind will make all the difference to the spirit of the full performance.

NYAYITO
PATTERN A

ATSIMEVU—MASTER DRUM

Eve Tribe, Ghana

SOGO

* When Master *first enters* on Pattern A, Sogo plays the phrase *Kiya* four times instead of twice and then adds *woya kpe daga na abuya* (see full score). After that, Sogo keeps playing as above.

KIDI

* See note on *Sogo*. Kidi does the same (see full score).

KAGAŊ

Kagaŋ uses this pattern continuously throughout the dance until he plays the ending pattern.

Pattern B

ATSIMEVU—MASTER DRUM

ga   ki - to   ga   ki - to   gaze krebe ki-
L   L R   L   L R   L R RLR   L L
C   C SM   C   C SM   C F FFF   M

- to, gaze   kre kre ki-to a-dza.
  R   L R   RL   R L R L L
  M CM F   FF   F M SM CM CM
                     RMD RMD

SOGO

a - dza   a - dza
L   R   L   R
F   F   F   F

KIDI

a - dza   a - dza
RL RL   RL RL
FF FF   FF FF

KAGAŋ as for Pattern A

PATTERN C

ATSIMEVU—MASTER DRUM

SOGO

KIDI

a - tsi-bla go glɔ̃
L RLR R R L R L
M FF F F F M M M

klo go dɔ̃
R RLR R
M FF M M

KAGAŊ as for PATTERN A

PATTERN D

ATSIMEVU—MASTER DRUM

♩ = 113

(R = Stick:
L = Hand)

ga krebe - gi kide, ga krebe - gi kide,
L RLR L R R L RLR L R R
C FFF M F F C FFF M F F

gaga kin - kin, gaa - ga kin - kin, gaga kin - kin gaa - ga
L L R R L L R R L L R R L L
C C SMC SMC C C SMC SMC C C SMC SMC C C

kin - kin.
R R
SMC SMC

SOGO

KIDI (*a*) Short Version

(*b*) Full Version

KAGAŊ as for PATTERN A

PATTERN E

ATSIMEVU—MASTER DRUM

- hi - ve
R RL
M FM

hi - ve,
R RL
SM FM

ma-tro-go-do matsoe
L R   R L RL
F F   F F FF

ma-tro-go-do matsoe
L R R R L RL
F F F F F FM

matrogodo   matsoe
L R   R L RL
F F   F F FF

matrogodo   matsoe.
L R R R LRL
F F F F FFM

REPEAT

&c.

KAGAŊ as for PATTERN A

PATTERN F

ATSIMEVU—MASTER DRUM

♩ = 113

Gankogui $\frac{12}{8}$ $\left[\frac{6}{8}\right]$

Atsimevu

(R = Stick:
L = Hand)

kito
L R
C SM

kito
L R
C SM

kito krebe kito
L RRLR L R
C SM FFF CM SM

kito
L R
C SM

kito ga
L R L
C SM C

REPEAT

&c.

kito.
L R
C SM

SOGO

Gankogui

Sogo
(2 sticks)

ke de
L R
F F

KIDI

Gankogui

Kidi
(2 sticks)

kre - be
R L R L
F F F F

KAGAƞ as for PATTERN A

CHANGING SIGNALS

ATSIMEƲU—MASTER DRUM

♩ = 113   Signal I

Gankogui

AtsimeƲu

(R = Stick:
L = Hand)

kre   kre   kre,   &c.
RL   RL   RL
FF   FF   FF

Signal II

Gankogui

AtsimeƲu

krebe krebe &c.
RLR   RLR
FFF   FFF

Signal III

Gankogui

AtsimeƲu

toŋ   toŋ   toŋ,   &c.
R   R   R
F   F   F

SOGO

For all three Signals

Gankogui $\begin{bmatrix} 12 \\ 8 \end{bmatrix} \begin{bmatrix} 6 \\ 8 \end{bmatrix}$

Sogo

(2 sticks)

kre   kre   &c.
R L L   R L L
F M M   F M M

KIDI

For all three Signals

Gankogui $\begin{bmatrix} 12 \\ 8 \end{bmatrix} \begin{bmatrix} 6 \\ 8 \end{bmatrix}$

Kidi

(2 sticks)

kre   kre   &c.
R L L   R L L
F M M   F M M

KAGAŊ as for PATTERN A

ENDING PATTERN

ATSIMEVU—MASTER DRUM

♩ = 113

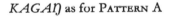

Gankogui $\begin{bmatrix} 12 \\ 8 \end{bmatrix} \begin{bmatrix} 6 \\ 8 \end{bmatrix}$

Atsimevu

(R = Stick: te - vlo   te - vlo   ga,   te - vlo   te - ga
L = Hand)   R L R   R L R   L   R L R   R L
            F F F   F   F F   CM   F F F   F   CM
                                   Hit with   Hit with
                                  side of Fist   side of Fist

SOGO

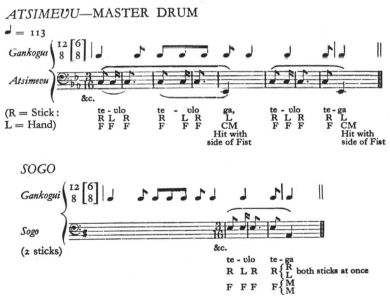

Gankogui $\begin{bmatrix} 12 \\ 8 \end{bmatrix} \begin{bmatrix} 6 \\ 8 \end{bmatrix}$

Sogo

(2 sticks)

&c.

te - vlo   te - ga
R L R   R { R / L } both sticks at once
F F F   F { M / M }

KIDI

Gankogui

Kidi
(2 sticks)

&c.

te - vlo   te - ga
R L R   R { R / L }   both sticks at once
F F F   F { M / M }

KAGAŊ

Gankogui

Kagaŋ
(2 sticks)

&c.

te - vlo   te - ga
R L R   R { R / L }   both sticks at once
F F F   F { M / M }

SOGBA OR SOGO
SOGBA SIGNAL

MASTER DRUM ONLY: _SOGO_ or _ATSIMEƲU_ [for Sogo transpose up to Key F]

Note. Gankogui is not played during this signal, but the master player keeps its beats in mind.

♩ = 204

Eve Tribe, Ghana

Gankogui
(not played)

Atsimevu

&c.

(R = Stick: gi - te - gi   ga-ga-ga,   gi - te - gi   gaa - ga-ga,   te-gi-de   ga te -
L = Hand)   L R L   L L L   L R L L   L L   R L R   L R
               M F M   C C C   M F M C   C C   F F F   C F

- gi-de   ga-ga   te-gi-de   ga   de   de   de   de   de   de   de*
  L R   L L   R L R   L   R   R   R   R   R   R   R
  F F   C C   F F F   C   F   F   F   F   F   F   F

* The beats 'de de' are continued until the entry of the first master pattern.

KIDI

While waiting for the first pattern, Kidi plays:

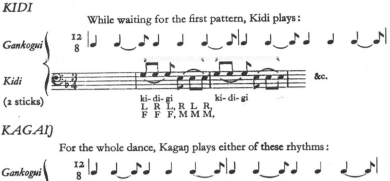

Gankogui

Kidi
(2 sticks)

ki- di- gi   ki- di- gi
L R L, R L R,
F F F, M M M,

KAGAŊ

For the whole dance, Kagaŋ plays either of these rhythms:

Gankogui

Kagaŋ
(2 sticks)

(a)   (b)
            OR

kagaŋ kagaŋ   kagaŋ kagaŋ
R R   R R   R R L R R L
F F   F F   F F F F F F

PATTERN A

SOGO or *ATSIMEVU*—MASTER DRUM [for Sogo transpose up
to Key F]

♩ = 204

Gankogui

Atsimevu

(R = Stick: vlo   vlo   vlo   vlo   ga-ga   to
L = Hand)   LR   LR   LR   LR   L L   R
              FF   FF   FF   FF   C C   SM

ga-ga   ga-te- gi- de ga-ga   vlo vlo vlo vlo
L L   L R L R L L   LR   LR   LR   LR
C C   C F F F C C   FF   FF   FF   FF

ga-ga   to   ga-ga   ga- ze- gree - te-te
L L   R   L L   L R LR   R R
C C   SM   C C   C F FF   F F

KIDI

(2 sticks)

PLATES

INDEX

PRINTED IN GREAT BRITAIN
BY COMPTON PRINTING LTD., LONDON AND AYLESBURY

PLATE II

The orchestra of the Ewe tribe

PLATE III

Playing the bell—*Gankogui*

PLATE IV

Playing the rattle—*Axatse*

PLATE V

Playing the high bell—*Atoke*

PLATE VI

Method of holding the *Atsimevu* (master drum) stick

PLATE VIII

Playing a secondary muted beat on *Kidi*
The left stick is muting: the right stick is about to strike

PLATE IX

Playing free stick beats on *Atsimevu* (master drum)
Note the stance and finger-control

PLATE X

Playing a secondary muted stick beat on *Atsimevu*
when using two sticks

The left fingers are muting: the right stick is about to strike

PLATE XI

Playing a secondary muted stick beat on *Atsimevu*
when using one stick
The left hand is muting in Zone 2

PLATE XII

Playing 'Ʊukɔgo' on *Atsimevu*
This is the nonsense syllable *dza*

PLATE XIII

Playing *Sogo* when it is used as master drum
The right hand is making a free beat in Zone 3

PLATE XIV

Sogo : a muted centre beat

PLATE XV

Sogo : a secondary muted beat in Zone 3
The left hand is muting : the right is striking

PLATE XVI

Sogo : a muted beat in Zone 2
The fingers are closed : compare PLATE XVII

PLATE XVII

Sogo : free beats in Zone 2 with fingers splayed to produce the
sound represented by the nonsense syllables *ga—tsya*

PLATE XVIII

Recording drum-patterns

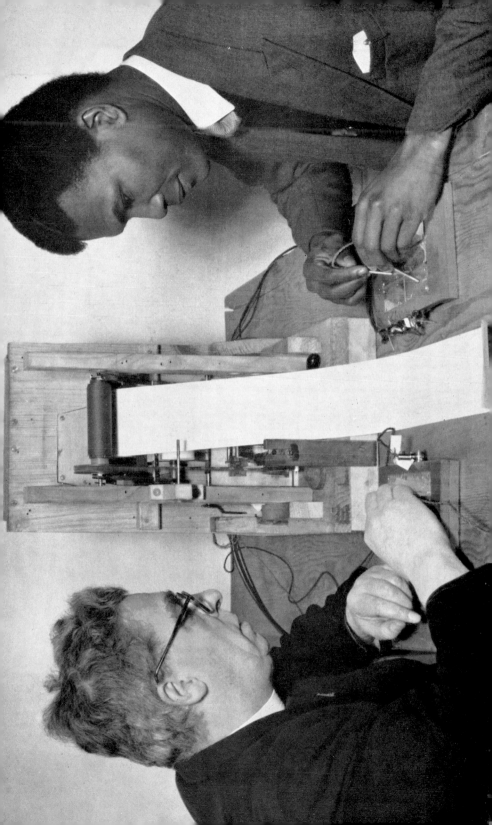